Wolfgang Amadeus Mozart

DON GIOVANNI

COMPLETE ORCHESTRAL AND VOCAL SCORE

DOVER PUBLICATIONS, INC., NEW YORK

This Dover edition, first published in 1974, is an unabridged republication of the edition by Georg Schünemann and Kurt Soldan, with German translation of the vocal text by Georg Schünemann, originally published by C. F. Peters, Leipzig, n.d. (editorial matter dated "Summer 1941"). In the present edition all the preliminary matter, editorial remarks in the score and the Editors' Commentary *(Revisionsbericht)*, originally in German, appear in a new English translation specially prepared by Stanley Appelbaum.

International Standard Book Number: 0-486-23026-0
Library of Congress Catalog Card Number: 73-91488

Manufactured in the United States of America
Dover Publications, Inc.
180 Varick Street
New York, N. Y. 10014

DON GIOVANNI

"DRAMMA GIOCOSO" IN TWO ACTS
TEXT BY LORENZO DA PONTE
MUSIC BY W. A. MOZART

CHARACTERS

DON GIOVANNI, a young nobleman of libertine habits . . . . *Baritone*
DONNA ANNA, ... *Soprano*
a lady betrothed to
DON OTTAVIO . . . . *Tenor*
COMMENDATORE . . . . *Bass*
DONNA ELVIRA, a lady of Burgos jilted by Don Giovanni . . . . *Soprano*
LEPORELLO, servant of Don Giovanni . . . . *Bass*
MASETTO, ... *Bass*
bridegroom of
ZERLINA, a peasant girl . . . . *Soprano*

Chorus of peasant men and girls. Musicians. House servants.
The action takes place in a city of Spain.

DRAMMA GIOCOSO IN DUE ATTI
POESIA DI LORENZO DA PONTE
MUSICA DI W. A. MOZART

PERSONAGGI

DON GIOVANNI, Giovane Cavaliere estremamente licenzioso . . . . *Baritono*
DONNA ANNA, ... *Soprano*
Dama promessa sposa di
DON OTTAVIO . . . . *Tenore*
COMMENDATORE . . . . *Basso*
DONNA ELVIRA, Dama di Burgos abbandonata da Don Giovanni . . . . *Soprano*
LEPORELLO, Servo di Don Giovanni . . . . *Basso*
MASETTO, ... *Basso*
Amante di
ZERLINA, Contadina . . . . *Soprano*

Coro di Contadini e di Contadine. Suonatori. Servitori.
La scena si finge in una città della Spagna.

Composed in 1787. First performance at the Count Nostitz National Theater in Prague on October 29, 1787, under the composer's direction.

INSTRUMENTATION

2 Flutes (Flauti), 2 Oboes (Oboi), 2 Clarinets (Clarinetti), 2 Bassoons (Fagotti), 2 Horns (Corni), 2 Trumpets (Trombe), 3 Trombones (Tromboni), 2 Kettledrums (Timpani), 1 Mandolin (Mandolino)
Violins (Violini) I & II, Violas (Viole), Cellos (Violoncelli), Basses (Contrabassi)

ON STAGE

In No. 13, Finale: Orchestra I: 2 Oboes, 2 Horns, Violins I & II, Violas, Cellos, Basses
Orchestra II: Violins, Cello, Bass
Orchestra III: Violins, Cello, Bass
In the Recitative preceding No. 22, Duet: 2 Oboes, 2 Clarinets, 2 Bassoons, 3 Trombones, Cello, Bass
In No. 24, Finale: 2 Oboes, 2 Clarinets, 2 Bassoons, 2 Horns, Cello

CONTENTS

SUPPLEMENT

PREFACE

Mozart's opera *The Marriage of Figaro* was cheered at its first performance in Prague in 1786 more enthusiastically than any other opera up to that time. "No one here talks about anything but—*Figaro*," Mozart wrote from Prague to Baron von Jaquin. "Nothing is played, tooted, sung or whistled but—*Figaro*. No opera is attended but—*Figaro* and always *Figaro*—certainly a great honor for me." Mozart had to be present at a performance on January 17, 1787; on January 20 he had to conduct the work personally and give a concert as well. The director of the theater, Pasquale Bondini, gave him a contract for a new opera for Prague at the usual fee of 100 ducats. Mozart discussed the assignment with the librettist of *Figaro*, Lorenzo da Ponte. Their choice fell on the theme of Don Giovanni, which had frequently been treated in literary works. The figure of the Don had been seen on the stage in Spain, France, Italy and Germany in tragedy, comedy, farce, spectacle and even opera. The most successful opera, Gazzaniga's *Convitato di pietra* (The Stone Guest), with text by Bertati, had come from Venice to Vienna. It was the direct model for Da Ponte's version. Da Ponte retained the characters and even the principal scenes, but he compressed the action and lifted it above the routine level of *opera buffa*. Mozart's influence made itself strongly felt in the drafting of the libretto. The music informs us to what an extent he swept the poet into his own world of profound humanity and dramatic truth.

There was little time left for the task of composition: Mozart could not begin to sketch the music until June 1787, when the libretto was finished. The score was completed in Prague on October 28, 1787. The opera was performed on the following day, October 29. *Il Dissoluto Punito o sia il Don Giovanni Dramma giocoso in due atti*—this is the full title of the work—was greeted "with the loudest acclaim," as Mozart reported. The audience already began to respond eagerly while the overture was being played, and the enthusiasm increased from one scene to the next. Mozart conducted four performances himself, then returned to Vienna.

The playbill of the first performance is lost. According to contemporary reports, the cast was as follows:

Don Giovanni	Luigi Bassi
Donna Anna	Teresa Saporiti
Don Ottavio	Antonio Baglioni
Donna Elvira	Caterina Micelli
Leporello	Felice Ponziani
Commendatore / Masetto	Giuseppe Lolli
Zerlina	Caterina Bondini

The opera was not performed in Vienna until May 7, 1788. For this performance Mozart wrote several new numbers, which he entered in his thematic catalogue on April 24, 28 and 30. These pieces, the tenor aria "Dalla sua pace," Elvira's aria "Mi tradì quel-l'alma ingrata" and the duet between Zerlina and Leporello "Per queste tue manine," with the corresponding recitatives, do not significantly intensify or supplement the plot, however beautiful the music may be and however superbly Mozart captured the words and the scenes in his recitatives and arias. The tenor was merely supplied with an additional aria, a humorous duet was provided for the spectators, and Elvira's entrance was explained. The Vienna performance was not a success. The singers were:

Don Giovanni	Francesco Albertarelli
Donna Anna	Aloisia Lange
Don Ottavio	Francesco Morella
Donna Elvira	Caterina Cavalieri
Leporello	Francesco Benucci
Commendatore / Masetto	Francesco Bussani
Zerlina	Luisa Mombelli

Only gradually did the Viennese come to appreciate the new work, which then began its triumphant career on the world's stages.

After the Prague performance it became necessary to translate the opera into German. Christian Gottlieb Neefe, the well-known composer of *Singspiele* and art songs and a teacher of Beethoven, wrote to his friend Grossmann: "Once more I have translated an opera, *Don Giovanni,* with its excellent music by Mozart, and my work is perhaps not without felicity" (May 23, 1789). At almost the same time Heinrich Gottlieb Schmieder did a translation for Mainz and Friedrich Ludwig Schroeder did one for Hamburg. Stage performances followed at short intervals, not only using the old translations but trying out new ones by Girzik and Spiess and, above all, revisions of the text. A new libretto was prepared in 1801 by Johann Friedrich Rochlitz. Despite all his liberties, he had done such a thorough job on the opera that his revision became the standard version for decades. Many turns of phrase of these older German texts, such as "Keine Ruh bei Tag und Nacht" or "Gib mir die Hand, mein Leben" (Schroeder), had become so firmly established that they held their own in stage performances and, sung everywhere, became as popular as folksongs.

Toward the middle of last century a new era in editing Mozart began. In 1850 Richard Wagner undertook a new version (unfortunately lost) for the Zurich theater. Eduard Devrient (1853), W. Viol (1858), Ludwig Bischoff (1860), B. v. Gugler (1869), Alfred von Wolzogen (1869) and C. H. Bitter (1871) attempted new solutions until in 1871 Franz Grandaur supplied the most felicitous version so far. Nevertheless many problems still remained unsolved, especially in the recitatives. After the score was published in the complete edition of Mozart's works with a translation by Karl Niese (1872), further editions once more began to appear. Max Staegemann, Max Kalbeck (1886), Ernst Heinemann (1906), Karl Scheidemantel (1914) and many others, up to Siegfried Anheisser (1935) and Herman Roth (1936), undertook translations, of which some were accurate in meaning, others close to the sound of the Italian and still others more or less free. None of these attempts offered a definitive solution.

The present German translation is based on the view that, in so far as the original Italian words and stage practice allow, the old texts, with their pleasing and popularly accepted phraseology that has been sung in German-speaking countries for a century, must be retained. They are much closer to Mozart's music than even the most accurate translation, to the extent that the latter neglects dramatic values and the nature of Mozart's music for the sake of the text. Therefore all available piano scores, librettos and full scores, beginning with the very earliest, were consulted and examined. Every passage and every expression in all the varied German revisions were compared against the Italian original. Only those passages have been newly translated in which the old versions are inadequate or in which an exact translation of the text set by Mozart is absolutely necessary. No excuse is offered for the deletion of the childish moralities that often used to be inserted. Numerous alterations in notation and other "improvements" that had become embedded in the arias and recitatives since Hermann Levi's revision, have been eliminated. Throughout, Mozart's notation and libretto have been restored with the greatest accuracy, and many errors that have persisted in piano and orchestral scores since Mozart's time have been rectified.

The present edition was prepared in very close collaboration with the conductor Kurt Soldan, whose rich experience and painstaking editorship were of great benefit to the project. For details, see the Editors' Commentary at the end of the volume.

Berlin, Summer 1941

GEORG SCHÜNEMANN

DON GIOVANNI

Ouvertura

W. A. Mozart
(1756-1791)

16
Fl.
Ob.
Clar. in A
Fag.
Cor. in D
Tr. in D
Timp.
16
I
Viol.
II
Viola
Vc.
Cb.
23
a 2
Fl.
cresc.
a 2
Ob.
Clar. in A
Fag.
Cor. in D
Tr. in D
Timp.
23
I
Viol.
II
Viola
Vc.
Cb.

27
Fl.
Ob.
Clar. in A
Fag.
Cor. in D
Tr. in D
Timp.
Viol. I
II
Viola
Vc.
Cb.
30
Molto Allegro
Fl.
Ob.
Clar. in A
Fag.
Cor. in D
Tr. in D
Timp.
Molto Allegro
Viol. I
II
Viola
Vc.
Cb.

38
Fl.
Ob.
Clar. in A
Fag.
Cor. in D
Tr. in D
Timp.
Viol. I
Viol. II
Viola
Vc.
46
Fl.
Ob.
Clar. in A
Fag.
Cor. in D
Tr. in D
Timp.
Viol. I
Viol. II
Viola
Vc.
Cb.
a 2

54
Fl.
Ob.
Clar. in A
Fag.
Cor. in D
Tr. in D
Timp.
a 2
54
I
Viol.
II
Viola
Vc.
Cb.
62
Fl.
Ob.
Clar. in A
Fag.
Cor. in D
Tr. in D
Timp.
62
I
Viol.
II
Viola
Vc.
Cb.
cresc.

70
Fl.
Ob.
Clar. in A
Fag.
Cor. in D
Tr. in D
Timp.
Viol. I
Viol. II
Viola
Vc.
Cb.
a 2
sf
p
79
I
f
[f]

88
Fl.
Ob.
Fag.
Viol. I II
Viola
Vc.
Cb.
96
Fl.
Ob.
Clar. in A
Fag.
Cor. in D
Tr. in D
Timp.
Viol. I II
Viola
Vc.
Cb.
a 2

103
Fl.
Ob.
Clar. in A
Fag.
Cor. in D
Tr. in D
Timp.
Viol. I II
Viola
Vc.
Cb.
a 2
110

117
a 2
Fl.
Ob.
Clar. in A
Fag.
Cor. in D
Tr. in D
Timp.
Viol.
I
II
Viola
Vc.
Cb.
127
I

137
Fl.
Ob.
Clar. in A
Fag.
Viol.
I
II
Viola
Vc.
Cb.
145
Cor. in D
Tr. in D
Timp.
p
f
[f]

154
Fl.
Ob.
Clar. in A
Fag.
Cor. in D
Tr. in D
Timp.
a 2
Viol. I
Viol. II
Viola
Vc.
Cb.
164

173
Fl.
Ob.
Clar. in A
Fag.
Cor. in D
Tr. in D
Timp.
173
Viol. I
Viol. II
Viola
Vc.
Cb.
182
Fl.
Ob.
Clar. in A
Fag.
Cor. in D
Tr. in D
Timp.
182
Viol. I
Viol. II
Viola
Vc.
Cb.

191
Fl.
Ob.
Clar. in A
Fag.
Cor. in D
Tr. in D
Timp.
191
Viol. I
Viol. II
Viola
Vc.
Cb.
p
199
Fl.
Ob.
Clar. in A
Fag.
Cor. in D
Tr. in D
Timp.
199
Viol. I
Viol. II
Viola
Vc.
f
p
I

207
Fl.
Ob.
Clar. in A
Fag.
Cor. in D
Tr. in D
Timp.
Viol. I II
Viola
Vc.
Cb.
a 2
215

223
Fl.
Ob.
Clar. in A
Fag.
Cor. in D
Tr. in D
Timp.
223
Viol. I
Viol. II
Viola
Vc.
Cb.
p
[p]
f
a2
[f]
cresc.
231
Fl.
Ob.
Clar. in A
Fag.
Cor. in D
Tr. in D
Timp.
231
Viol. I
Viol. II
Viola
Vc.
Cb.
a2

240
Fl.
Ob.
Clar. in A
Fag.
Cor. in D
Tr. in D
Timp.
Viol. I
Viol. II
Viola
Vc.
Cb.
250

259
Fl.
Ob.
Clar. in A
Fag.
Cor. in D
Tr. in D
Timp.
Viol.
I
II
Viola
Vc.
Cb.
a 2
267

*) For the concert ending of the Overture, see Supplement I, page 459.

ERSTER AKT

[Garten.] Nacht.

Erste Szene

Leporello (in einen Mantel gehüllt, geht vor dem Haus der Donna Anna auf und ab). Dann Don Giovanni und Donna Anna. Später der Komtur.

ATTO PRIMO

[Giardino.] Notte.

Scena I

Leporello (con ferrajuolo, che passeggia davanti la casa di Donna Anna); poi Don Giovanni, Donna Anna; indi il Commendatore.

Nº 1. Introduzione

14
a 2
Ob.
a 2
Fag.
Cor. in F
14
I
Viol.
II
Viola
L.
macht, schma-le Kost und we-nig Geld, das er-tra-ge, wem's ge - fällt. Ich will
dir, pio-va e ven-to sop-por-tar, mangiar ma-le e mal dor - mir. Vo - glio
Vc.
Cb.

21
Ob.
Fag.
Cor. in F
21
I
Viol.
II
Viola
L.
selbst den Her-ren ma-chen, mag nicht län-ger Die-ner sein, mag nicht län-ger Die-ner
far il gen-til - uo - mo, e non vo-glio più ser - vir, e non vo-glio più ser -
Vc.
Cb.

28
Ob.
Fag.
I
p
sfp
Cor. in F
Viol.
II
Viola
L.
sein, nein, nein, nein, nein, ich mag nicht län - ger Die - ner sein.
vir; no, no, no, no, no, no, non vo - glio più ser - vir.
So ein gro - ßer Herr kann lachen!
Oh che ca - ro ga - lant-uomo!
Vc.
Cb.
37
a 2
Tändelt er mit einer Schönen, dann muß ich als Schildwach stöhnen, als Schildwach stöhnen, als Schildwach stöhnen!
Voi star dentro colla bel - la, ed io far la sen - ti - nel - la, la sen - ti - nel - la, la sen - ti - nel-la!

45
Ob.
Fag.
Cor. in F
Viol. I II
Viola
L.
Ich will selbst den Her-ren ma - chen, mag nicht län-ger Die-ner
Vo - glio far il gen-til - uo - mo, e non vo-glio più ser -
Vc.
Cb.
50
sein, mag nicht län-ger Die-ner sein, nein, nein, nein, nein, ich mag nicht län-ger Die - ner sein. Doch was gibt's, ich hö-re
vir, e non vo-glio più ser - vir, no, no, no, no, no, no, non vo-glio più ser-vir. Ma mi par, che venga

59
Ob.
Fag.
Cor. in F
Viol. I II
Viola
L.
kommen, doch was gibt's, ich hö-re kommen; fort ins Dunkel schnell hin-ein, ja, fort ins Dunkel schnell hin-ein, fort ins Dun-kel
gen-te, ma mi par, che ven-ga gen-te; non mi vo-glio far sen-tir, ah non mi vo-glio far sen-tir, non mi vo-glio
Vc.
Cb.
cresc.
a 2
65
Fl.
[Verbirgt sich]
[S'asconde]
schnell hin - ein, ja, ja, ja, ja, fort, fort ins Dun-kel schnell hin-ein.
far sen - tir, no, no, no, no, no, non mi vo-glio far sen-tir.

73
Fl.
Ob.
Fag.
Cor. in F
Viol. I
II
Viola
Donna Anna [Don Giovanni am Arm festhaltend]
[tenendo forte pel braccio Don Giovanni]
D.A.
Hoffe nicht, so lang ich at - me, un - er-kannt zu_fliehn von hier.
Non spe-rar, se non m'uc-ci - di, ch'io ti la - sci_fug - gir mai.
Vc.
Cb.
79
Donna Anna
Hof-fe nicht, so lang ich
Non spe - rar, se non m'uc-
Don Giovanni [immer sein Gesicht zu verbergen suchend]
[cercando sempre di celarsi]
D.G.
Wer ich bin, du tö - richt Mädchen, nie er-fährst du das von mir.
Don-na fol - le, in-dar - no gri-di, chi son io tu non sa - prai.
Wer ich
Don-na
Leporello
L.
Welch ein Lär-men, o
Che tu - mul - to, oh

85
Fl.
Ob.
Fag.
a 2
Cor. in F
a 2
85
I
Viol.
II
Viola
D.A.
at - me, un-er-kannt zu fliehn von hier, hof - fe nicht, un - er-kannt zu fliehn von hier. Helft, o
ci - di, ch'io ti la - sci fug - gir mai, non spe - rar, ch'io ti la - sci fug - gir mai. Gen - te,
D.G.
bin, du tö - richt Mäd-chen, nie erfährst du das von mir, nein, er - fährst es nie.
fol - le, in - dar - no gri - di, chi son io tu non sa - prai, no, tu non sa - prai.
L.
Gott, welch Schrei-en, ach, mein Herr in neu - er Not.
ciel, che gri - di, il pa - dron in nuo - vi guai.
Vc.
Cb.
91
Fl.
Ob.
Fag.
Cor. in F
91
I
Viol.
II
Viola
D.A.
Leu - te, helft mir Ar - men! Ehr - ver - geß - ner! Ehr - ver - geßner!
ser - vi, al tra - di - to - re! Scel - le - ra - to! Scel - le - ra - to!
D.G.
Still, sonst kenn ich kein Er - barmen. Fort, Ver - weg - ne! Fort, Verwegne!
Ta - ci e tre - ma al mio fu - ro - re. Scon - si - glia - ta! Scon - si - gliata!
L.
Sei - ne
Sta a ve -
Vc.
Cb.

99
Fl.
Ob.
Fag.
Cor. in F
Viol. I II
Viola
D. A.
Hört mich niemand? Gleich der Furie sieh mich rasen, dein Verderben werd ich
Gente, servi! Come furia disperata ti saprò persegui-
D. G.
Schweig und zittre! Dieser Furie tolles Rasen, mein Ver-
Tacie trema! Questa furia disperata mi vuol
L.
tollen Abenteuer werden mein Verderben sein. Welch ein Lärmen,
der che il libertino mi farà precipitar. Che tumulto,
Vc.
Cb.
105
a 2
[div.]
sein, gleich der Furie sieh mich rasen, sieh mich rasen, dein Ver-
tar, come furia disperata, disperata ti sa-
derben wird es sein, dieser Furie tolles Rasen, mein Ver-
far precipitar, questa furia disperata mi vuol
o Gott, welch Schreien! Seine tollen Abenteuer werden mein Verderben
oh ciel, che gridi! Sta a veder che il libertino mi farà precipi-

110
Fl.
Ob.
Fag.
a 2
Cor. in F
Viol. I II
Viola
D.A.
der - - ben werd ich sein. Bleib, Ver-räter! Ehr-vergeßner!
prò per - se - - gui - tar. Scel - le - ra-to! Scel - le - ra-to!
D.G.
der - - ben wird es sein. Fort, Verwegne! Fort, Verwegne!
far pre - ci - - pi - tar. Scon - si-gliata! Scon - si-gliata!
L.
sein, sei-ne tol-len A-ben-teu-er werden mein Verderben sein. Sei - ne
tar, sta a ve-der che il li-ber-ti-no mi fa-rà preci-pi-tar. Sta a ve -
Vc.
Cb.
117
Hört mich niemand? Gleich der Fu-rie sieh mich ra - sen, dein Ver-der - ben werd ich
Gen - te, ser-vi! Co-me fu-ria dis - pe - ra - ta ti sa-prò per - se - gui -
Schweig und zit-tre! Dieser Fu - rie tol - les Ra - sen, mein Ver -
Ta - ci e tre - ma! Questa fu - ria dis - pe - ra - ta mi vuol
tol-len A-ben-teu-er wer-den mein Ver-der-ben sein. Welch ein Lär - men,
der che il li-ber - ti - no mi fa - rà pre-ci - pi - tar. Che tu-mul - to,

123
Fl.
Ob.
Fag.
Cor. in F
Viol. I II
Viola
D. A.
D. G.
L.
Vc.
Cb.
a 2
[div.]
sein, gleich der Fu - rie — sieh mich ra - sen, sieh mich ra - sen, dein Ver -
tar, co - me fu - ria — dis - pe - ra - ta, — dis - pe - ra - ta ti sa -
der - ben — wird es — sein, dieser Fu - rie tol - les Ra - sen, mein Ver -
far pre - ci - pi - tar, questa fu - ria dis - pe - ra - ta mi vuol
o Gott, welch Schrei - en! Seine tol - len A - ben - teuer werden mein Verderben
oh ciel, che gri - di! Sta a veder che il liber - ti - no mi fa - rà preci - pi -
128
der - ben werd ich sein, dein Ver -
prò per - se - gui - tar, ti sa -
der - ben wird es sein, mein Ver -
far pre - ci - pi - tar, mi vuol
sein, sei - ne tol - len A - ben - teu - er wer - den mein Ver - der - ben sein, sei - ne tol - len A - ben - teu - er wer - den mein Ver - der - ben
tar, sta a ve - der che il li - ber - ti - no mi fa - rà pre - ci - pi - tar, sta a ve - der che il li - ber - ti - no mi fa - rà pre - ci - pi -

132
Fl.
Ob.
Fag.
a 2
Viol.
I
II
Viola
(Läßt Don Giovanni los und geht ins Haus [da sie den Komtur kommen hört])
([Sentendo il Commendatore] lascia Don Giovanni ed entra in casa)
D.A.
der - ben werd ich sein.
prò per - se - - - gui - tar.
D.G.
der - ben wird es sein.
far pre - ci - - - pi - tar.
L.
sein, sei-ne tol-len A-ben-teu-er werden mein Verderben sein.
tar, sta a ve-der che il li-ber-ti-no mi fa-rà preci-pi-tar.
Vc.
Cb.
138
cresc.
Don Giovanni
Nein, mit dir kämpfen wär wenig Ehre!
Va, non mi de-gno di pugnar te-co.
Komtur
Il Commendatore
K.
Laß sie, Verwegner, stell dich zur Wehre!
La-sciala, indegno, bat - ti - ti me-co!
Mit eitlem
Così pre-

147
Fl.
Ob.
Fag.
Cor. in F
Viol. I
Viol. II
Viola
D.G.
K.
L.
Vc.
Cb.
a 2
Don Giovanni
Ich mit dir käm - pfen? Nein!
Va, non mi de - gno, no.
Vor - wand willst du entfliehn, mit eit-lem Vor-wand willst du ent-
ten - di da me fug-gir, co-sì pre-ten-di da me fug-
Leporello
(Ach könnt ich lei - se zurück mich ziehn!)
(Po-tes-si al-me - no di qua par-tir!)
155
G.P.
mezza voce
più voce
We-he dir! We-he dir! Wohl - an, so sei es, du
Mi-se-ro! Mi-se-ro! Mi - se - ro, at - ten - di, se
fliehn? Her zu mir!
gir? Bat - ti-ti!
(Ach könnt ich lei - se zu-rück mich ziehn!)
(Po-tes-si al-me - no di qua par-tir!)

164
Fl.
Ob.
a 2
[p]
Fag.
Cor. in F
Viol. I
Viol. II
Viola
D.G.
(Sie fechten)
(Combattono)
wählst den Tod!
vuoi mo-rir!
Vc.
Cb.
172
Andante
K.
(Der Komtur ist tödlich getroffen)
(Il Commendatore mortalmente ferito)
Komtur
Il Commendatore
Ach, zu
Ah soc -
pizz.

177
Fag.
[pp]
Cor. in F
177
I
Viol.
II
Viola
Don Giovanni
sotto voce
D. G.
Ha, da liegt der_ Un - glück - sel'ge, win-det schwer sich in To - des -
Ah già ca - de il scia - gu - ra - to, af - fan - no - sa e a - go - niz -
K.
Hil-fe... ach, zu Hil-fe... weh, mich fas - sen... To - des-schmerzen...
cor-so... son tra-di-to... l'as - sas - si - no... m'ha fe - ri - to...
Leporello
L.
Welch Ver - bre - chen, welch ein Fre - vel!
Qual mis - fat - to, qual ec - ces - so!
Vc.
Cb.
181
Fag.
Cor. in F
181
I
Viol.
II
Viola
D. G.
schmerzen, bald aus tief - durch-bohr - tem Herzen wird sein schwaches Le-ben fliehn, wird sein
zan - te già dal se - no pal - pi - tan-te veg-go l'a - ni - ma par - tir, veg - go
K.
aus dem tief - durch-bohr - ten Herzen fühl ich
e dal se - no pal - pi - tan-te sen - to
L.
Ach, vor Schrecken und vor Za - gen fühl ich al - le Pul - se schla - gen, soll ich blei - ben, soll ich
Entro il sen dal-lo spa-ven-to pal-pi-tar il cor mi sen - to, io non sò che far, che
Vc.
Cb.

185
Fag.
Cor. in F
185
I
Viol.
II
Viola
D. G.
schwa - ches Le - ben fliehn, bald aus tief - durch-bohr - tem Herzen wird sein
l'a - ni - ma par - tir, già dal se - - no pal - pi - tan-te veg - - go
K.
schon das Le - ben fliehn, fühl ich schon das
l'a - ni - ma par - tir, sen - - - - - - to l'a - ni -
L.
fliehn, soll ich blei-ben, soll ich fliehn, ach, vor Schrecken und vor Za-gen fühl ich al - le Pul - se schlagen, soll ich bleiben, soll ich
dir, io non sò che far, che dir, en-tro il sen dal-lo spa-ven-to pal-pi-tar il cor mi sen-to, io non sò che far, che
Vc.
Cb.
189
Fl.
Ob.
Fag.
Cor. in F
189
I
Viol.
II
Viola
D. G.
schwa - ches Le - ben fliehn.
l'a - ni - ma par - tir.
(Stirbt)
(Muore)
K.
Le - ben fliehn.
ma par - - tir.
L.
fliehn, soll ich blei-ben, soll ich fliehn?
dir, io non sò che far, che dir.
Vc.
Cb.

Zweite Szene

[Don Giovanni. Leporello.]

Scena II

[Don Giovanni. Leporello.]

Recitativo

Dritte Szene

Don Ottavio und Donna Anna mit Dienern (welche Fackeln tragen).

Scena III

Don Ottavio, Donna Anna, con servi (che portano diversi lumi).

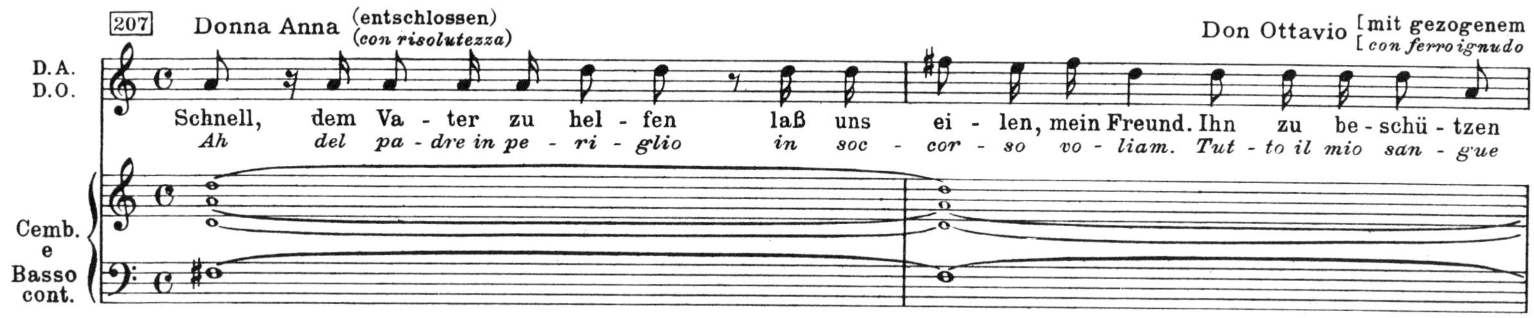

attacca subito Istromentato [*No. 2*]

No. 2. Recitativo e Duetto

8
Fl.
Ob.
a 2
Fag.
Cor. in F
8
I
Viol.
II
Viola
D.A.
Himmel!
mie-i!
Mein Va-ter... o mein Va-ter... teu-er-ster Va-ter...
Il pa-dre... pa-dre mi-o... mio ca-ro pa-dre...
D.O.
Don Ottavio
Dein
Si-
Vc.
Cb.
sf
15
a 2
I
f
p
Ach, tödlich traf ihn des Mörders Stahl.
Ah l'as-sas-si-no mel tru-ci-dò.
Dies Blut... die-se Wunde... dies
Quel sangue... quel-la pia-ga... quel
Va-ter...
gno-re...

23
Fl.
Ob.
Fag.
Cor. in F
Viol. I
Viol. II
Viola
D.A.
Vc.
Cb.
Antlitz... bleich und er-kal-tet durch den Hauch des Todes. Kein O-dem hebt die
vol-to... tin-to e co-per-to dei co-lor di mor-te. Ei non re-spi-ra
31
Brust... kalt sei-ne Glieder... O mein Vater... lieber Vater... teu-er-ster Vater...
più... fred-de ha le membra... Pa-dre mi-o... ca-ro padre... pa-dre a-ma-to...

39
Fl.
Ob.
Fag.
a 2
Maestoso
Viol.
Viola
Donna Anna
D.A.
Ich wanke...
io manco...
ich sterbe...
io mo-ro...
Don Ottavio
D.O.
Freunde, kommt schnell zu Hil-fe der Heißge - lieb-ten. O
Ah soc - cor - re - te, a-mi-ci, il mio te - so-ro. Cer-
Vc.
Cb.
46
Andante
zögert nicht, bringt Stärkung ihr, steht ihr bei... welch ein Jammer... ach eilt, ich bit-te... O An-na... Freundin...
ca-te-mi... re - ca-te-mi... qual-che o-dor... qual-che spir-to... ah non tar-da-te... Donn' An-na... spo-sa...
50
Ach...
Ahi...
Ge-lieb-te...
a - mi - ca...
Des Schmerzes Ü-ber-maß wird die Ärm-ste tö-ten...
il duo-lo e-stre-mo la me-schi-nel-la uc-ci-de...
Sie er-holt sich...
Già rin-vie-ne...

54
Viol. I II
Viola
D.A.
D.O.
Vc.
Cb.
Ach, mein Vater...
Pa - dre mi-o...
bringt ihr noch wei-tre Stärkung...
da - te - le nuo-vi a-ju - ti...
Ihr Freunde, entfernet schnell aus ih - ren Augen, was so tief sie er-
Ce - la - te, al-lon-ta - na - te a-gli oc-chi suo-i quell'og-get - to d'or-
58
Fl.
Ob.
Fag.
Cor. in F
schüttert.
ro - re.
Teure Ge-lieb-te...
A-ni-ma mi-a...
er-ho-le dich...
con-so-la-ti...
erwache...
fa co-re...
[Duetto]
63 Allegro
Donna Anna (verzweifelt)
(disperatamente)
Flie - he, Ver-rä-ter, flie-he, laß mich mein Le - ben enden, er fiel von Mör-der-händen, der mir das Le - ben
Fug - gi, cru-de-le, fug-gi, la - scia ch'io mo-ra anch'i - o, o-ra ch'è mor-to, oh Di - o, chi a me la vi - ta

72
Ob.
[p]
Fag.
[p]
72
I
Viol.
II
Viola
D.A.
gab.
diè.
Don Ottavio
D.O.
Hör mich, o hör, Ge - lieb - te, der dir sein Le - ben weihte, der Freund steht dir zur
Sen - ti, cor mio, deh sen - ti, guar - da - mi un so - lo i-stan - te, ti par - la il ca - ro a -
Vc.
Cb.
80
Fl.
I
sfp
p
Fag.
I
sfp
p
80
I
Viol.
II
sfp
p
Viola
sfp
p
D.A.
Bist du's... mein Freund... ver - zeih _ mir... der Schmerz, der Jammer be -
Tu sei... per - don... mio be - ne... l'af - fan - no mi - o, le
D.O.
Sei - te, dein Ei - gen bis zum Grab.
man - te, che vi - ve sol per te.
Vc.
sfp
p
Cb.
sfp
p

89
Fl.
Ob.
Fag.
Cor. in F
Viol. I II
Viola
D. A.
D. O.
Vc.
Cb.
[p]
cresc.
f
[f]
sfp
täubt mich...
pe - ne...
Wo ist mein Va-ter, sprich?
Ah il pa-dre mio dov' è?
Dein Va-ter...
Il pa-dre...
laß, Ge-lieb-te,
la-scia, o ca-ra,
99
mf
p
Ach... mein
Ah... il
laß der Er-inn-rung Leiden...
la rimembran-za a-ma-ra...
dein Gat-te beschirmt als Va-ter dich.
hai spo-so e pa - dre in me.

109
Fl.
Ob.
Fag.
Cor. in F
Viol. I II
Viola
D. A.
Va-ter, wo ist mein Vater, sprich?
pa-dre... il pa-dre mio dov' è?
D. O.
Laß, Ge-liebte, laß der Er-inn-rung Leiden... dein Gat - te, dein
La-scia, o ca-ra, la rimembran-za a-ma-ra... hai spo - so e
Vc.
Cb.
120
Recitativo
Auf, schwöre ew'ge Rache für dies vergoß - ne
Ah, ven-di-car, se il puo-i, giu-ra quel san-gue o-
Gat - te, dein Gat - te be-schirmt als Va-ter dich.
pa - dre, hai spo-so e pa - dre in me.

128
Maestoso
Adagio in tempo
Viol. I II
Viola
D.A.
D.O.
Vc.
Cb.
Blut!
gnor!
Ich schwöre… ich schwöre… ich schwör's bei dei - nen Tränen, bei un - srer Lie - be
Lo giu - ro… lo giu - ro… lo_ giu - ro agl'oc - chi tuo - i, lo giu - ro al no - stro a-
134
Tempo I
Fl.
Ob.
Fag.
Cor. in F
a 2
Glut!
mor.
Ver - nimm den Schwur, o Himmel, am
Che giu - ra - men - to, oh De - i, che
cresc.
sfp

141
Fl.
Ob.
Fag.
Cor. in F
a 2
Viol. I
Viol. II
Viola
D. A
D. O
Vc.
Cb.
cresc.
sfp
p
Tag des blut'- gen Grauens! In tausend schweren Qua-len schlägt bang mein armes Herz, in
bar - ba-ro mo-men-to! Fra cento af-fet-ti e cen-to vam-mi on-deggiando il cor, fra
149
f
[p]
tau-send schwe-ren Qua - len schlägt bang mein ar - mes Herz. Schwör, dies Blut zu
cen - to af - fet - ti e cen - to vam-mi on - deg - gian - do il cor. Ven - di - car quel
tau - send schwe - ren Qua - len schlägt bang mein ar - mes Herz.
cen - to af - fet - ti e cen - to vam-mi on - deg - gian - do il cor.

158
Fl.
Ob.
Fag.
Cor. in F
Viol. I II
Viola
D.A.
rächen, schwö-re!
sangue giu-ra!
D.O.
Ich schwöre bei dei- nen Tränen, bei un- srer Liebe Glut!
Lo giu-ro agl' oc- chi tuo-i, al no- stro a-mor.
Vc.
Cb.
169
D.A.
Ver-nimm den Schwur, o Himmel, am Tag des blut'-gen Grauens!
Che giu-ra-men-to, oh De-i, che bar-ba-ro mo-men-to!
D.O.
Ver-nimm den Schwur, o Himmel, am Tag des blut'-gen Grauens!
Che giu-ra-men-to, oh De-i, che bar-ba-ro mo-men-to!
cresc.
sfp

177
Fl.
Ob.
Fag.
Cor. in F
Viol. I
Viol. II
Viola
D.A.
D.O.
Vc.
Cb.
In tau-send schweren Qua-len schlägt bang mein ar-mes Herz, in tau - send
Fra cen-to af-fet-tie cen - to vam-mi on-deg-giando il cor, fra cen - to af -
184
schwe-ren Qua - len schlägt bang mein ar - mes Herz, schlägt bang mein ar - - - - - - -
fet - ti e cen - to vam-mi on-deg - gian - do il cor, vam - mi on-deg-gian - - - - - -
schwe-ren Qua - len schlägt bang mein ar - mes Herz, schlägt bang mein ar - - mes
fet - ti e cen - to vam-mi on-deg - gian - do il cor, vam - mi on-deg - gian - do il
cresc.
sfp
[p]
p
f

192
Ob.
Fag.
Cor. in F
Viol. I
Viol. II
Viola
D.A.
- mes, mein ar - mes Herz, schlägt bang mein ar - - - - - - - mes, mein ar - mes
- do, on-deg-gian - do il cor, vam - mi on-deg - gian - - - - - - - do, on-deg-gian - do il
D.O.
Herz, schlägt bang mein ar - mes Herz, schlägt bang mein ar - mes Herz, schlägt bang mein ar - mes
cor, vam - mi on-deggian-do il cor, vam - mi on-deg - gian - do il cor, vam - mi on-deggian-do il
Vc.
Cb.
cresc.
199
Fl.
Ob.
Fag.
Viol. I
Viol. II
Viola
D.A.
Herz, schlägt bang mein ar - mes Herz, schlägt bang mein ar - mes Herz, schlägt bang mein ar - mes Herz,
cor, vam - mi on-deg - gian-do il cor, vam-mi on-deg-gian-do il cor, vam - mi on-deg - gian-do il cor,
D.O.
Herz, schlägt bang mein ar - mes Herz, schlägt bang mein ar - mes Herz, schlägt bang mein ar - mes Herz,
cor, vam - mi on-deg - gian-do il cor, vam-mi on-deg-gian-do il cor, vam - mi on-deg - gian-do il cor,
Vc.
Cb.

208
Fl.
Ob.
Fag.
Viol. I II
Viola
D. A.
schlägt bang mein ar - mes Herz, schlägt bang mein ar - mes Herz, schlägt bang mein ar - mes
vam-mi on-deg-gian-do il cor, vam - mi on-deg-gian-do il cor, vam - mi on-deg-gian-do il
D. O.
schlägt bang mein ar - mes Herz, schlägt bang mein ar - mes Herz, schlägt bang mein ar - mes
vam-mi on-deg-gian-do il cor, vam - mi on-deg-gian-do il cor, vam - mi on-deg-gian-do il
Vc.
Cb.
215
cresc.
a 2
Cor. in F
[p] cresc.
(Vorhang zu)
[Sie gehen ab]
[Partono]
Herz, bang mein ar - mes Herz.
cor, on - deg-gian - do il cor.

Verwandlung

Straße. Nacht.

Vierte Szene

Don Giovanni. Leporello.

Mutazione

Strada. Notte.

Scena IV

Don Giovanni. Leporello.

Recitativo

segue l'Aria di Donn' Elvira [Nº. 3]

Fünfte Szene

[Die Vorigen (beiseite). Donna Elvira (in Reisekleidern).]

Scena V

[I suddetti (in disparte); Donna Elvira (in abito da viaggio).]

Nº 3. Aria

12
Clar. in B
Fag.
a 2
Cor. in Es
Viol. I
Viol. II
Viola
Donna Elvira
D. E.
Ach, werd ich ihn wohl finden, der Lie - be mir ver - hieß, der schmeichelnd mich be -
Ah chi mi di - ce ma - i, quel bar - ba - ro dov' è, che per mio scor - no a -
Vc.
Cb.
18
Clar. in B
Fag.
Cor. in Es
Viol. I
Viol. II
Viola
D. E.
tör - te und treu - los dann ver - ließ, treu - los mich dann ver - ließ?
ma - i, che mi man - cò di fè, che mi man - cò di fè?
Vc.
Cb.
cresc.
sfp
[f]

23
Clar. in B
Fag.
Cor. in Es
Viol. I
Viol. II
Viola
D. E.
Find ich den Un - ge - treu - en, rührt ihn nicht mehr mein
Ah se ri - tro - vo l'em - pio e a me non tor - na an -
Vc.
Cb.
30
Schmerz, dann soll er's schwer be - reu - en, mein Zorn zermalmt sein Herz, mein Zorn zermalmt sein Herz,
cor, vo' far - ne or - ren - do scem - pio, gli vo' ca - va reil cor, gli vo' ca - va - reil cor,
D. Giov.
D. G.
Ei
U -
cresc.

38
Clar. in B
Fag.
Cor. in Es
Viol. I
Viol. II
Viola
D. E.
dann soll er's schwer be-reu-en, mein Zorn zermalmt sein
vo' far-ne or-ren-do scempio, gli vo' ca-va-re il
D. G.
hörst du's, ei-ne Schö-ne, ver-las-sen vom Ge-liebten.
di-sti, qualche bel-la dal va-go ab-ban-do-na-ta.
Vc.
Cb.
45
a 2
Herz, mein Zorn zer-malmt sein Herz, ja, mein Zorn zer-malmt sein
cor, gli vo' ca-va-re il cor, sì, gli vo' ca-va-re il
Ar-mes Mädchen, ar-mes Mädchen!
Po-ve-ri-na, po-ve-ri-na!

53
Clar. in B
Fag.
a 2
Cor. in Es
Viol. I II
Viola
D. E.
Herz.
cor.
Ach, werd ich ihn wohl
Ah chi mi di - ce
Don Giovanni
D. G.
Ich wer-de trösten al - le ih - re Schmerzen.
Cerchiam di con-so - lare il suo tor - men - to.
Leporello
L.
So hat er schon ge-tröstet tausend Her-zen.
Co-sì ne con-so-lò mille e ot-to - cen - to.
Vc.
Cb.
60
fin-den, der Lie - be mir ver-hieß, der schmei-chelnd mich be - tör - te und
ma - i, quel bar - ba-ro dov' è, che per mio scor - no a-ma - i, che

65
Clar. in B
Fag.
a 2
Cor. in Es
Viol. I
II
Viola
D. E.
Vc.
Cb.
cresc.
treu - los dann ver - ließ, treu - - los mich dann ver - ließ? Find ich den
mi man - cò di fè, che mi man - cò di fè? Ah se ri -
71
Un - ge - treu - en, rührt ihn nicht mehr mein Schmerz, dann soll er's schwer be -
tro - vo l'em - pio e a me non tor - na an - cor, vo' far - ne or - ren - do

78
Clar. in B
Fag.
Cor. in Es
a 2
Viol. I
Viol. II
Viola
D. E.
reu-en, mein Zorn zermalmt sein Herz,
scempio, gli vo' ca-va-re il cor,
mein Zorn zer-malmt sein Herz, ja,
gli vo' ca-va-re il cor, sì,
Don Giovanni
D. G.
Ar-mes Mädchen, ar-mes Mädchen!
Po-ve-ri-na, po-ve-ri-na!
Vc.
Cb.
86
Donna Elvira
mein Zorn zer-malmt sein Herz.
gli vo' ca-va-re il cor.
Don Giovanni
Ich wer-de trö-sten al-le ih-re Schmerzen.
Cerchiam di con-so-la-re il suo tor-men-to.
Leporello
L.
So hat er schon ge-tröstet tau-send
Così ne con-so-lò mil-le e ot-to-

92
Clar. in B
Fag.
Cor. in Es
Viol. I
II
Viola
D. E.
Donna Elvira
Mein Zorn zermalmt sein Herz, mein Zorn zermalmt sein
Gli vo' ca-va - reil cor, gli vo' ca-va - reil
L.
Herzen.
cen-to.
Vc.
Cb.
100
a 2
cresc.
[cresc.]
[f]
Herz, mein Zorn zermalmt sein Herz, zer - malmt sein Herz.
cor, gli vo' ca-va-reil cor, ca - va - reil cor.
Wer
Chi è
D. G.
Don Giovanni
Schö-ne Donna, schöne Don-na!
Si-gno-ri-na, Si-gno-ri-na!

Recitativo

109
Don Giovanni
Leporello
Donna Elvira
D. E.
D. G.
L.
naht? Him-mel, was seh ich! O herr-lich, Don-na El-vi-ra! Don Gio-van-ni! Du hier, treu-lo-ser Mann, fre-cher Be-
là? Stel-le, che ve-do! O bel-la, Don-na El-vi-ra! Don Gio-van-ni! Sei qui mo-stro, fel-lon, ni-do d'in-
Cemb. e Basso cont.
113
Leporello
Don Giovanni
D. E.
L.
D. G.
trü-ger. (Ei, was für schö-ne Ti-tel, die kennt ja mei-nen Herrn ganz vor-treff-lich.) Ach, teu-re Don-na El-
gan-ni. (Che ti-to-li cru-scan-ti, man-co ma-le che lo co-no-sce be-ne.) Via, ca-ra Don-na El-
Cemb. e Basso cont.
116
Donna Elvira
D. G.
D. E.
vi-ra, wie könnt Ihr nur so zür-nen... ich bit-te... ver-gönnt mir nur ein Wort... Was kannst du sa-gen
vi-ra, cal-ma-te que-sta col-le-ra... sen-ti-te... la-scia-te-mi par-lar... Co-sa puoi di-re
Cemb. e Basso cont.
119
D. E.
nach so schwe-rer Un-tat? Du drängtest schmeichelnd gleich dich in mei-ne Nä-he, mit tau-send Kün-sten, mit fal-schem Eid ge-
do-po a-zion sì ne-ra? In ca-sa mi-a en-tri fur-ti-va-men-te, a for-za d'ar-te, di giu-ra-men-ti e
Cemb. e Basso cont.
122
D. E.
lang es, Frev-ler, dir end-lich, die-ses Herz zu be-tö-ren und es ganz zu ge-win-nen; du nann-test mich Gat-tin, und dann, miß-
di lu-sin-ghe ar-ri-vi a se-dur-re il cor mi-o; m'in-na-mo-ri, o cru-de-le, mi di-chia-ri tua spo-sa, e poi, man-
Cemb. e Basso cont.
126
D. E.
ach-tend heil'-ge Rech-te des Him-mels und der Er-de, hast du dich nach drei Ta-gen still wie ein Dieb aus Bur-gos gleich ent-
can-do del-la ter-ra e del cie-lo al san-to drit-to con e-nor-me de-lit-to do-po tre dì da Bur-gos t'al-lon-
Cemb. e Basso cont.

129
D. E.
fernt, mich ver-las-send, ent-flohst du und gabst der Reu-e mich preis und hei-ßen Trä-nen, mich, die so treu und
ta-ni, m'ab-ban-do-ni, mi fug-gi, e la-sci in pre-da al ri-mor-so ed al pian-to, per pe-na for-se
Cemb. e Basso cont.
132
D. E. L. D. G.
Leporello
Don Giovanni
[Zu Lep
[A Lep.]
in-nig dich ge-liebt hat! (Wie ein Buch kann sie re-den.) O, wenn Ihr wüß-tet, wie ich hier-zu ge-zwun-gen. Du
che t'a-mai co-tan-to! (Pa-re un li-bro stam-pa-to.) Oh in quan-to a que-sto eb-bi le mie ra-gio-ni: è
135
D. G. L. D. E.
Leporello [ironisch] [ironicamente]
Donna Elvira
weißt es? Wahr-haf-tig, ge-zwun-gen durch wicht'-ge Grün-de! Und wel-che Grün-de, dein zü-gel-lo-ser
ve-ro? È ve-ro, e che ra-gio-ni for-ti! E qua-li so-no, se non la tua per-
138
Leichtsinn, dein Herz ohn Lieb und Treue? Doch wars des Him-mels Wil-le; ich fand dich wie-der und werd Ver-gel-tung an dir
fi-dia, la leg-ge-rez-za tu-a? Ma il giu-sto cie-lo vol-le ch'io ti tro-vas-si, per far le sue, le mie ven
141
D. E. D. G.
Don Giovanni
neh-men. O hör auf mich und sei ver-nünf-tig jetzt. (Wahr-haf-tig, das Weib macht mir heiß.) Willst mei-nen Wor-ten du nicht
det-te. Eh vi-a, sia-te più ra-gio-ne-vo-le. (Mi po-ne a ci-men-to co-stei.) Se non cre-de-te al lab-bro
144
D. G. L.
Leporello
Don Giovanni (laut) (forte)
Leporello (leise) (piano)
D. Gio
(laut) (forte)
glau-ben, so glau-be doch die-sem Eh-ren-mann. (Doch nicht im-mer.) Komm und er-zäh-le... Was soll ich ihr denn sa-gen? Ja,
mi-o, cre-de-te a que-sto ga-lant-uo-mo. (Sal-vo il ve-ro.) Via, dil-le un po-co... E co-sa de-vo dir-le? Sì,

Donna Elvira (zu Leporello, Don Giovanni benutzt die Gelegenheit zur Flucht)
(a Leporello, in questo fra tempo Don Giovanni fugge)
Leporello
147
D. G.
D. E.
L.
ja, sag ihr nur al - les. Wohl - an, so re - de... Wahr - haf - tig... schö - ne Don - na... nun sin - te -
sì, dil - le pur tut - to. Eb - ben, fa pre - sto... Ma - da - ma... ve - ra - men - te... in que - sto
Cemb. e Basso cont.
150
L.
D. E.
Donna Elvira (zu Leporello) (a Leporello)
ma - len und all - die - weil es je - der - mann be - kannt, daß ein Vier - eck nicht rund ist... Ha, Ver -
mon - do con - cios - sia co - sa quan - do fos - se che il qua - dro non è ton - do... Scia - gu -
Cemb. e Basso cont.
152
D. E.
[Zu Don Giovanni, den sie noch anwesend glaubt]
[Verso Don Giovanni, che non crede partito]
meß - ner, du wagst es, mei - ner Lei - den noch zu spot - ten? Und du... Him - mel, der Fal - sche ent -
ra - to, co - sì del mio do - lor gio - co ti pren - di? Ah voi... stel - le, l'i - ni - quo fug -
Cemb. e Basso cont.
155
D. E.
L.
Leporello
wich, we - he mir Ar - men, wo - hin floh er... Ach, so laßt ihn nur lau - fen, nein, er ver - dient nicht,
gì, mi - se - ra me, do - ve, in qual par - te... Eh la - scia - te che va - da: e - gli non mer - ta
Cemb. e Basso cont.
158
L.
D. E.
Donna Elvira
Leporello
daß Ihr sein noch ge - den - ket... O, der Ver - bre - cher übt Ver - rat und Be - trug! Gebt euch zu - frie - den nur, ich weiß, Ihr
che di lui ci pen - sia - te... Il scel - le - ra - to m'in - gan - nò, mi tra - dì! Eh con - so - la - te - vi; non sie - te
Cemb. e Basso cont.
161
L.
seid, Ihr wa - ret und Ihr wer - det nicht die er - ste noch letz - te sein; hier seht nur
voi, non fo - ste, e non sa - re - te nè la pri - ma, nè l'ul - ti - ma; guar - da - te
Cemb. e Basso cont.

attacca l'Aria di Leporello [Nº 4]

Nº 4. Aria

7
I
Viol.
II
Viola
L.
fä-ren; der Ver-fas - ser des Werks steht vor Ih-nen, wenn's ge-fäl-lig, so gehn wir es durch, wenn's ge-
mi-o, un ca-ta - lo-go e-gli è che ho fatt' i - o, os-ser-va-te, leg-ge - te con me, os-ser-
Vc.
Cb.
14
Fl.
Ob
Fag.
Cor. in D
a 2
f
p
fäl-lig, so gehn wir es durch. In I - ta-lien sechshundert und vierzig,
va-te, leg-ge - te con me. In I - ta-lia sei-cen-to e qua-ran-ta,

Fl.
Ob.
Fag.
Cor. in D
Viol.
Viola
L.
Vc.
Cb.
hier in Deutschland zweihun-dert und dreißig, hun-dert in
in La - ma - gna due-cen-to e trent' u - na, cen-to in
Frankreich und neun-zig in Persien, a - ber in Spanien, ja, in Spanien schon tausend und drei, tausend und drei,
Fran-cia, in Turchia novant' u - na, ma in I - spagna, ma in I - spagna son già mil-le e tre, mil-le e tre,

36
Fl.
Ob.
Fag.
Cor. in D
a 2
Viol. I II
Viola
L.
Vc.
Cb.
[p]
tausend und drei. Hier ein schmuckes Kammerkätzchen, dort ein net-tes Bür-ger-
mil-le e tre. V'han fra que-ste con-ta-di-ne, ca-me-rie-re e cit-ta-
41
schätzchen, Kammerzofen, Ba-ro-nessen, hochge-bo-re-ne Prin-zessen, Mädchen sind's von je-dem
di-ne, v'han con-tes-se, ba-ro-nesse, marche-sa-ne, prin-ci-pes-se, e v'han don-ne d'ogni
cresc.

46
Fl.
Ob.
Fag.
Cor. in D
a 2
Viol. I II
Viola
L.
Vc.
Cb.
Stan-de, je-der Gat-tung und Ge-stalt, schön und häß-lich, jung und alt. In I-ta-lien
gra-do, d'o-gni for-ma, d'o-gni e-tà, d'o-gni for-ma, d'o-gni e-tà. In I-ta-lia
52
sechs-hun-dert und vierzig, hier in Deutschland zwei-hun-dert und drei-ßig,
sei-cen-to e qua-ran-ta, in La-ma-gna due-cen-to e trent' u-na,

58
Fl.
Ob.
Fag.
Cor. in D
Viol. I II
Viola
L.
Vc.
Cb.
hun - - dert in Frank-reich und neun - zig in Persien, a - ber, a - ber in Spanien, ja, in Spanien schon tausend und
cen - - to in Fran-cia, in Tur-chia no - vant' u-na, ma, ma, ma in I-spa-gna, ma in I-spa-gna son già mil-le e
67
drei, tausend und drei, tausend und drei. Hier ein schmuckes Kammerkätzchen, dort ein nettes Bürger-
tre, mil-le e tre, mil-le e tre. V'han fra que-ste con-ta-di-ne, ca-me-riere e cit-ta-

73
Fl.
Ob.
Fag.
Cor. in D
Viol. I
Viol. II
Viola
L.
Vc.
Cb.
a 2
cresc.
[div.]
schätzchen, Kammerzofen, Baro - nessen, hoch-ge-bo-re-ne Prin-zessen, Mädchen sind's von jedem Stande, jeder Gattung und Ge -
di - ne, v'han con-tesse, ba-ro - nes-se, mar-che-sa-ne, princi - pes-se, e v'han don - ne d'o-gni gra-do, d'ogni for-ma, d'o-gni e -
77
stalt, schön und häß - lich, jung und alt, schön und
tà, d'o - - gni for - - ma, d'o - - gni e - - tà, d'o - gni

81
Fl.
Ob.
Fag.
Cor. in D
Viol. I II
Viola
L.
Vc.
Cb.
a 2
cresc.
Andante con moto
Andante con moto
[div.]
häß - lich, jung und alt. Bei Blon - di - nen preist er als Ken-ner hol - de
for - ma, d'o - gni e - tà. Nel - la bion-da e - gli ha l'u - san - za, di lo -
90
An - mut und sanf - tes We - sen, bei Brü - net - ten fe - ste Treu - e, bei den
dar la gen - ti - lez - za, nel - la bru - na, la co - stan - za, nel - la

98
Fl.
Ob.
Fag.
Cor. in D
Viol. I
Viol. II
Viola
L.
Vc.
Cb.
Blas - sen sü - ßes Schmachten. Vol - le sucht er für den Win - ter, für den
bian - ca la dol - cez - za; vuol d'in-ver - no la gras-sot - ta, vuol d'e-
104
Som - mer schlanke Kin-der. Gro - ße liebt er gra - vi - tä - tisch,
sta - te la ma-grot-ta; è la gran-de ma - e - sto - sa,
cresc.

110
Fl.
Ob.
Fag.
Cor. in D
Viol. I
Viol. II
Viola
L.
Vc.
Cb.
p
cresc.
f
a 2
I
ernst und vor - nehm, ma - je - stä - - - - - - - tisch. Doch die
è la gran - de ma - e - sto - - - - - - - - sa, la pic-
116
Klei-ne, doch die Kleine, doch die Kleine, ja die Kleine, ja die Kleine, ja die Kleine, ja die Kleine, ja die Kleine, ja die
ci - na, la pic-ci - na, la pic - ci - na, la pic - ci - na, la pic - ci - na, la pic - ci - na, la pic-ci - na, la pic-ci - na, la pic-

Fl.
Ob.
Fag.
Cor. in D
Viol. I II
Viola
L.
Klei-ne, die sei pos-sier-lich, die sei ma-nier-lich, sei fein und zierlich. Daß dies Büchlein Stoff er-hal-te,
ci-na è o-gnor vez-zo-sa, è o-gnor vez-zo-sa, è o-gnor vez-zo-sa; del-le vec-chie fa con-qui-sta,
Vc.
Cb.
schwärmt er manchmal auch selbst für Al-te; doch wofür er immer glühte, ist der Ju-gend er-ste
pel pia-cer di por-le in li-sta; ma passion predomi-nan-te è la gio-vin prin-ci-

135
Fl.
Ob.
Fag.
Cor. in D
Viol. I
Viol. II
Viola
L.
Vc.
Cb.
cresc.
mfp
mf
Blü-te. Da's ihm gleich ist, ob sie bleich ist, ob sie bet - telt o - der
pian-te; non si pic - ca, se sia ric - ca, se sia brut - ta, se sia
140
reich ist, ob sie bet-telt, o-der ob sie reich ist, nimmt er Wei-ber je - der Sor - te. Nun, Ihr
bel - la, se sia ric-ca, brut-ta, se sia bel - la, pur - chè por-ti la gon-nel - la, voi sa-

148
Fl.
Ob.
Fag.
Cor. in D
148
I
Viol.
II
Viola
L.
wißt ja, wie's da geht, nun, Ihr wißt ja, wie's da geht. Doch wo-zu noch all die Wor-te, kennt ja
pe-te quel che fa, voi sa-pe-te quel che fa, pur-chè por-ti la gon-nel-la, voi sa-
Vc.
Cb.
157
Fl.
Ob.
Fag.
Cor. in D
157
I
Viol.
II
Viola
L.
selbst ihn ganz ge-nau, kennt ja selbst ihn, kennt ja selbst ihn ganz ge-nau, ganz ge-nau,
pe-te quel che fa, voi sa-pe-te, voi sa-pe-te quel che fa, quel che fa,
Vc.
Cb.

Sechste Szene

Donna Elvira (allein).

Scena VI

Donna Elvira (sola).

Recitativo

segue Coro № 5

Siebente Szene

Masetto. Zerlina. Chor der Bauern und Bäuerinnen
[welche spielen, tanzen und singen].

Scena VII

Masetto, Zerlina e Coro di contadini e contadine
[che suonano, ballano e cantano].

Nº 5. Coro

15
a 2
Fl.
Ob.
Fag.
Cor. in G
Viol. I II
Viola
[div.]
Zerlina
Z.
O ihr Mädchen, zur Lie-be ge-bo-ren, zur Lie-be ge-bo-ren, auf, be-
Gio-vi-net-te che fa-te all' a-mo-re, che fa-te all' a-mo-re, non la-
Vc.
Cb.
p
21
nü-tzet die blühende Zeit, die blühende Zeit, die blühende Zeit! Wenn ihr schmachtet, in Sehnsucht ver-loren, in Sehnsucht ver-
scia-te che pas-si l'e-tà, che pas-si l'e-tà, che pas-si l'e-tà! Se nel se-no vi bu-li-ca il co-re, vi bu-li-ca il

27
Fl.
Fag.
Viol. I
Viol. II
Viola
Z.
lo-ren, seht die Hil-fe, sie ist schon be - reit.
co-re, il ri-me-dio ve-de-te-lo quà.
O die Freu-de, die Freu-de ist
Che pia-cer, che pia-cer che sa-
Vc.
Cb.
33
a 2
Ob.
Cor. in G
da!
rà!
Chor der Bäuerinnen
Coro di contadine
Soprano
Alto
Coro
Ah,
A
o die Freude, die Freude ist da, tra la le ra la, tra la le ra la!
che pia-cer, che pia-cer che sa - rà, la la la ra la, la la la ra la!

40
Fl.
a 2
I
p
Ob.
Fag.
Cor. in G
Viol. I
Viol. II
[div.]
Viola
Masetto
M.
O ihr Bursche, mit Leichtsinn im Her-zen, mit Leichtsinn im Herzen, flattert ja nicht zu lan-ge um-her, so hin und
Gio-vi-net-ti leg-gie-ri di te-sta, leg-gie-ri di te-sta, non an-da-te gi-ran-do quà e là, e quà e
Vc.
Cb.
46
her, so hin und her! Freude bringt wohl das Tändeln und Scherzen, das Tändeln und Scherzen, doch ein Weibchen erfreut euch noch
là, e quà e là. Po-co du-ra de' mat-ti la fe-sta, de' mat-ti la fe-sta, ma per me co-min-cia-to non

52
Fl.
Ob.
Fag.
Cor. in G
Viol. I II
Viola
M.
mehr, es erfreut euch noch mehr.
ha, comin-cia - to non ha.
O die Freu-de, die Freu-de ist da!
Che pia - cer, che pia-cer che sa - rà!
Chor der Bauern
Coro di contadini
Tenore
Coro
Basso
Ah,
A
Vc.
Cb.
a 2
59
Z.
Zerlina
Komm, o kom-me, Ge-lieb-ter, zum
Vie - ni, vie - ni, ca-ri-no e go-
Masetto
Komm, o kom-me, Ge-lieb-te, zum
Vie - ni, vie - ni, ca-ri-na e go-
o die Freu-de, die Freu-de ist da, tra la le ra la, tra la le ra la!
che pia - cer, che pia-cer che sa - rà, la la la ra la, la la la ra la!

65
Fl.
Ob.
Fag.
Cor. in G
65
I Viol. II
Viola
[div.]
Z.
Fe-ste, laßt uns tan-zen und sin-gen, ihr Gä-ste, laßt uns tan-zen und sin-gen, ihr Gä-ste; o die Freu-de, die Freu-de ist
dia-mo, e can-tia-mo, e bal-lia-mo, e sal-tia-mo, vie-ni, vie-ni, ca-ri-no e go-dia-mo; che pia-cer, che pia-cer che sa-
M.
Fe-ste, laßt uns tan-zen und sin-gen, ihr Gä-ste, laßt uns tan-zen und sin-gen, ihr Gä-ste; o die Freu-de, die Freu-de ist
dia-mo, e can-tia-mo, e bal-lia-mo, e sal-tia-mo, vie-ni, vie-ni, ca-ri-na e go-dia-mo; che pia-cer, che pia-cer che sa-
Vc.
Cb.
71
a 2
71
da! Ah, o die Freude, die Freu-de ist da!
rà! A che pia-cer, che pia-cer che sa-rà!
Chor der Bauern und Bäuerinnen
Coro di contadini e contadine
Coro
Soprano
Alto
Ah, o die Freude, die Freu-de ist
A che pia-cer, che pia-cer che sa-
Tenore
Basso

Achte Szene

Masetto. Zerlina. Chor der Bauern und Bäuerinnen.
Don Giovanni und Leporello (von der Seite).

Scena VIII

Masetto, Zerlina, Coro di contadini e contadine.
Don Giovanni e Leporello (da parte).

Recitativo

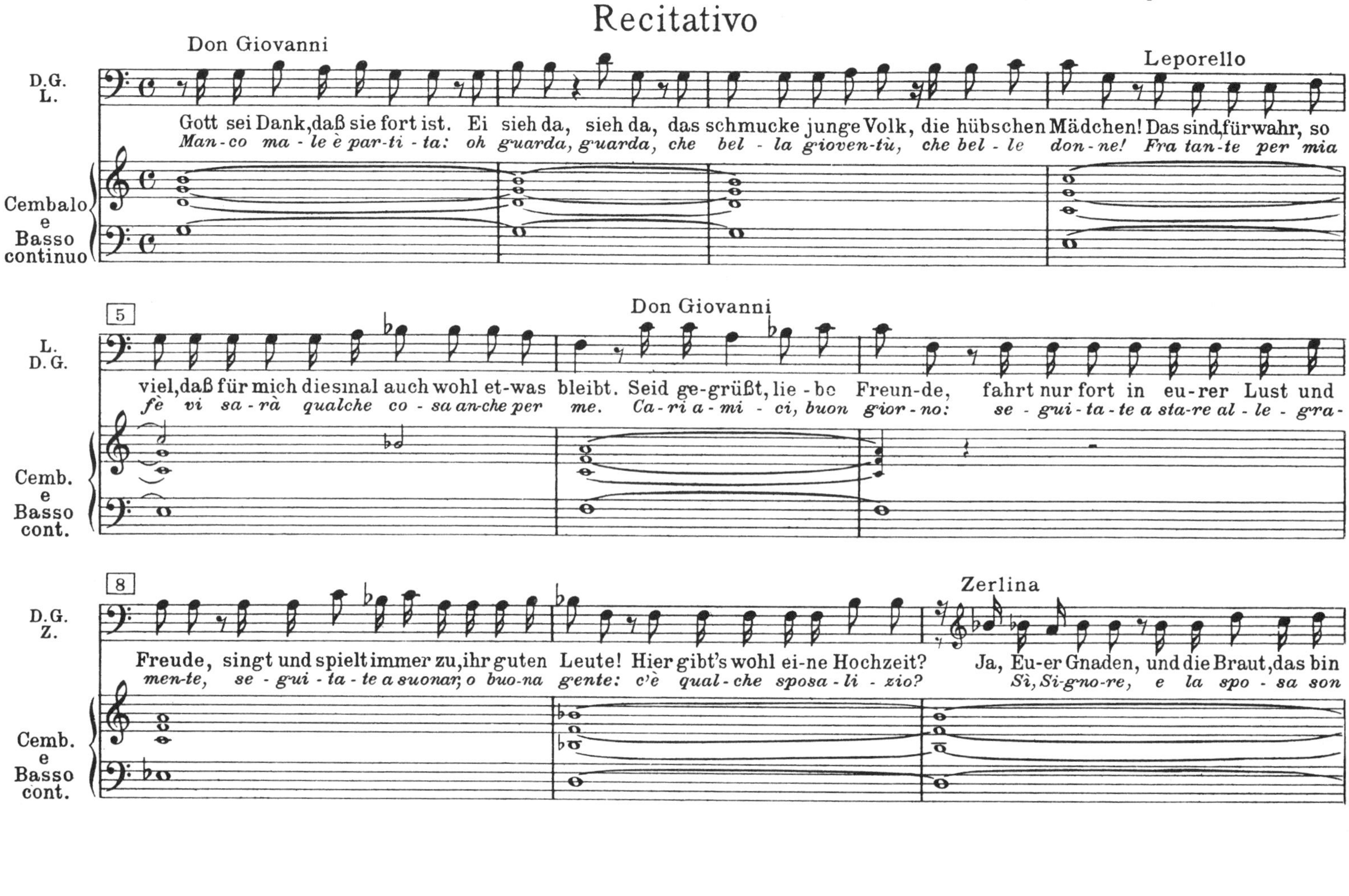

11 Don Giovanni Masetto Don Giovanni
Z. D.G. M.
ich. Wahr-lich, das freut mich. Der Bräut'-gam? Ich, euch zu die-nen. Vor-treff-lich, „Mir zu die-nen." Gut ge-
i-o. Me ne con-so-lo. Lo spo-so? Io, per ser-vir-la. Oh bra-vo, per ser-vir-mi: que-sto è
Cemb. e Basso cont.
14 Leporello Zerlina Don Giovanni
D.G. L. Z.
sprochen, ganz wie ein Mann von Stande! Ja, wie ein guter E-hemann. O, mein Ma-set-to hat das beste Herz. Ganz wie ich
ve-ro par-lar da ga-lant-uo-mo. Ba-sta che sia ma-ri-to. Oh il mio Ma-set-to è un uom d'ot-ti-mo co-re. Oh anch' io, ve-
17 Zerlina Don Giovanni Masetto
D.G. Z. M.
sel-ber, sei-en wir dar-um Freun-de; wie ist dein Na-me? Zer-li-na. Der dei-ne? Ma-
de-te, vo-glio che sia-mo a-mi-ci; il vo-stro no-me? Zer-li-na. E il tu-o? Ma-
20 Don Giovanni
M. D.G.
set-to. Nun, lie-ber Freund Ma-set-to, und lie-be Braut Zer-li-na, ich ver-sich-re euch mei-ner Huld und
set-to. O ca-ro il mio Ma-set-to, ca-ra la mia Zer-li-na, v'e-si-bi-sco la mi-a pro-te-
[Zu Leporello, der mit den anderen Bauernmädchen scherzt]
[A Leporello che fa dei scherzi alle altre contadine]
23 Leporello
D.G. L.
Gna-de. Le-po-rel-lo... Was machst du da, du Schlin-gel? Auch ich, gnä-di-ger Herr, ich ver-
zio-ne. Le-po-rel-lo... co-sa fai lì, bir-bo-ne? Anch' io, ca-ro pa-dro-ne, e-si-
26 Don Giovanni
L. D.G.
sich-re die Leutchen meiner Gnade. Hur-tig, füh-re sie fort und geh mit ih-nen so-gleich zu mei-nem Schlosse,
bi-sco la mia pro-te-zi-o-ne. Pre-sto, va con co-stor: nel mio pa-laz-zo con-du-ci-li sul fat-to:
29
D.G.
sor-ge aufs be-ste für Scho-ko-la-de, Kaf-fee, Wein und für Spei-sen, sor-ge für Un-ter-
or-di-na ch'ab-bia-no cioc-co-lat-ta, caf-fè, vi-ni, pro-sciut-ti; cer-ca di-ver-tir

segue Aria di Masetto Nº

Nº 6. Aria

Allegro di molto
2 Flauti
2 Fagotti
2 Corni in F
Allegro di molto
Violino I
II
Viola
Masetto
Violoncello
Contrabasso
a 2
[f]
f
p
tr
Masetto
Hab's verstanden, gnäd'-ger Herr,
Ho ca-pi-to, Si-gnor, sì,
8
Fl.
Fag.
Cor. in F
Viol.
M.
Vc.
Cb.
gnäd'-ger Herr, höf-lich dankend geh ich fort. Weil es euch denn so be-
Si-gnor sì, chi-no il ca-po, e me ne vo. Già che piace a voi co-

15
Fl.
Fag.
Cor. in F
Viol. I
Viol. II
Viola
M.
Vc.
Cb.
cresc.
f
p
[f]
tr
liebt, sag ich nicht ein ein-zig Wort, ich sa-ge nicht ein ein-zig Wort. O, wie könnt ich euch miß-
sì, al-tre re-pli-che non fo, no, no, no, no, no, no, non fo. Ca-va-lier voi sie-te
23
[p]
traun, seid Ihr doch ein Ka-va-lier; deut-lich sagt mir eu-re Huld, was Ihr ha-ben wollt von
già, du-bi-tar non pos-so af-fè; me lo di-ce la bon-tà che vo-le-te a-ver per

31
Fl.
Fag.
Cor. in F
Viol.
I
II
Viola
M.
Vc.
Cb.
cresc.
f
[f]
p
fp
[div.]
(Beiseite zu Zerlina)
(Da parte a Zerlina)
mir, ja was Ihr ha-ben wollt von mir. Ha, du Fal-sche, Un-ge-treu-e, mich be-törst du nicht aufs neu - e, mich be -
me, a - ver per me, a - ver per me. Bric-co-nac-cia, ma-lan-dri-na, fo-stio-gnor la mia ru - i - na, fo-stio -
38
sf
(Zu Leporello [der ihn fortzubringen sucht])
(A Leporello [che lo vuol condur seco])
(Zu Zerlina)
(A Zerlina)
törst du nicht aufs neu - e. Nun, ich komm schon. Bleib nur, blei-be, Eh - re
gnor la mia ru - i - na. Ven - go, ven - go. Re - sta, re - sta, è u - nu

45
Fl.
Fag.
Cor. in F
Viol. I
Viol. II
Viola
M.
sol - chem bra - ven Wei-be; mag der gnäd'ge Herr dich ma-chen nur recht bald zur gnäd'gen
co - sa mol - to o - ne-sta; fac-cia il no-stro ca - va - lie - re ca - va - lie-ra an-co - ra
Vc.
Cb.
53
cresc.
[div.]
(Beiseite zu Zerlina)
(Da parte a Zerlina)
Frau, nur recht bald zur gnäd'gen Frau! Ha, du Fal-sche, Un-ge-treu-e, mich be-törst du nicht aufs neu - e, mich b
te, ca - va - lie-ra an-co - ra - te! Bric-con-nac - cia, ma-lan-dri-na, fo-sti o-gnor la mia ru - i - na, fo - sti

60
Fl.
Fag.
Cor. in F
Viol. I
II
Viola
M.
Vc.
Cb.
f
p
cresc.
(Zu Leporello [der ihn fortzubringen sucht])
(A Leporello [che lo vuol condur seco])
(Zu Zerlina)
(A Zerlina)
törst du nicht aufs neu-e. Nun, ich komm schon. Bleib nur, blei-be, Eh - re
gnor la mia ru-i-na. Ven - go, ven - go. Re - sta, re-sta, è u - na
67
sol - chem bra - ven Wei-be; mag der gnäd'ge Herr dich ma chen nur recht
co - sa mol - to o - ne-sta; fac-cia il no-stro ca - va - lie - re ca - va -

74
Fl.
Fag.
Cor. in F
Viol. I
Viol. II
Viola
M.
bald zur gnäd'gen Frau, nur recht bald zur gnäd'gen Frau, mag der gnäd'ge Herr dich ma-chen nur recht bald zur gnäd'gen Frau, mag der
lie-ra an-co-ra te, ca-va-lie-ra an-co-ra te, fac-cia il no-stro ca-va-lie-re ca-va-lie-ra an-co-ra te, fac-cia il
Vc.
Cb.
82
gnäd'-ge Herr dich ma-chen nur recht bald zur gnäd'gen Frau, nur recht bald zur gnäd'gen Frau, nur recht bald zur gnäd'gen
no-stro ca-va-lie-re ca-va-lie-ra an-co-ra te, ca-va-lie-ra an-co-ra te, ca-va-lie-ra an-co-ra

Neunte Szene

Don Giovanni. Zerlina.

Scena IX

Don Giovanni e Zerlina.

Recitativo

segue il Duettino
di Zerlina e Don Giovanni Nº 7

No. 7. Duettino

16
Fl.
Ob.
Fag.
Cor. in A
Viol. I
Viol. II
Viola
Z.
schwer, bald wie-der bang und schwer.
cor, ma può bur-lar-mi an-cor.
Ma-set-to wür-de-ster-ben.
Mi fà pie-tà Ma-set-to.
D. G.
Laß nicht umsonst mich wer-ben;
Vie-ni, mio bel di-let-to;
Vc.
Cb.
28
23
a 2
Kaum kann ich wi-der-stre-ben, kaum wi-der-stre-ben, kaum wi-der-stre-ben.
Pre-sto non son più for-te, non son più for-te, non son più for-te.
Glück soll dich stets um-ge-ben.
io can-gie-rò tua sor-te.
Komm, o folg mir.
Vie-ni, vie-ni.

30
Fl.
Ob.
Fag.
Cor. in A
Viol. I
Viol. II
Viola
Z.
D. G.
Vc.
Cb.
p cresc.
p
Ach, kann ich wohl es wagen,
Vor - rei, e non vor - re - i,
mein Herz klopft gar zu_sehr;
mi tre-ma un po-co il cor;
Reich mir die Hand, mein Le-ben,
Là ci da-rem la ma-no,
komm auf mein Schloß mit mir;
là mi di - re - te sì;
es ist nicht weit von
partiam, ben mio, da
38
mf
bald wie-der bang und schwer.
ma può bur-la - mi an-cor.
Ma - set - to würde - ster - ben.
Mi fà pie - tà_ Ma - set - to.
Kaum kann ich wi - der-
Pre - sto non son più
hier.
qui.
Laß nicht umsonst mich wer-ben;
Vie - ni, mio bel di - let - to;
Glück soll dich stets um-ge-ben.
io can-gie-rò tua sor-te.

44
Fl.
Ob.
Fag.
Cor. in A
Viol. I
II
Viola
Z.
D.G.
Vc.
Cb.
streben, kaum wi-der-streben, kaum wi-der-streben.
for-te, non son più for-te, non son più for-te.
O komm, o komm!
An-diam, an-diam!
Wohl-an!
An-diam!
So dein zu sein auf e-wig, wie
An-diam, an-diam, mio be-ne, a
52
[div.]
glücklich, o wie se-lig, wie se-lig werd ich sein,
ri-sto-rar le pe-ne d'un in-no-cen-te a-mor,
so dein zu sein auf e-wig,
an-diam, an-diam, mio be-ne,

60
Fl.
Ob.
Fag.
Cor. in A
Viol. I II
Viola
Z.
D. G.
Vc.
Cb.
[div.]
pizz.
arco
glücklich, o wie se-lig, wie se - lig werd ich sein!
ri - sto-rar le pe-ne d'un in - no - cen - te a - mor!
Wohl -
An -
O komm!
An - diam!
68
an!
diam!
Wohl - an!
An - diam!
Komm, laß uns glücklich sein, komm,
An-diam, mio ben, an-diam, le

Zehnte Szene

Die Vorigen. Donna Elvira [die mit verzweifelter Gebärde Don Giovanni anhält].

Scena X

I suddetti e Donn' Elvira [che ferma con atti disperatissimi Do Giovanni].

Recitativo

11
Zerlina
Don Giovanni (leise zu Zerlina)
(piano a Zerlina)
D.E.
Z.
D.G.
worf - ner, wie grausam du scherzest... A-ber sprecht, Eu-er Gna-den... ist's Wahr-heit, was sie sag-te? Ach, die-se Un-glück-sel'-ge
de-le, co-me tu ti di-ver-ti... Ma, Si-gnor Ca-va-lie-re... è ver quel ch'el-la di-ce? La po-ve-ra in-fe-li-ce
Cemb. e Basso cont.
14
D.G.
ist ver-liebt bis zum Wahnsinn, und nur aus Mit-leid spiel ich den Ver-liebten; war-um, ach, ist mein Herz so weich nur ge-schaf-fen.
è di me in-na-mo-ra-ta, e per pie-tà deg-gio fin-ge-re a-mo-re; ch'io son per mia dis-gra-zia uom di buon co-re.
Cemb. e Basso cont.
attacca l'Aria di Donna Elvira Nº8

Nº 8. Aria

Allegro
Violino I
II
Viola
Donna Elvira
O flieh, Be-trog-ne, flieh und trau dem Fal-schen
Ah fug - gi il tra-di-tor, non lo la-sciar più
Cembalo e Basso continuo
Violoncello
Contrabasso
7
Viol. I II
Viola
D.E.
nicht; sein Blick ist Heu-che-lei, und Lü - ge, was er spricht.
dir; il lab-bro è men-ti-tor, fal-la - ce il ci-glio.
Vc.
Cb.

14
I
Viol.
II
Viola
D. E.
Mein Kum - mer, mei - ne Zäh-ren, sie sa - gen dir ge - nug, sie mö - gen vor Be -
Da miei tor-men - ti im - pa - ra a cre - der a quel cor, e na - scail tuo ti -
Vc.
Cb.
p
20
trug dir Schutz ge-wäh - ren. O flie-he, flie - he, o flieh, Be-trog-ne,
mor dal mio pe-ri - glio. Ah fug-gi, fug - gi, ah fug - gi il tra-di-
26
flieh und trau dem Fal - schen nicht; sein Blick ist Heu - che-lei, und Lü - ge, was er
tor, non lo la-sciar più dir; il lab-bro è men - ti - tor, fal-la - ce il ci -
tr

Elfte Szene

Don Giovanni (allein). Dann Don Ottavio und Donna Anna.

Scena XI

Don Giovanni (solo); poi Don Ottavio e Donna Anna.

Recitativo

Zwölfte Szene

Die Vorigen. Donna Elvira.

Scena XII

I suddetti. Donna Elvira.

No. 9. Quartetto

8
Fl.
Clar. in B
Fag.
Cor. in B
Viol. I II
Viola
D.A.
D.E.
D.O.
Vc.
Cb.
Donna Anna
Himmel, welch edles Frauenbild, welch hol-de Ma-je-stät! Wie mir ihr Schmerz, ihr
Cie-li, che a-spetto no-bi-le, che dol-ce ma-e-stà! Il suo pal-lor, le
nun droht auch dir Ver-rat.
te vuol tra-di-re an-cor.
Don Ottavio
Himmel, welch edles Frauenbild, welch hol-de Ma-je-stät! Wie mir ihr Schmerz, ihr
Cie-li, che a-spetto no-bi-le, che dol-ce ma-e-stà! Il suo pal-lor, le
15
Fl.
Clar. in B
Fag.
Cor. in B
Viol. I II
Viola
D.A.
D.O.
D.G.
Vc.
Cb.
Trä-nenblick tief in die See-le geht, tief in die See-le geht!
la-gri-me m'empiono di pie-tà, m'empiono di pie-tà.
Trä-nenblick tief in die See-le geht, tief in die See-le geht!
la-gri-me m'empiono di pie-tà, m'empiono di pie-tà.
Don Giovanni [beiseite, Donna Elvira horcht auf]
[a parte, Donna Elvira ascolta]
Das ar-me, gu-te Mädchen, ihr Freun-de, ist von
La po-ve-ra ra-gaz-za è paz-za, a-mi ci

21
Fl.
Clar. in B
Fag.
Cor. in B
Viol. I II
Viola
D.G.
Sinnen, ihr Freunde, ist von Sinnen, ich bit - te, geht von hinnen, dann wird sie ru-hig sein, dann wird sie ru-hig
mie-i, è pazza, a-mi - ci miei; la-scia - te-mi con le-i, for - se si cal-me-rà, for - se si cal-me-
Vc.
Cb.
cresc.
28
Donna Elvira
D.E.
O glaubt dem frechen Lügner nicht, verwei - let hier, ver-wei-let,
Ah non cre-de-te al per-fi-do, re-sta - te, ancor, re - sta - te,
Donna Anna
D.A.
Auf wen ist hier zu baun, wem sollen wir ver-
A chi si cre-de-rà, a chi si cre-de-
Don Ottavio
D.O.
Auf wen ist hier zu baun, wem sollen wir ver-
A chi si cre-de-rà, a chi si cre-de-
sein! Von Sinnen ist die Ar-me. O ei-let!
rà! È paz-za, non ba-da-te. È pazza!

33
Fl.
Clar. in B
Fag.
Cor. in B
Viol. I II
Viola
D.A.
D.E.
D.O.
D.G.
Vc.
Cb.
p cresc.
f
a 2
tr
cresc.
traun, auf wen ist hier zu baun, wem hier zu traun? Wie er-greift mich un-nenn-ba-res
rà, a chi si cre-de-rà, si cre - de - rà. Cer-to mo - to d'i-gno-to tor-
verweilet, o glaubt dem frechen Lügner nicht, ver - wei - let!
re-state, ah non cre-de-te al per-fi - do, re - sta - te!
traun, auf wen ist hier zu baun, wem hier zu traun? Wie er-greift mich un-nenn-ba-res
rà, a chi si cre-de-rà, si cre - de - rà. Cer-to mo - to d'i-gno-to tor-
Wie er-greift mich un-nenn-ba-res
Cer-to mo - to d'i-gno-to tor-
37
p
Ban - gen, o wie fühlt sich die See-le be - fan - gen,
men - to dentro l'al - ma gi - ra-re mi sen - to,
Ha, von Ab-scheu, Ver-ach-tung und Bangen fühl ich ganz meine See-le be-
Sde-gno, rab-bia, dis-pet-to, tor-men-to den-tro l'al - ma gi-ra - re mi
Ban - gen, o wie fühlt sich die See-le be - fan - gen,
men - to dentro l'al - ma gi - ra-re mi sen - to,
Ban - gen, o wie fühlt sich die See-le be - fan - gen,
men - to dentro l'al - ma gi - ra-re mi sen - to,

40
Cor. in B
Viol. I II
Viola
D.A.
was in mir für die Ar - me sich re - get, ach, zu deu - ten, zu deu - ten ver-mag ich es
che mi di - ce per quell' in - fe - li - ce cen - to co - se che in-ten - der, che inten - der non
D.E.
fangen, was noch hält mich, den Frevler zu scho - nen, ach, zu deu - ten ver-mag ich es
sento, che mi di - ce di quel tradi - to - re cen - to co - se che in-ten - der non
D.O.
was in mir für die Ar - me sich re - get, ach, zu deu - ten ver-mag ich es
che mi di - ce per quell' in - fe - li - ce cen - to co - se che in-ten - der non
D.G.
was in mir für die Ar - me sich re - get, ach, zu deu - ten ver-mag ich es
che mi di - ce per quell' in - fe - li - ce cen - to co - se che in-ten - der non
Vc.
Cb.
44
Fl.
Clar. in B
Fag.
a 2
Cor. in B
Viol. I II
Viola
D.A.
nicht, nein, nein, was in mir sich
sà, no, no, che in - ten - der non
D.E.
nicht, nein, was noch hält mich, den Frevler zu schonen, den Frevler zu scho - nen, ach, zu deu-ten ver-mag ich es
sà, no, che mi di - ce di quel tra-di - to - re, di quel tra-di - to - re cen - to co - se che in-ten - der non
D.O.
nicht, nein, nein, was in mir sich
sà, no, no, che in - ten - dor non
D.G.
nicht, nein, nein, ach, zu deu - ten ver-mag ich es
sà, no, no, cen - to co - se che in-ten - der non
Vc.
Cb.

47
Fl.
Clar. in B
Fag.
I
Cor. in B
47
I
Viol.
II
Viola
D.A.
regt,
sà,
ich deut es mir nicht.
che in - ten - der non sà.
D.E.
nicht, was noch hält mich, den Frevler, den Frev-ler zu scho-nen, ach, zu deu-ten ver-mag ich es nicht.
sà, che mi di-ce, mi di-ce di quel tra-di-to-re cen-to co-se che in-ten-der non sà.
D.O.
regt,
sà,
ich deut es mir nicht.
che in - ten - der non sà.
D.G.
nicht,
sà,
ach, zu deu - ten ver-mag ich es nicht.
cen - to co - se che in-ten - der non sà.
Vc.
Cb.
50
Fl.
Clar. in B
Fag.
50
I
Viol.
II
Viola
Donna Anna (beiseite) (a parte)
D. A.
Nein, für Wahn-sinn spricht kein
Non ha l'a-ria di paz-
Don Ottavio (beiseite) (a parte)
D.O.
Nein, nicht e-her will ich weichen, bis mir Klarheit wird und Licht.
Io di quà non va-do vi-a, se non sco-pro questo af-far.
Vc.
Cb.

54
Fl.
Clar. in B
Fag.
Cor. in B
54
I
Viol.
II
Viola
D.A.
Zeichen aus dem ed-len An-ge-sicht.
zi-a il suo volto, il suo par-lar.
D.E.
D. Elvira
Die-ser
Da quel
D.G.
Don Giovanni
Um dem Arg-wohn zu ent-weichen, gilt es ke-cke Zu-ver-sicht.
Se men va-do, si po-tri-a qualche co-sa so-spet-tar.
Vc.
Cb.
59
Fl.
Clar. in B
Fag.
Cor. in B
59
I
Viol.
II
Viola
D.A.
Donna Anna (zu Donna Elvira)
(a Donna Elvira)
Al-so je-ner?
Dun-que que-gli?
D.E.
Blick, sein fal-sches Au-ge kün-det euch den Bö-se-wicht.
cef-fo si do-vri-a la ner' al-ma giu-di-car.
Ist ein Ver-
È un tra-di-
D.O.
Don Ottavio (zu Don Giovanni)
(a Don Giovanni)
Sie von Sin-nen?
Dunque quel-la?
D.G.
Don Giovanni
Ja ganz von Sin-nen.
È paz-za-rel-la.
Vc.
Cb.

63
Fl.
Clar. in B
Fag.
Cor. in B
63
I
Viol.
II
Viola
[div.]
D.A.
D.E.
D.O.
D.G.
Vc.
Cb.
Zwei - fel re - gen sich in
In - co - min - cio a du - bi -
rä-ter!
to-re.
Mis-se-tä-ter, Mis-se-tä-ter, fre-cher Lügner!
Men-ti - to-re, men-ti-to-re, men-ti - to-re!
Zwei - fel re - gen sich in
In - co - min - cio a du - bi -
Un - glück-sel'ge!
In - fe - li-ce!
68
Fl.
Cor. in B
68
I
Viol.
II
Viola
D.A.
mir.
tar.
D.O.
mir.
tar.
Don Giovanni (leise zu Donna Elvira)
(piano a Donna Elvira)
D.G.
Stil-le, still, es na-hen Leu-te, o ver-su-che, dich zu fas-sen, läßt du nicht von die-sem Streite, droht für dich und mich Ge-
Zit - to, zit - to, che la gen-te si ra-duna a noi d'in-tor-no, sia-te un po - co più pru-den-te, vi fa - re - te cri - ti -
Vc.
Cb.

70
Fl.
Clar. in B
Fag.
Cor. in B
Viol. I II
Viola
Donna Elvira (laut zu Don Giovanni) (forte a Don Giovanni)
D.E.
Nein, ich schweig nicht, du Vermeßner, hoffe nichts, du Ehrvergeßner, mein Geschick und dein Verbrechen,
Non spe - rar - lo, o scel-le-ra - to, ho per-du - ta la prudenza, le tue col-pe ed il mio sta-to
D.G.
fahr!
car!
Vc.
Cb.
73
[div.]
Donna Anna [beiseite, Don Giovanni beobachtend]
[a parte, guardando Don Giovanni]
D.A.
Die - ses
Que - gli ac -
Donna Elvira
al - len werd es of - fen - bar, al - len werd es of - fen - bar,
vo - glio a tut - ti pa - le - sar, vo - glio a tut - ti pa - le - sar,
Don Ottavio [beiseite, Don Giovanni beobachtend]
[a parte, guardando Don Giovanni]
D.O.
Die - ses
Que - gli ac -
Don Giovanni
D.G.
Stil - le, still, es na - hen
Zit - to, zit - to, che la

75
Fl.
Clar. in B
Fag.
Cor. in B
75
I
Viol.
II
Viola
D.A.
Flü - stern, die - ses Schmei - cheln, sein Er-
cen - ti sì som - mes - si, quel can-
D.E.
schweige, schweige, du Ver-meß-ner, hof-fe nichts, du Ehr-ver-geß-ner,
non spe-rar-lo, o scel-le-ra-to, ho per-du-ta la pru-den-za,
D.O.
Flü - stern, die - ses Schmei - cheln, sein Er-
cen - ti sì som - mes - si, quel can-
D.G.
Leu-te, o ver-su-che, dich zu fas-sen, läßt du nicht von die-sem
gen-te si ra-du-na a noi d'in-tor-no, sia-te un po - co più pru-
Vc.
Cb.
77
Fl.
Clar. in B
Fag.
Cor. in B
77
I
Viol.
II
Viola
D.A.
cresc.
f
p
rö - - - - ten, sein Er - blei-chen, al - les sind ganz sich - re
giar - - - - si di co - lo - re, son in - di - zi trop - po es-
D.E.
cresc.
f
p
mein Geschick und dein Verbrechen, al - len werd es of - fen - bar,
le tue col-pe ed il mio sta-to vo-glio a tut - ti pa - le - sar,
D.O.
cresc.
f
p
rö - - - - ten, sein Er - blei-chen, al - les sind ganz sich - re
giar - - - - si di co - lo - re, son in - di - zi trop - po es-
D.G.
cresc.
f
p
Strei-te, droht für dich und mich Ge-fahr, lei - se, lei - se, nur ge-
den-te, vi fa-re-te cri-ti-car, sia-te un po - co più pru-
Vc.
Cb.

80
Clar. in B
Fag.
Cor. in B
Viol. I II
Viola
D.A.
Zei - chen, sei-ne Schuld wird of - fen-bar, sei - ne
pres - si, che mi fan de-ter - mi - nar, che mi
D.E.
schweige, schweige, du Vermeßner, schweig, Ver-meßner, hof-fe nichts, du Ehrver-
ho per-du - ta la prudenza, non spe-rar-lo, ho per-du - ta la pru-
D.O.
Zei - chen, sei-ne Schuld wird of - fen-bar, sei - ne
pres - si, che mi fan de-ter - mi - nar, che mi
D.G.
las - sen, nur ge-las-sen, o ver-su-che, dich zu fas-sen,
den - te, zit - to, zit - to, si ra-du-na a noi la gen-te,
Vc.
Cb.
83
Schuld wird of - fen - bar, sei - ne
fan de - ter - mi - nar, che mi
geß-ner, hof-fe nichts, du Ehr-ver-geß-ner, mein Ge-schick und dein Ver-
den - za, non spe-rar - lo, o scel-le - ra - to, le tue col-pe ed il mio
Schuld wird of - fen - bar, sei - ne
fan de - ter - mi - nar, che mi
o ver-su-che, dich zu fas-sen, läßt du nicht von diesem Strei - te,
zit - to, zit - to, zit - to, zit - to, sia-te un po - co più pru-den - te,

85
Fl.
Clar. in B
Fag.
Cor. in B
Viol. I
II
Viola
D.A.
D.E.
D.O.
D.G.
Vc.
Cb.
pp
pizz.
Schuld wird of - fen - bar.
fan de - ter - mi - nar.
[Geht ab]
[Parte]
bre-chen, al - len werd es of - fen - bar.
sta - to vo - glio a tut - ti pa - le - sar.
Schuld wird of - fen - bar.
fan de - ter - mi - nar.
droht für dich und mich Ge - fahr, droht uns Ge - fahr.
vi fa - re - te, vi fa - re - te cri - ti - car.

Recitativo

Don Giovanni
D.G.
Ar - mes be - tör - tes Mäd - chen, sie zu be - schü - tzen, folg ich ihr nach; es
Po - ve - ra sven - tu - ra - ta, i pas - si suo - i vo - glio se - guir: non
Cembalo e Basso continuo
3
könn - te sie leicht ein Un - glück tref - fen: Drum ver - gebt mir, o schö - ne Don - na An - na; kann ich
vo - glio che fac - cia un pre - ci - pi - zio: Per - do - na - te, bel - lis - si - ma Donn' An - na; se ser -
Cemb. e Basso cont.

attacca Recitativo coi stromenti Nº 10

Dreizehnte Szene

[Don Ottavio. Donna Anna.]

Scena XIII

[Don Ottavio e Donna Anna.]

Nº 10. Recitativo ed Aria

7
Fl.
Ob.
Fag.
Cor. in Es
Tr. in C
7
I
Viol.
II
Viola
D. A.
Hab Erbarmen, o rette mich!
Per pietà, soccorretemi!
O Himmel!
Oh Dei!
D. O.
Geliebte, Mut nur und Fassung!
Mio bene... fate coraggio!
Vc.
Cb.
12
Fl.
Ob.
Fag.
Cor. in Es
Tr. in C
12
I
Viol.
II
Viola
D. A.
O Himmel!
Oh Dei!
Er hat den Mord verübt an meinem Vater!
Quegli è il carnefice del padre mio.
O zweifle länger
Non dubitate
D. O.
Was sagst du...
Che dite...
Vc.
Cb.

17
D.A.
nicht: Die letz-ten Wor-te, die der Ver-rä-ter sprach, Hal-tung und Stim-me, al-les die-ses ver-riet mir den Ver-
più: gli ul-ti-mi ac-cen-ti, che l'em-pio pro-fe - rì, tut-ta la vo - ce ri-chia-mar nel cor mio di quell' in -
Cemb. e Basso cont.
20
D.A.
worf-nen, der jüngst in mei-ner Wohnung...
de-gno, che nel mio ap-par-ta-men-to...
Don Ottavio
D.O.
O Gott, wär's möglich denn, daß unterm heil'gen Mantel treu-er Freundschaft... Doch was ge-
Oh ciel, pos-si-bi-le che sot-to il sa-cro man-to d'a-mi-ci - zia... Ma co-me
Cemb. e Basso cont.
23
Andante
Viol. I II
f
p
Viola
D.A.
Schon warf der A-bend sei-ne Schlei-er her-nie-der, als in mei-ne Ge-
E - ra già al-quanto a-van - za - ta la not-te, quando nel-le mie
D.O.
schah? Er-zäh-le mir den son-der-ba-ren Her-gang.
fu, nar-ra-te-mi lo stra-no av-ve-ni - men-to.
Andante
Cemb. e Basso cont.
Vc.
Cb.

27
Viol. I
II
Viola
D. A.
mä-cher, wo ich zu meinem Un-heil völ-lig al - lein war, ein Mann her-ein-trat, ge-hüllt in ei - nen Man-tel. Im er - sten Au-gen-
stan-ze, o-ve so-let-ta mi tro-vai per sven - tu - ra, en-trar io vi-di in un man-tel-lo av - vol - to un uom che al pri-mo i-
Vc.
Cb.
30
Andante
p
bli-cke wähnt ich dich, Freund, mir nah, doch nur zu bald er-kannt ich die schreck-li-che Täu-schung.
stan-te a - vea pre - so per voi: ma ri-co-nob-bi poi che un in - gan - no e-ra il mi - o.
Don Ottavio (leidenschaftlich) (con affanno)
D.O.
Him-mel, sprich
Stel - le, se -
33
stringendo il tempo
cresc.
Schweigend schleicht er mir nä-her, schlingt um mich sei-nen Arm; ich will ent - flie-hen, er hält mich
Ta - ci - to a me s'ap-pres-sa, e mi vuo-le ab-brac-ciar: scio-gler-mi cer - co, ei più mi
wei-ter!
gui-te!

37
Tempo I
Andante
Fl.
Ob.
Fag.
Cor. in Es
in D
Tr. in C
a 2
37
Tempo I
Andante
I
Viol.
II
Viola
D.A.
fe - ster, ich ru - fe;
strin-ge; gri-do:
doch nie-mand kommt.
Non vie-ne al - cun.
Mit ei-ner Hand ver-
Con u - na ma - no
Vc.
Cb.
41
I
Viol.
II
Viola
D.A.
sucht er, mei-ne Ru-fe zu hin-dern,
cer - ca d'im-pe - di - re la vo - ce,
mit der an-dern um - faßt er hef - ti - ger mich,
e coll' al - tra m'af - fer - ra stret - ta co - sì,
schon glaubt ich mich ver-
che già mi cre - do
Vc.
Cb.

44
Viol. I II
Viola
D.A.
lo - ren. Die To - des - angst, der Ab-scheu vor dem furcht-ba-ren
vin - ta. Al - fi - ne il duol, l'or - ro - re dell' in - fa - me at-ten-
D.O.
Don Ottavio
Schänd-li-cher, und dann?
Per - fi - do, e al - fin?
Vc.
Cb.
47
Fre-vel er - höh-te so mir mei-ne Kräf-te, daß ich mich durch heft'-ges Weh-ren, Rin - gen
ta - to ac-creb-be sì la le - na mi - a, che a for-za di vin - co - lar-mi, tor-cer-mi
50
Donna Anna
und Ent-win-den end-lich be-frei-te. Be-freit raff ich al - le Kraft zu
e pie-gar-mi da lui mi sciol-si. Al - lo - ra rin-for-zo i stri - di
Don Ottavio
Mein Herz wird leich-ter.
Ohi - me, re - spi - ro.

54
Tempo I
Fl.
Ob.
Fag.
in D
Cor. in D
Tr. in C
a 2
Viol. I II
Viola
D.A.
Vc.
Cb.
sam-men, ru-fe nach Hil-fe, er a-ber flieht; in
mie-i, chia-mo soc-cor-so, fug-ge il fel-lon, ar-
59
flam-men-der Em-pö-rung folg ich ihm nach bis auf die Stra-ße und wer-de aus der Ver-folg-ten die Ver-
di-ta-men-te il se-guo fin nel-la stra-da per fer-mar-lo, e so-no as-sa-li-tri-ce d'as-sa-

62
Fl.
Ob.
Fag.
Cor. in D
62
I
Viol.
II
Viola
D.A.
fol-ge-rin.
li - ta.
Da naht mein Va-ter, stellt zur Re-de ihn, doch der Bu-be, ü-ber-le-gen an
Il pa-dre v'ac-cor-re, vuol co-no-scer-lo, e l'i - ni-quo, che del po - ve-ro
Vc.
Cb.
FORTE SUO SUO
66
Ob.
Fag.
a 2
Cor. in D
a 2
66
I
Viol.
II
Viola
D.A.
Kräften dem schwachen Greise, häuft noch das Maß der Schande, häuft noch das Maß der Schande, raubt ihm das Leben.
vec-chio e - ra più for-te, com-pie il mis-fat-to su - o, com-pie il mis-fat-to su - o, col dar-gli morte.
Vc.
Cb.
attacca subito l' Aria di Donna Ann

Aria
Andante
Ob.
Fag.
Cor. in D
Viol. I
Viol. II
Viola
D. A.
Du kennst nun den Frev - ler, der
Or sai chi l'o - no - re ra -
Vc.
Cb.
Schan - de mir droh - te, mit mörd - - - ri - schem
pi - - - re a me vol - se, chi fu il tra - - - di -

76
Ob.
Fag.
I
Cor. in D
p
Viol. I
Viol. II
Viola
D.A.
Stahle den Va-ter, den Va-ter mir raub-te; zur Ra - che ruft
to-re che il pa-dre, che il pa-dre mi tol - se; ven - det - ta ti
Vc.
Cb.
81
al - les, wohl - auf denn zur Tat,
chie - do, la chie - de il tuo cor,

84
Fag.
or. in D
84
I
Viol.
II
Viola
D. A.
— wohl - auf denn zur Tat! Ge - den - ke der Wun - de im
— la chie - de il tuo cor. Ram - men - ta la pia - ga del
Vc.
Cb.
89
Ob.
Fag.
r. in D
89
I
iol.
II
iola
). A.
Her zen des To - ten, ge - den - ke des Blu - tes, des
mi - se - ro se - no, ri - mi - ra di san - gue co -
Vc.
Cb.

98
Ob.
Fag.
Cor. in D
Viol. I II
Viola
D. A.
Blu - tes, das tränk-te den Boden, es feu-re aufs neu-e zur Ra - che dich an, zur Ra-che dich
per - to, co-per - to il ter - re-no, se l'i-ra in te lan-gue d'un giu - sto fu - ror, d'un giu-sto fu -
Vc.
Cb.
100
an. Du kennst nun den Frev - ler, der
ror. Or sai chi l'o - no - re ra -

103
Ob.
Fag.
Viol. I
Viol. II
Viola
D. A.
Schan - de mir droh - te, mit mörd - ri - schem
pi - rea me vol - se, chi fu il tra - di -
Vc.
Cb.
106
Ob.
Fag.
Cor. in D
Viol. I
Viol. II
Viola
D. A.
Stah-le den Va-ter, den Va-ter mir raub-te; zur Ra-che ruft
to-re che il pa-dre, che il pa-dre mi tol-se; ven-det-ta ti
Vc.
Cb.

111
Ob.
Cor. in D
Viol. I II
Viola
D. A.
al - les, wohl - auf denn zur Tat,
chie - do, la chie - de il tuo cor,
Vc.
Cb.
114
Ob.
Fag.
Cor. in D
Viol. I II
Viola
D. A.
wohl - auf denn zur Tat! Ge - den - ke der Wun - de, ge
la chie - de il tuo cor. Ram - men - ta la pia - ga ri
Vc.
Cb.

118
Ob.
Fag.
Cor. in D
118
I
Viol.
II
Viola
D.A.
den-ke des Blu-tes. Zur Ra - che ruft al - les, wohl -
mi-ra di san-gue. Ven - det - ta ti chie - do, la
Vc.
Cb.
121
Ob.
Fag.
I
Cor. in D
121
I
Viol.
II
Viola
D.A.
auf denn zur Tat, wohl-auf denn zur
chie - de il tuo cor, la chie-de il tuo
Vc.
Cb.

125
Ob.
Fag.
Cor. in D
Viol. I
Viol. II
Viola
D. A.
Tat, zur Ra - che ruft al - les, wohl-auf denn zur Tat, zur Ra - che ruft
cor, ven - det - ta ti chie - do, la chie - de il tuo cor, ven - det - ta ti
Vc.
Cb.
128
al - les, wohl - auf denn zur Tat, wohl- auf denn zur Tat, wohlauf denn zur
chie - do, la chie - de il tuo cor, la chie - de il tuo cor, la chie - de il tuo

132
Ob.
Fag.
Cor. in D
Viol. I
Viol. II
Viola
D. A.
Vc.
Cb.
cresc.
a 2
Tat, wohl - auf denn zur Tat, wohl - auf denn zur Tat, ge - denk dei - nes
cor, la chie - de il tuo cor, la chie - de il tuo cor, ven - det - ta ti
135
f
p
[Geht ab]
[Parte]
Schwures, ge denk mei - ner Schmach!
chie - do, la chie - de il tuo cor.

Vierzehnte Szene

[Don Ottavio (allein).]

Scena XIV

[Don Ottavio (solo).]

Recitativo

Mozart composed the following aria on April 24, 1788, and inserted it in this place, for the tenor Morella. The aria "Il mio tesoro" (No. 21) was not performed at the Vienna première of the opera.

Nr. 10a. Aria

Fl.
Fag.
Cor. in G
Viol. I
II
Viola
D. O.
doch ih-re Lei-den bre-chen mein Herz, bre - chen, bre-chen mein Herz. Ja, ih-re
quel che le in-cre-sce mor-te mi dà, mor - te, mor-te mi dà. S'el-la so-
Vc.
Cb.
cresc.
mf
p cresc.
stacc.
Fl.
Ob.
Fag.
Viol. I
II
Viola
D. O.
Seuf-zer sind auch die mei-nen, und mein ihr Zür-nen, und
spi - ra, so - spi - ro anch'i - o; è mia quell' i - ra, quel
Vc.
Cb.

24
Fl.
Ob.
Fag.
Cor. in G
Viol. I
Viol. II
Viola
D. O.
mein ihr Wei-nen; kein Glück auf Er-den kenn ich al-lein,
pian-to è mi-o; e non ho be-ne, s'el-la non l'ha,
Vc.
Cb.
29
Fl.
Ob.
Fag.
Cor. in G
Viol. I
Viol. II
Viola
D. O.
kein Glück auf Erden kenn ich al-lein, kein Glück auf Er-den kenn ich allein! Nur ih-rem Frieden
e non ho be-ne, s'el-la non l'ha, e non ho be-ne, s'el-la non l'ha! Dal-la sua pa-ce
Vc.
Cb.

39
Cor. in G
Viol. I II
Viola
D.O.
weih ich mein Le - ben, nur ih-re Freu - de kann Glück mir ge-ben, doch ih-re Lei-den bre-chen mein
la mia di - pen - de; quel che a lei pia - ce vi - ta mi ren-de, quel che le in-cre-sce mor-te mi
Vc.
Cb.
cresc.
mf
f
48
Fl.
Ob.
Fag.
p
[p]
p cresc.
Herz, bre - - chen, bre-chen mein Herz, nur ih-rem Frieden weih ich mein Leben, nur ih-re Freu-de kann Glück mir
dà, mor - - te, mor-te mi dà, dal-la sua pa-ce la mia di-pen-de; quel che a lei pia-ce vi-ta mi

56
Fl.
Ob.
Fag.
Cor. in G
Viol. I
Viol. II
Viola
D.O.
ge-ben, doch ih-re Lei-den bre-chen mein Herz, bre - - chen, bre-chen mein Herz,
ren-de, quel che le in-cre-sce mor-te mi dà, mor - - te, mor-te mi dà,
Vc.
Cb.
66
Fl.
Ob.
Fag.
Cor. in G
Viol. I
Viol. II
Viola
D. O.
[Geht ab]
[Parte]
brechen mein Herz, doch ih-re Lei-den bre-chen mein Herz.
mor-te mi dà, quel che le in-cre-sce mor-te mi dà.
Vc.
Cb.

Fünfzehnte Szene

Leporello (allein). Dann Don Giovanni.

Scena XV

Leporello (solo), poi Don Giovanni.

Recitativo

segue l'Aria di Don Giovanni Nº 11

Nº 11. Aria

Presto
2 Flauti
2 Oboi
2 Clarinetti in B
2 Fagotti
2 Corni in B
Violino I II
Viola
[div.]
Don Giovanni
Violoncello
Contrabasso
Auf zu dem Fe - ste, froh soll es werden, bis meine Gä - ste glü - hen von Wein. Siehst du ein Mädchen na - hen dem Garten, laß sie nicht
Finch'han dal vi - no cal - da la te - sta, u - na gran fe - sta fa pre - pa - rar. Se tro - vi in piaz - za qual - che ra - gaz - za, te - co ancor
Fl.
Clar. in B
Viol.
Viola
D. G.
Vc.
Cb.
11

22
Fl.
Clar. in B
Fag.
Viol. I II
Viola
D. G.
war - ten, führ sie her - ein, laß sie nicht war - ten, führ sie her - ein, führ sie her - ein, führ sie her-
quel - la cer - ca me - nar; te - co ancor quel - la cer - ca me - nar; cer - ca me - nar; cer - ca me-
Vc.
Cb.
32
Fl.
Ob.
Clar. in B
Fag.
Cor. in B
Viol. I II
Viola
D. G.
ein. Tan - zen laß al - le sie wild durchein - an - der, hier Me - nu - et - te, da Sa - ra - banden, dort Al - le-
nar. Sen - za al - cun or - di - ne la dan - za si - a, chi'l mi - nu - et - to, chi la fol - li - a, chi l'a - le-
Vc.
Cb.

42
Fl.
Ob.
Clar. in B
Fag.
Cor. in B
Viol.
I
II
Viola
D.G.
manden, ord-ne die Reihn, hier Me-nu-et-te, ord-ne die Reihn, da Sa-ra-ban-den, ord-ne die
ma-na, fa-rai bal-lar, chi'l mi-nu-et-to, fa-rai bal-lar, chi la fol-li-a, fa-rai bal-
Vc.
Cb.
52
Reihn, dort Al-le-man-den, ord-ne die Reihn. Ich a-ber lei-se nach al-ter Wei-se führ mein Feins-
lar, chi l'a-le-ma-na, fa-rai bal-lar. Ed io fra tan-to dall' al-tro can-to con que-sta e

62
Fl.
Ob.
Clar. in B
Fag.
Cor. in B
Viol. I II
Viola
D. G.
lieb-chen ins Kämmer-lein, ins Käm-mer - lein, ins Käm-mer - lein. Fort mit den Sorgen,
quel-la vo'a - mo-reg-giar, vo'a - mo - reg - giar, vo'a - mo-reg - giar. Ah la mia li-sta
Vc.
Cb.
72
a 2
[f]
wahrlich, schon morgen soll mein Re-gi-ster stär-ker noch sein, wahrlich, schon morgen soll mein Re-
do-man mat-ti-na d'u-na de-ci-na de-vi aumen-tar, ah la mia li-sta d'u-na de-

83
Fl.
Ob.
Clar. in B
Fag.
Cor. in B
Viol. I
Viol. II
Viola
D.G.
gi-ster stär-ker noch sein. Siehst du ein Mäd-chen na-hen dem Gar-ten, laß sie nicht war-ten, führ sie her-ein.
ci-na de-vi aumen-tar. Se trovi in piaz-za qual-che ra-gaz-za, te-co an-cor quel-la cer-ca me-nar.
Vc.
Cb.
94
Fort mit den Sorgen, wahr-lich, schon morgen soll mein Re-gi-ster stär-ker noch sein.
Ah la mia li-sta do-man mat-ti-na d'u-na de-ci-na de-viau-men-tar.

105
Fl.
Ob.
Clar. in B
Fag.
Cor. in B
Viol. I
Viol. II
Viola
D. G.
Tan-zen laß al-le sie wild durch-ein-an-der, hier Me-nu-et-te, da Sa-ra-ban-den, dort Al-le-man-den,
Sen-za al-cun or-di-ne la dan-za si-a; chi'l mi-nu-et-to, chi la fol-li-a, chi l'a-le-ma-na
Vc.
Cb.
115
ord-ne die Reihn. Fort mit den Sor-gen, wahr-lich, schon morgen soll mein Re-gi-ster
fa-rai bal-lar. Ah la mia li-sta do-man mat-ti-na d'u-na de-ci-na

126
Fl.
Ob.
Clar. in B
Fag.
Cor. in B
Viol. I
Viol. II
Viola
D.G.
stär - ker noch sein, soll — mein Re - gi - ster stär-ker noch sein, soll — mein Re - gi - ster stär-ker noch sein, — stär-ker noch
de - vi au-men-tar, d'u - na de - ci - na de - vi au-men-tar, d'u - na de - ci - na de - vi au-men-tar, — de - vi au-men-
Vc.
Cb.
137
a 2
cresc.
sein, — stär-ker noch sein, — stär - ker, stär - ker noch sein.
tar, — de - vi au - men - tar, — de - vi, de - vi au - men - tar.
[Sie gehen ab]
[Partono]

Verwandlung

[Garten mit zwei Pforten, die von außen zu schließen sind.
Zwei Nischen (Lauben).]

Mutazione

[Giardino con due porte chiuse a chiave per di fuori.
Due nicchie.]

Sechzehnte Szene

[Masetto. Zerlina. Chor der Bauern und Bäuerinnen
(die hier und da auf Rasenbänken schlafen oder sitzen).]

Scena XVI

[Masetto e Zerlina; Coro di contadini e contadine
(sparse quà e là, che dormono e sedono sopra sofà d'erbe).]

Recitativo

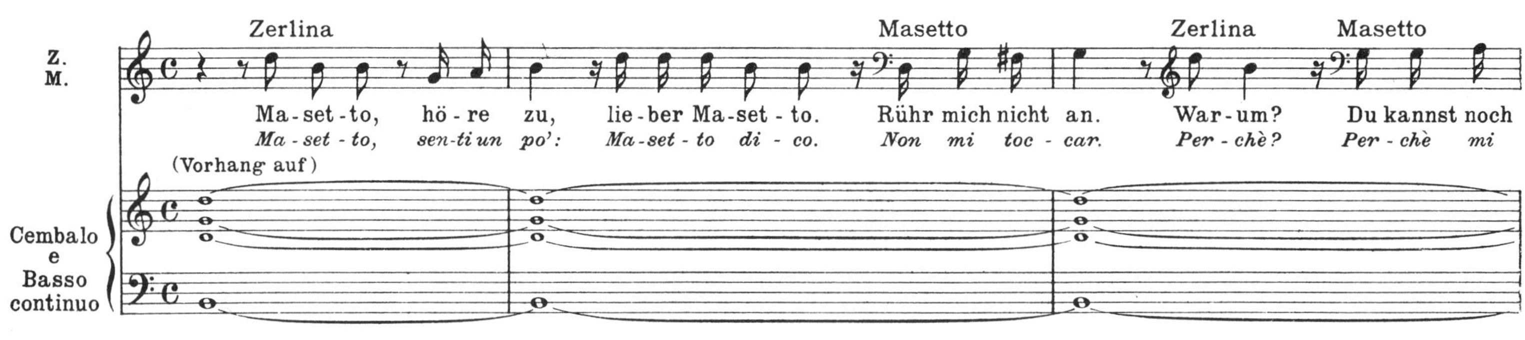

attacca subito l'Aria di Zerlina №12

Nº 12. Aria

Andante grazioso
1 Flauto
1 Oboe
1 Fagotto
2 Corni in F
Andante grazioso
Violino I
II
Viola
Zerlina
Schmäle, to-be, lie-ber Jun-ge, wie ein Lamm will ich's er-tra-gen, fromm, er-ge-ben, oh-ne Kla-gen, oh-ne
Bat-ti, bat-ti, o bel Ma-set-to, la tua po-ve-ra Zer-li-na, sta-rò quì co-me a-gnel-li-na, le tue
Violoncello obligato
Violoncello
Contrabasso
7
Fl.
Ob.
Fag.
Cor. in F
Viol.
Viola
Z.
je-den Wi-der-stand, schmä-le, to-be, ich will's er-tra-gen wie ein Lamm, wie ein
bot-te ad a-spet-tar, bat-ti, bat-ti, la tua Zer-li-na, sta-rò quì, sta-rò
Vc. oblig.
Vc.
Cb.

14
Fl.
Ob.
Fag.
14
I
Viol.
II
tr
[div.]
Viola
Z.
Lamm, oh-ne je-den Wi-der-stand.
quì, — le tue bot-te ad a-spet-tar.
Je-de Stra-fe will ich
La-scie-rò straziar-mi il
Vc. oblig.
Vc.
Cb.
20
Fl.
Ob.
Fag.
Cor. in F
a 2
p
20
I
Viol.
II
Viola
Z.
dul-den,
cri-ne,
schelten kannst du mich und schlagen, Dank da-für will ich dir
la-scie-rò ca-var-mi gli oc-chi, e — le — ca-re tue ma-
Vc. oblig.
Vc.
Cb.

26
Fl.
Ob.
Fag.
a 2
Cor. in F
26
Viol. I
Viol. II
Viola
Z.
sa - gen und noch küs - sen dei - ne Hand, die lie - be Hand, dir küs - sen
ni - ne lie - ta_ poi sa - prò ba - ciar, sa - prò ba - ciar, ba - ciar, sa -
Vc. oblig.
Vc.
Cb.
sfp
32
Fl.
Ob.
Fag.
Cor. in F
32
Viol. I
Viol. II
Viola
Z.
dei - ne lie - be Hand. Schmäle, to - be, lie - ber Jun - ge, will es_
prò, sa - prò ba - ciar. Bat - ti, bat - ti, o bel Ma - set - to, la_ tua
Vc. oblig.
Vc.
Cb.

39
Fl.
Ob.
Fag.
39
I
Viol.
II
Viola
Z.
wie ein Lamm er - tra - gen, fromm, er - ge - ben, oh - ne Kla - gen, oh - ne je - den Wi - der - stand,
po - ve - ra Zer - li - na, sta - rò quì co - me a - gnel - li - na, le tue bot - te ad a - spet - tar,
Vc. oblig.
Vc.
Cb.
45
Fl.
Ob.
Fag.
Cor. in F
45
I
Viol.
II
Viola
Z.
ja schmä - le, to - be, will's er - tra - gen wie ein Lamm, wie ein Lamm, oh - ne je - den Wi - der -
o bel Ma - set - to, bat - ti, bat - ti, sta - rò quì, sta - rò quì, le tue bot - te ad a - spet -
c. oblig.
Vc.
Cb.

52
Fl.
Ob.
Fag.
Cor. in F
Viol. I II
Viola
Z.
stand.
tar.
Ja, ich seh es, kannst nicht
Ah lo ve - do, non hai
Vc. oblig.
Vc.
Cb.
56
cresc.
f
[cresc.]
[f]
zür-nen, ja, ja, nicht zür - nen, kannst nicht zür - nen, kannst nicht zür-nen.
co - re, ah non hai co - re, ah— lo ve - do non— hai co - re.

60
Ob.
Fag.
or. in F
Viol. I II
Viola
z.
Frie-de, Frie - de laß_ uns schlie - ßen, Frie-de, Frie - de laß_ uns schlie - ßen, laß_ der Lie - be Glück ge -
Pa - ce, pa - ce,o vi - ta mi - a, pa - ce, pa - ce,o vi - ta mi - a, in_ con - ten - ti ed al - le -
. oblig.
Vc.
Cb.
66
nie - ßen uns_ in Won - ne Tag_ für Tag, uns_ in
gri - a not - te e dì_ vo - gliam pas - sar, not - te e

71
Fl.
Ob.
Fag.
Cor. in F
71
Viol. I
II
Viola
Z.
Won - ne Tag — für Tag, uns in Won - ne Tag — für Tag,
dì — vo - gliam pas - sar, not - te e dì — vo - gliam pas - sar,
Vc. oblig.
Vc.
Cb.
76
Fl.
Ob.
Fag.
Cor. in F
76
Viol. I
II
Viola
Z.
— uns in Won - ne Tag — für Tag. Frie-de, Frie - de laß — uns schlie-ßen, Frie-de,
— not - te e dì — vo - gliam pas - sar. Pa - ce, pa - ce, o vi - ta mi - a, pa - ce,
Vc. oblig.
Vc.
Cb.

81
Fl.
Fag.
or. in F
81
I
Viol.
II
Viola
z.
Frie - de laß uns schlie - ßen, laß der Lie - be Glück ge - nie - ßen uns in Won - ne Tag für
pa - ce, o vi - ta mi - a, in con - ten - ti, in al - le - gri - a not - te e dì vo - gliam pas -
.oblig.
Vc.
Cb.
86
Fl.
Ob.
Fag.
r. in F
86
I
Viol.
II
Viola
z.
Tag, ja, ja, ja, ja, ja, ja, uns in Won - ne Tag für Tag, ja, ja, ja, ja, ja, ja, uns in
sar, sì, sì, sì, sì, sì, sì, not - te e dì vo - gliam pas - sar, sì, sì, sì, sì, sì, sì, not - te e
oblig.
Vc.
Cb.

91
Fl.
Ob.
Fag.
Cor. in F
91
I
Viol.
II
Viola
Z.
Won - ne Tag für Tag, in Won - ne Tag für Tag, in
dì vo - gliam pas - sar, vo - gliam pas - sar, vo
Vc. oblig.
Vc.
Cb.
95
Fl.
p
Ob.
p
Fag.
p
Cor. in F
pp
95
I
Viol.
II
pp
pp
Viola
pp
Z.
Won - ne Tag für Tag.
gliam pas - sar.
Vc. oblig.
Vc.
pp
Cb.
pp

Recitativo

segue Finale [Nº 13]

№ 13. Finale

Allegro assai
Orchester I (Auf der Bühne, von weitem)
Orchestra I (Sopra il teatro, da lontano)
2 Oboi
2 Corni in F
Allegro assai
Violino I
II
Viola
Violoncello e Contrabasso
Allegro assai
2 Flauti
2 Oboi
2 Clarinetti in C
2 Fagotti
2 Corni in C
2 Trombe in C
Timpani [in C und G]
Allegro assai
Violino I
II
Viola
Donna Anna
Donna Elvira
Zerlina
Don Ottavio
Don Giovanni
Leporello
Masetto
Masetto
Hur-tig, hur-tig, eh er na-het will ich auf die Sei - te ge-hen; in der Ni - sch
Pre - sto, pre-sto, pria ch'ei ven-ga, por mi vo' da qual - che la - to; c'è u - na nic - chia
Coro
Tenore
Basso
Violoncello
Contrabasso

8
a 2
Fl.
Ob.
Clar. in C
Fag.
Cor. in C
Tr. in C
8
I
Viol.
II
Viola
Z.
Zerlina
Ach, Ma-set-to, was beg-innst du? Ach hör mein Fle-hen, nicht ver-
Sen-ti, sen-ti... do-ve va-i? Ah non t'a-sconder, o Ma-
M.
Masetto
kann ich hö-ren, mäuschen-still ver-weil ich dort.
quì ce-la-to, che-to, che-to mi vo' star.
Vc.
Cb.
mfp
p
16
Fl.
Ob.
Fag.
Cor. in C
16
I
Viol.
II
Viola
Z.
stecken! Soll-te er dich dort ent-decken, ach, dann ist's um dich ge-schehn, ach, dann ist's um dich ge-schehn, um dich ge-
set-to, se ti tro-va, po-ve-ret-to, tu non sai quel che può far, po-ve-ret-to, tu non sai quel che può
Vc.
Cb.
I

24
Fl.
Ob.
Fag.
Cor. in C
Tr. in C
Viol. I II
Viola
Z.
M.
Vc.
Cb.
cresc.
a 2
schehn.
far.
Masetto
Ach, er hört mich nicht, der Tol - le!
Ah non gio - van le pa - ro - le!
Er ist
Che ca
Sag und mach er was er wol - le.
Fac - cia, di - ca quel che vuo - le.
Re - de laut und bleib hier ste - hen,
Par - la for - te, e quì t'ar - re - sta,
31
Clar. in C
taub für all mein Fle - hen, er ist taub für all mein Fle - hen!
pric - cio, ha nel - la te - sta, che ca - pric - cio ha nel - la te - sta!
sotto voce
O wie grausam,
Quell' in - gra - to,
wie
que
re - de laut und bleib hier ste - hen!
par - la for - te, e quì t'ar - re - sta!
Ich will sehn, ob sie mir treu ist,
Ca - pi - rò se m'è fe - de - le,

37
Fl.
Ob.
Fag.
Cor. in C
a 2
Viol. I
II
Viola
Z.
scheulich, ach, er will mein Unglück nur, o wie grausam, wie abscheulich, er will mein Verderben
de - le ogg-gi vuol pre-ci - pi - tar, quell'in - gra - to, quel cru - de - le og-gi vuol pre-ci-pi-
M.
so nur komme ich auf die Spur, ich will sehn, ob sie mir treu ist,
e in qual mo - do an - dò l'af - far, ca - pi - rò, se m'è fe - de - le,
Vc.
Cb.
43
a 2
Fl.
Ob.
Clar. in C
Fag.
Cor. in C
Tr. in C
p
I
Viol. I
II
Viola
Z.
nur, o wie grau - sam, wie ab - scheulich, er will mein Ver - der - ben
tar, quell'in - gra - to, quel cru - de - le og-gi vuol pre - ci - pi -
M.
ob sie mir treu ist, so nur komm ich auf die Spur, so nur komm ich auf die
se m'è fe - de - le, e in qual mo - do an - dò l'af - far, in qual mo - do an - dò l'af
Vc.
Cb.

Siebzehnte Szene

[Zerlina. Don Giovanni mit vier reichgekleideten Dienern.]

Scena XVII

[Zerlina; Don Giovanni con quattro servi nobilmente vestiti.]

63
Fl.
Ob.
Clar. in C
Fag.
Cor. in C
Viol. I II
Viola
D.G.
schwinde mir die Leute hier zum Mahle, fül-let al-le Wein-po-ka-le, Freu-de herrsch in die-ser Nacht, Freu-de herrsch in die-ser
dan-za con-du-ce-te tut-ti quan-ti, ed a tut-ti in ab-bon-dan-za gran rin-fre-schi fa-te dar, gran rin-fre-schi fa-te
Vc.
Cb.
cresc.
68
Tr. in C
Timp.
Nacht!
dar.
Chor der Diener
Coro di servi
Tenore
Coro
Basso
Auf, ihr Freun-de, mun-ter, mun-ter,
Sù, sve-glia-te-vi da bra-vi,
nicht ver-le-gen, lie-be
sù, co-rag-gio, o buo-na

76
a 2
Fl.
Ob.
Clar. in C
Fag.
Cor. in C
Tr. in C
Timp.
Viol. I II
Viola
Coro
Leu-te, nur die Freu-de herrsche heu-te, tanzt und scherzet, trinkt und lacht, nur die Freu-de herrsche heu-te, tanzt und scherzet, trinkt und
gen-te, vo-gliam sta-re al-le-gra-mente, vo-gliam ri-de-re e scher-zar, vo-gliam sta-re al-le-gra-mente, vo-gliam ri-de-re e scher
Vc.
Cb.
84
poco a poco piano
(Im Abgehen)
(Partendo)
(Gehen hinein)
(Entrano)
lacht, tanzt und scher-zet, trinkt und lacht, tanzt und scher-zet, trinkt und lacht, tanzt und scher-zet, trinkt und
zar, vo-gliam ri-de-re e scher-zar, vo-gliam ri-de-re e scher-zar, vo-gliam ri-de-re e scher-

Achtzehnte Szene

[Don Giovanni. Zerlina. Masetto (in der Nische).]

Scena XVIII

[Don Giovanni, Zerlina; Masetto (nella nicchia).]

103
Fl.
Ob.
Fag.
Cor. in F
Viol. I
II
Viola
Z.
ei - len!
vi - a!
Wenn Ihr Mit - leid wür-det ken-nen...
Se pie - ta - de a-ve-te in co - re...
D. G.
Nein, bei mir sollst du ver - wei-len!
No, no, re - sta, gio-ja mi - a!
Sieh mein Herz vor Lie - be
Sì, ben mio, son tut-to a -
Vc.
Cb.
109
[div.]
Ach, wenn er Ma-set - - to
Ah s'ei ve-de il spo - - so
brennen. Komm zur Lau-be, sü - - ße Tau-be, komm, dort sollst du glücklich sein, komm mit mir_ in je - ne
mo-re. Vie - ni un po-co in que - - sto lo - co, for - - tu - na-ta io ti vo' far, vie-ni un po - - co in que-sto

115
Fl.
Ob.
Fag.
Cor. in F
Viol. I II
Viola
Z.
fin-det,wer - den wir ver-lo-ren sein,ach,dann werden,dann werden wir ver-lo-ren sein,ach,dann werden,dann werden
mi-o, so ben io quel che può far, so ben io, so ben io, so quel che può far, so ben io, so ben io, so
D. G.
Lau - be,komm,dort sollst du glück-lich sein, komm,dort sollst du glücklich sein, komm,dort
lo - co, for-tu-na-ta io ti vo' far, for-tu-na-ta io ti vo' far, for-tu-
Vc.
Cb.
120
a 2
wir verlo - ren sein!
quel che può far!
[Entdeckt beim Betreten der Nische Masetto und fährt zurück]
[Don Giovanni, nell' aprire la nicchia e vedendo Masetto, fa un moto di stupore]
[Etwas verwirrt]
[Un poco confuso]
sollst du glücklich sein!
na-ta io ti vo' far!
Ma-set-to!
Ma-set-to!
Ver-bor-gen hier, war-um?
E chiu-so là, per-chè?
M.
Masetto
Ja, Ma-set-to!
Sì, Ma-set-to!

128
Fl.
Ob.
Fag.
a 2
Cor. in F
Viol. I II
tr
Viola
Don Giovanni [wieder gefaßt] [riprende ardire]
D. G.
Zer-lin - chen war voll Ban-gen, nach dir hatt sie Ver-lan - gen, du
La bel - la tua Zer-li - na non può, la po-ve-ri - na, più
Vc.
Cb.
133
cresc.
p
f
[Zu Zerlina] [A Zerlina]
warst zu lang nicht hier, drum führt ich selbst sie her zu dir. Nun vorwärts, fort zum
star sen-za di te, non può più star sen-za di te. A-des-so fa-te
Masetto [etwas ironisch] [un poco ironico]
M.
Ja, ich ver-steh, Eu'r Gna - den.
Ca-pi-sco, sì, Si-gno - re.

139
Allegretto
(Auf der Bühne, von weitem)
(Sopra il teatro, da lontano)
Ob.
Cor. in F
a 2
Viol.
Viola
Vc. e Cb.
Fag.
Z.
D. G.
Vc.
Cb.
Zerlina
[Man hört das Vorspiel des Tanzes]
[Si sente il preludio della danza]
Fe-ste, fort zum Fe-ste! Die Geigen hört ihr klingen, zum Tan-ze kommt mit mir.
co-re, fa-te co-re! I suo-na-to-ri u-di-te, ve-ni-te o-mai con me.
Zum
Sì,
148
Fl.
cresc.
Fe-ste laßt uns ei-len, zum Fe-ste laßt uns ei-len, der an-dern Lust zu tei-len, zu-sam-men ge-hen
sì, fac-cia-mo co-re, sì, sì, fac-cia-mo co-re, ed a bal-lar co-gli al-tri an-dia-mo tut-ti
Don Giovanni
Auf, auf und kommt, zu-sam-men ge-hen
Ve-ni-te o-mai, ve-ni-te o-mai con
Masetto
M.
Zum Fe-ste laßt uns ei-len, der an-dern Lust zu tei-len, zu-sam-men ge-hen
Sì, sì, fac-cia-mo co-re, ed a bal-lar co-gli al-tri an-dia-mo tut-ti

155
Fl.
Ob.
Fag.
a 2
Cor. in F
Viol. I
Viol. II
Viola
Z.
wir, zum Fe - ste, zum Tan - ze laßt uns gehn, zum Fe - ste, zum Tan - ze
tre, an - dia - mo, an - dia - mo tut - ti tre, an - dia - mo, an - dia - mo
D. G.
wir, zum Fe - ste, zum Tan - ze laßt uns gehn, zum Fe - ste, zum Tan - ze
me, ve - ni - te, ve - ni - te o - mai con me, ve - ni - te, ve - ni - te o -
M.
wir, zum Fe - ste, zum Tan - ze laßt uns gehn, zum Fe - ste, zum Tan - ze
tre, an - dia - mo, an - dia - mo tut - ti tre, an - dia - mo, an - dia - mo
Vc.
Cb.
162
(Sie gehen ab)
(Partono)
laßt uns gehn, zum Tan-ze laßt uns gehn, zum Tan-ze laßt uns gehn!
tut - ti tre, an - dia-mo tut-ti tre, an - dia-mo tut - ti tre.
laßt uns gehn, zum Tan-ze laßt uns gehn, zum Tan-ze laßt uns gehn!
mai con me, ve - ni-te o-mai con me, ve - ni-te o-mai con me.
laßt uns gehn, zum Tan-ze laßt uns gehn, zum Tan-ze laßt uns gehn!
tut - ti tre, an - dia-mo tut-ti tre, an - dia-mo tut - ti tre.

Neunzehnte Szene

[Don Ottavio, Donna Anna und Donna Elvira (maskiert). Dann Don Giovanni und Leporello (am Fenster).]

Scena XIX

[Don Ottavio, Donna Anna e Donna Elvira (in maschera); poi Leporello e Don Giovanni (alla finestra).]

182
Fl.
Ob.
Fag.
Cor. in F
182
Viol. I II
Viola
D. E.
sein!
lor.
Don Ottavio
D. O.
So hör der Freun-din Wor-te, sei mu-tig, o, Ge-lieb-te, das Ziel, nach dem wir
L'a-mi-ca di-ce be-ne, co-rag-gio a-ver con-vie-ne; dis-cac-cia, o vi-ta
Vc.
Cb.
188
a 2
Fl.
Ob.
Fag.
Cor. in F
188
Viol. I II
Viola
Donna Anna
D. A.
Ge-fahr-voll
Il pas-so è
D. O.
stre-ben, es mag dir Kraft ver-leihn.
mi-a, l'af-fan-no ed il ti-mor.
Vc.
Cb.

194
Fl.
Ob.
Fag.
Cor. in F
in Es
194
Viol. I
Viol. II
Viola
D. A.
Un - ter - fan - gen, mich faßt ein- tie - fes Ban - gen;
pe - ri - glio - so, può na - scer- qual - che im - bro - glio;
Vc.
Cb.
200
Viol. I
Viol. II
Viola
D. A.
du bist's, für den ich fürch - te, für den ich
te - mo pel ca - ro spo - so, pel ca - ro
Vc.
Cb.
205
Fag.
205
Viol. I
Viol. II
Viola
D. A.
fürch - te, laß uns nicht hier al - lein, du
spo - so, e per noi te - mo an - cor, te
Vc.
Cb.

210
Fl.
Ob.
Fag.
a 2
Viol. I
Viol. II
Viola
D. A.
bist's, für den ich fürch-te, für den ich fürchte, laß uns nicht hier al-
-mo pel ca-ro spo-so, pel ca-ro spo-so, e per noi te-mo an-
Vc.
Cb.
Menuetto
(Auf der Bühne, von weitem)
(Sopra il teatro, da lontano)
217
Cor. in F
Vc. e Cb.
lein.
cor.
D. G.
L.
(Leporello öffnet das Fenster)
(Leporello apre la finestra)
Leporello [zum Fenster heraus]
[fuori dalle finestre]
Ach, gnäd'ger Herr, o seht doch die al-ler-lieb-sten Masken!
Si-gnor, guarda-te un po-co, che masche-re ga-lan-ti!
Don Giovanni
Laß sie mir nicht ent-
Fal-le pas-sar a-

225
Ob.
Cor. in F
a 2
Viol. I II
Viola
Vc. e Cb.
D. A.
Donna Anna
p
(Wie Mie - nen doch und Bli - cke den Schänd-li-chen ver - ra - ten.)
(Al vol - to ed al - la vo - ce si sco - pre il tra - di - to - re.)
D. E.
Donna Elvira
p
(Wie Mie - nen doch und Bli - cke den Schänd-li-chen ver - ra - ten.)
(Al vol - to ed al - la vo - ce si sco - pre il tra - di - to - re.)
D. O.
Don Ottavio
p
(Wie Mie - nen doch und Bli - cke den Schänd-li-chen ver - ra - ten.)
(Al vol - to ed al - la vo - ce si sco - pre il tra - di - to - re.)
D. G.
ge-hen, la-de zum Ball sie ein.
van-ti, dì che ci fan-no o-nor.
L.
Leporello
Hol - la, ihr schönen
Zi, zi, Si-gno-re
233
Donna Anna ([leise] zu Don Ottavio)
(a Don Ottavio [piano])
Gib du ihm Antwort!
Via, ri-spon-de-te!
Donna Elvira ([leise] zu Don Ottavio)
(a Don Ottavio [piano])
Gebt ihr ihm Antwort!
Via, ri-spon-de-te!
Don Ottavio
Sagt, was be-
Co - sa chie-
Mas-ken dort, hol - la! Hol - la, ihr schönen Mas-ken dort!
ma-sche-re, zi, zi! Zi, zi, Si-gno-re ma-sche-re!

239
Ob.
Cor. in F
239
Viol. I II
Viola
Vc. e Cb.
239
D. O.
gehrt Ihr?
de - te?
Dank für so gro-ße Eh - re; wohl-
Gra - zie di tan-to o - no - re; an-
Leporello
L.
Zum Tanz lädt mein Ge - bie - ter euch al-le freundlich ein.
Al bal - lo, se vi pia - ce, v'in - vi-ta il mio Si-gnor.
246
Adagio
Ob.
Cor. in F
246
Adagio
Viol. I II
Viola
Vc. e Cb.
246
Adagio
Viol. I II
Viola
D. O.
an, wir werden kom-men.
diam, com-pa-gne bel - le.
(Zieht sich zurück [und schließt das Fenster])
(Entra [e chiude])
L.
Mein Freund wird bald euch zei - gen, wie er die Lieb ver - steht.
L'a - mi - co an-che su quel - le pro-ve fa-rà d'a - mor.
Vc.
Cb.
p

252
Fl.
Ob.
Clar. in B
Fag.
Cor. in Es
in B
in Es
p
Viol. I
Viol. II
Viola
D. A.
D. E.
D. O.
Vc.
Cb.
Donna Anna
Der Him - mel mag be - wah - ren uns all in der Ge -
Pro - teg - ga il giu - sto cie - lo il ze - lo del mio
Donna Elvira
Ra - che, ihr Him - mels - mäch - te,
Ven - di - chi il giu - sto cie - lo
Don Ottavio
Der Him - mel mag be - wah - ren uns all in der Ge -
Pro - teg - ga il giu - sto cie - lo il ze - lo del mio
256
I
fahr, der Him - mel, er mag be - wah - ren uns
cor, pro - teg - ga il giu - sto cie - lo il
für mein ver - rat - nes Herz, Ra - che, ihr Him - mels - mäch - te, für mein ver - rat - nes
il mio tra - di - to a - mor, ven - di - chi il giu - sto cie - lo il mio tra - di - to a -
fahr, der Him - mel mag be - wah - ren uns all in der Ge -
cor, pro - teg - ga il giu - sto cie - lo il ze - lo del mio

259
Fl.
Ob.
Clar. in B
Fag.
Cor. in Es
a 2
D. A.
all in der Ge - fahr, der Him - mel, er mag be -
ze - lo del mio cor, pro - teg - ga il giu - sto
D. E.
Herz, für mein ver - rat - nes, ver - rat - nes Herz, Ra - che, ihr Him - mels -
mor, il mio tra - di - to, tra - di - to a - mor, ven - di - chi il giu - sto
D. O.
fahr, uns all, uns all in der Ge - fahr, der Him - mel mag be -
cor, il ze - lo, il ze - lo del mio cor, pro - teg - ga il giu - sto
263
Fl.
Ob.
Clar. in B
Fag.
Cor. in Es
D. A.
wah - ren uns all in der Ge -
cie - lo il ze - lo del mio
D. E.
mäch - te, für mein ver - rat - nes Herz, für mein, für mein ver - rat - nes
cie - lo il mio tra - di - to a - mor, il mio, il mio tra - di - to a -
D. O.
wah - ren uns all in der Ge - fahr, uns all, uns all in der Ge -
cie - lo il ze - lo del mio cor, il ze - lo, il ze - lo del mio

266
Clar. in B
Fag.
Cor. in Es
D. A.
fahr, der Him - mel mag be - wah-ren uns
cor, pro - teg - ga il giu - sto_ cie - lo il
D. E.
Herz, Ra-che, o Ra-che, ihr Him-mels-mäch - te, für mein ver-rat-nes, ver-rat-nes
mor, ven-di-chi, ven-di-chi il giu-sto_ cie - lo il mio_ tra-di-to, tra-di-to a-
D. O.
fahr, der Him - mel mag be - wah-ren uns
cor, pro - teg - ga il giu - sto_ cie - lo il
269
Fl.
Ob.
Clar. in B
Fag.
Cor. in Es
I
a 2
sfp
D. A.
[Sie gehen ab]
[Partono]
(Vorhang zu)
all_ in der_ Ge - fahr!
ze - lo del_ mio cor!
D. E.
Herz, ver-rat - nes Herz!
mor, tra-di - to a - mor!
D. O.
all in der Ge - fahr!
ze - lo del mio cor!

Verwandlung

[Glänzend erleuchteter, für ein großes Ballfest hergerichteter Saal.]

Zwanzigste Szene

[Don Giovanni. Masetto. Zerlina. Leporello.
Bauern und Bäuerinnen. Diener (mit Erfrischungen).
Dann Don Ottavio, Donna Anna und Donna Elvira (maskiert).]

[Ein Tanz ist soeben beendet; Don Giovanni fordert die Mädchen, Leporello die Burschen zum Sitzen auf]

Mutazione

[Sala illuminata e preparata per una gran festa di ballo.]

Scena XX

[Don Giovanni. Masetto. Zerlina. Leporello;
contadini e contadine, servitori (con rinfreschi); poi
Don Ottavio, Donna Anna e Donna Elvira (in maschera).]

[Don Giovanni fa seder le ragazze, e Leporello i ragazzi, che saranno in atto di aver finito un ballo]

281
Fl.
Clar. in B
Fag.
Cor. in Es
Viol. I II
Viola
Don Giovanni
D.G.
Ru-het aus nun, ihr rei-zen-den Kin-der, dann be-
Ri-po-sa-te, vez-zo-se ra-gaz-ze! Tor-ne-
Leporello
L.
Kommt, erfrischt euch, ihr ar-ti-gen Burschen, dann be-
Rin-fre-sca-te-vi, bei gio-vi-not-ti! Tor-ne-
Vc.
Cb.

288
Fl.
Clar. in B
Fag.
Cor. in Es
Viol. I II
Viola
D.G.
gin-nen wir wie-der zu tan-zen, wirbeln lu-stig im Krei-se her-um, wir-beln lu-stig her-um. He, Kaf-
re-te a far pre-sto le paz-ze, tor-ne-re-te a scher-zar, e bal-lar, a scher-zar, e bal-lar. Ehi Caf-
L.
gin-nen wir wie-der zu tan-zen, wirbeln lu-stig im Krei-se her-um, wir-beln lu-stig her-um.
re-te a far pre-sto le paz-ze, tor-ne-re-te a scher-zar, e bal-lar, a scher-zar, e bal-lar.
Vc.
Cb.

295
Clar. in B
Fag.
Cor. in Es
Viol. I
Viol. II
Viola
D.G.
L.
M.
Vc.
Cb.
p
[Man bringt Erfrischungen]
[Si portano i rinfreschi]
fee!
fè!
Leporello
Scho - ko - la - de!
Cioc - co - la - ta!
Masetto
Ach, Zer - li - na, be - hut - sam,
Ah Zer - li - na, giu - di - zio,
Ge - fror - nes!
Sor - bet - ti!
Ko
Con
303
Z.
Zerlina [beiseite]
[a parte]
Zwar recht ar - tig be - gin - net das Spiel hier,
Trop - po dol - ce co - min - cia la sce - na,
fekt her!
fet - ti!
Masetto
ach, Zer - li - na, be - hut - sam!
ah Zer - li - na, giu - di - zio!
[Beiseite]
[A parte]
Zwar recht ar - tig be - gin - net das Spiel hier,
Trop - po dol - ce co - min - cia la sce - na,

310
Fl.
Clar. in B
Fag.
Cor. in Es
Viol. I
Viol. II
Viola
Z.
D.G.
M.
Vc.
Cb.
a 2
Zerlina
doch das En - de, wer sieht es vor-aus, doch, doch das En - de, wer sieht es vor-aus.
in a-ma - ro po-tria ter-mi-nar, sì, in a-ma - ro po-tria ter-mi-nar.
D. Giov.
O, wie
Sei pur
Masetto
doch das En - de, wer sieht es vor-aus, doch, doch das En - de, wer sieht es vor-aus.
in a-ma - ro po-tria ter-mi-nar, sì, in a-ma - ro po-tria ter-mi-nar.
318
[div.]
L.
Zerlina
Ei, Ihr scherzt.
Sua bon - tà.
[zärtlich zu Zerlina]
[fa carezze a Zerlina]
bist du so rei-zend, Zer - li - na!
va-ga, bril-lan-te Zer - li - na!
Leporello
O, wie
Sei pur
Masetto (wütend) (fremendo)
Wie die Schel - min ver-gnügt ist!
La bric - co - na fa fe - sta!

324
Fl.
Clar. in B
Fag.
Cor. in Es
Viol. I
Viol. II
Viola
Z.
L.
M.
Vc.
Cb.
a 2
Zerlina [beiseite] [a parte]
Ach, Ma - set - to ver - dreht schon die
Quel Ma - set - to mi par stra - lu -
[ahmt seinen Herrn mit den anderen Mädchen nach]
[imita il padrone colle altre ragazze]
bist du so rei - zend, Gia - not - ta!
ca - ra, Gia - not - ta, San - dri - na!
Masetto
Rühr sie an, und es soll dich ge - reu - en!
Toc - ca pur, che ti ca - da la te - sta!
329
cresc.
f
p
I
D.G.
Au - gen, die - ser Han - del, er en - det nicht gut,
na - to; brut - to, brut - to si fa quest' af - far,
ach, Ma - set - to ver - dreht schon die
quel Ma - set - to mi par stra - lu
Don Giovanni
Ach, Ma - set - to ver - dreht schon die Au - gen,
Quel Ma - set - to mi par stra - lu - na - to,
Leporello
Ach, Ma - set - to ver - dreht schon die Au - gen,
Quel Ma - set - to mi par stra - lu - na - to,

335
Fl.
Clar. in B
Fag.
Cor. in Es
Viol. I II
Viola
Z.
Au-gen,
na-to,
die-ser Han-del, er en-det nicht gut,
brut-to, brut-to si fa quest' af-far,
Don Giovanni
D.G.
die-ser Han-del, er en-det nicht gut,
qui bi-so-gna cer-vel-lo a-do-prar,
Leporello
L.
die-ser Han-del, er en-det nicht gut,
qui bi-so-gna cer-vel-lo a-do-prar,
Masetto
M.
Wie die Schel-min ver-gnügt ist!
La bric-co-na fa fe-sta!
Rühr sie
Toc-ca
Vc.
Cb.
342
ach, Ma-set-to ver-dreht schon die Au-gen, die-ser Han-del, er en-det nicht
quel Ma-set-to mi par stra-lu-na-to, brut-to, brut-to si fa quest' af-
ach, Ma-set-to ver-dreht schon die Au-gen, die-ser Han-del, er en-det nicht
quel Ma-set-to mi par stra-lu-na-to, qui bi-so-gna cer-vel-lo a-do-
ach, Ma-set-to ver-dreht schon die Au-gen, die-ser Han-del, er en-det nicht
quel Ma-set-to mi par stra-lu-na-to, qui bi-so-gna cer-vel-lo a-do-
an, und es soll dich ge-reu-en!
pur, che ti ca-da la te-sta!

347
Fl.
Clar. in B
Fag.
Cor. in Es
Viol. I
Viol. II
Viola
Z.
D.G.
L.
M.
Vc.
Cb.
cresc.
gut, er en - det nicht gut, ach, Ma - set - to ver - dreht schon die Au - gen, die - ser Han - del, er en - det nicht
far, si fa quest' af - far, quel Ma - set - to mi par stra - lu - na - to, brut - to, brut - to si fa quest' af -
gut, er en - det nicht gut, ach, Ma - set - to ver - dreht schon die Au - gen, die - ser Han - del, er en - det nicht
prar, cer - vel - lo a - do - prar, quel Ma - set - to mi par stra - lu - na - to, qui bi - so - gna cer - vel - lo a - do -
Ha, die Fal - sche, ha, die Fal - sche, ha, die
Toc - ca, toc - ca, ah bric - co - na, ah bric -
353
a 2
in C
gut, er en - det nicht gut, die - ser Han - del, er en - det nicht gut!
far, si fa quest' af - far, brut - to, brut - to si fa quest' af - far!
prar, cer - vel - lo a - do - prar, qui bi - so - gna cer - vel - lo a - do - prar!
Fal - sche, wie beb ich vor Wut, ha, die Fal - sche, wie beb ich vor Wut!
co - na, mi vuoi dis - pe - rar, ah bric - co - na, mi vuoi dis - pe - rar!

360 Maestoso
Fl.
Ob.
Clar. in B
Fag.
Tr. in C
Timp.
Viol. I
II
Viola
[Don Ottavio, Donna Anna und Donna Elvira treten maskiert ein]
[Entrono Don Ottavio, Donna Anna e Donna Elvira mascherate]
D.G.
L.
Leporello
Nur nä-her, schö-ne Mas-ken, will-kommen hier zum Fe-ste!
Ve - ni - te pur a - van - ti, vez - zo - se ma-sche-ret-te!
D. Giov.
Will-
E a-
Vc.
Cb.
369
a 2
[div.]
D.A.
Donna Anna
Wir dan-ken eu-rer Groß-mut und schätzen frei-en Sinn, und
Siam gra-ti a tan-ti se - gni di ge - ne - ro - si - tà, di
D.E.
Donna Elvira
Wir dan-ken eu-rer Groß-mut und schätzen frei-en Sinn, und
Siam gra-ti a tan-ti se - gni di ge - ne - ro - si - tà, di
D.O.
Don Ottavio
Wir dan-ken eu-rer Groß-mut und schätzen frei-en Sinn, und
Siam gra-ti a tan-ti se - gni di ge - ne - ro - si - tà, di
D.G.
kommen, lie-be Gä-ste, hoch leb die Freiheit, hoch!
per-to a tut-ti quanti; vi - va la li - ber - tà!

877
Fl.
Ob.
Clar. in B
Fag.
Tr. in C
Timp.
877
Viol. I
Viol. II
Viola
D.A.
schätzen frei-en Sinn, wir dan - ken für eu-re Groß-mut, für eu-re Gast-lich-keit!
ge - ne - ro - si - tà, siam gra - ti a tan-ti se - gni di ge - ne - ro - si - tà!
D.E.
schätzen frei-en Sinn, wir dan - ken für eu-re Groß-mut, für eu-re Gast-lich-keit!
ge - ne - ro - si - tà, siam gra - ti a tan-ti se - gni di ge - ne - ro - si - tà!
D.O.
schätzen frei-en Sinn, wir dan - ken für eu-re Groß-mut, für eu-re Gast-lich-keit!
ge - ne - ro - si - tà, siam gra - ti a tan-ti se - gni di ge - ne - ro - si - tà!
D.G.
Will-kom-men al - le, seid mei-ne Gä-ste, Frei - heit
E a-per-to a tut - ti, a tut - ti quan-ti; vi - va,
Vc.
Cb.

385
Fl.
Ob.
Clar.in B
Fag.
a 2
[f]
Tr.in C
Timp.
Viol.
I
II
Viola
Donna Anna
D.A.
Hoch leb die Freiheit, hoch, sie le-be hoch,
Vi - va la li-ber-tà, la li-ber-tà,
Donna Elvira
D.E.
Hoch leb die Freiheit, hoch, sie le-be hoch,
Vi - va la li-ber-tà, la li-ber-tà,
Don Ottavio
D.O.
Hoch leb die Freiheit, hoch, sie le-be hoch,
Vi - va la li-ber-tà, la li-ber-tà,
D.G.
Freiheit, sie le - be hoch!
vi-va la li-ber-tà,
Hoch leb die Freiheit, hoch, sie le-be hoch,
vi - va la li-ber-tà, la li-ber-tà,
Leporello
L.
Hoch leb die Freiheit, hoch, sie le-be hoch, hoch leb die Freiheit,
Vi - va la li-ber-tà, la li-ber-tà, vi - va la li-ber-
Vc.
Cb.

393
Fl.
Ob.
Clar. in B
Fag.
a 2
Tr. in C
Timp.
393
I
Viol.
II
Viola
D. A.
hoch leb die Freiheit, hoch, sie le - be hoch, Frei - heit, Freiheit, sie le - be hoch, Frei-heit, Frei-heit, sie le - be
vi - va la li - ber - tà, la li - ber - tà, vi - va, vi - va la li - ber - tà, vi - va, vi - va la li - ber
D. E.
hoch leb die Freiheit, hoch, sie le - be hoch, Frei - heit, Freiheit, sie le - be hoch, Frei-heit, Frei-heit, sie le - be
vi - va la li - ber - tà, la li - ber - tà, vi - va, vi - va la li - ber - tà, vi - va, vi - va la li - ber
D. O.
hoch leb die Freiheit, hoch, sie le - be hoch, Frei - heit, Freiheit, sie le - be hoch, Frei-heit, Frei-heit, sie le - be
vi - va la li - ber - tà, la li - ber - tà, vi - va, vi - va la li - ber - tà, vi - va, vi - va la li -
D. G.
hoch leb die Freiheit, hoch, sie le - be hoch, Frei - heit, Freiheit, sie le - be hoch, Frei-heit, Frei-heit, sie le - be
vi - va la li - ber - tà, la li - ber - tà, vi - va, vi - va la li - ber - tà, vi - va, vi - va la li - be
L.
hoch, sie le - be hoch, Frei - heit, Freiheit, sie le - be hoch, Frei-heit, Frei-heit, sie le - be
tà, la li - ber - tà, vi - va, vi - va la li - ber - tà, vi - va, vi - va la li - be
Vc.
Cb.

400
Fl.
a 2
Ob.
a 2
Clar. in B
a 2
Fag.
a 2
Tr. in C
a 2
Timp.
400
I
Viol.
II
Viola
D. A.
hoch, sie le-be hoch, sie le-be hoch!
tà, la li-ber - tà, la li-ber - tà!
D. E.
hoch, sie le-be hoch, sie le-be hoch!
tà, la li-ber - tà, la li-ber - tà!
D. O.
hoch, sie le-be hoch, sie le-be hoch!
tà, la li-ber - tà, la li-ber - tà!
[Zu Leporello]
[A Leporello]
D. G.
hoch, sie le-be hoch, sie le-be hoch! Laßt die Mu-sik be - gin-nen! Du ord - ne schnell die
tà, la li-ber - tà, la li-ber - tà! Ri - co-min-cia-te il suo-no! Tu ac-coppia i bal - le-
L.
hoch, sie le-be hoch, sie le-be hoch!
tà, la li-ber - tà, la li-ber - tà!
Vc.
Cb.

Menuetto
Orchester I
Orchestra I
406
Ob.
Cor. in G
a 2
Viol. I II
Viola
Vc. e Cb.
(Don Ottavio tanzt mit Donna Anna Menuett)
(Don Ottavio balla Menuetto con Donna Anna)
D. G.
Tänzer!
ri-ni!
L.
Leporell
Nu
Da
416
Donna Anna
D. A.
Ich ster-be!
Io mo-ro!
Donna Elvira (zu Donna Anna)
(a Donna Anna)
D. E.
Das ist die jun-ge Bäu-rin.
Quel-la è la con-ta-di-na.
Don Ottavio (zu Donna Anna)
(a Donna Anna)
D. O.
Still, nur Fas-sung!
Si-mu-la-te!
D. Giova
Ni
[Sie tanzen]
[Qui ballano]
flink zum muntern Tan-ze!
bra-vi, via bal-la-te!
Lepor
Ni

424
Orchester II
Orchestra II
Viol.
Vc. e Cb.
(Stimmend)
(Accordano)
424
Orchester I
Orchestra I
Ob.
Cor. in G
Viol. I II
Viola
Vc. e Cb.
424
D.G.
bes- ser könntes gehn!
be- ne in ve- ri- tà!
[Zu Leporello]
[A Leporello]
Ma-set-to schaff bei Sei-te!
A ba-da tien Ma-set-to!
L.
bes- ser könntes gehn!
be- ne in ve- ri- tà!
Masetto (spöttisch)
(ironicamente)
M.
Vor- treff-lich, vor- treff-lich, vor-trefflich, muß ge-stehn!
Va be- ne, va be- ne, va be-ne in ve- ri- tà!
431
Orchester II
Orchestra II
Viol.
Vc. e Cb.
pizz.
arco
pizz.
arco
431
Orchester I
Orchestra I
Ob.
Cor. in G
Viol. I II
Viola
Vc. e Cb.
431
Don Giovanni (zu Zerlina)
(a Zerlina)
D.G.
Reich mir die Hand zum Tan - ze, Zer- li - na, Zer-
Il tuo com-pagno io so - no, Zer- li - na, Zer-
Leporello [zu Masetto]
[a Masetto]
L.
War-um willst du nicht tan-zen, ar-mer Jun-ge?
Non bal- li, po- ve - ret- to, po- ve - ret- to!
Komm her, mein Freund Ma- set - to, tan - ze,
Vien quà, Ma - set - to ca - ro, ca - ro,

436 Orchester II
Orchestra II
Viol.
Vc. e Cb.
(Gibt das Zeichen)
(Dà il segno)
(Don Giovanni-Zerlina)
436 Orchester I
Orchestra I
Ob.
Cor. in G
a 2
Viol. I II
Viola
Vc. e Cb.
436
(Beginnt mit Zerlina einen Kontertanz)
(Si mette a ballar con Zerlina una contradanza)
D.G.
li - na, komm mit mir!
li - na, vien pur quà!
Leporello
L.
so wie's die an-dern tun.
facciam quel ch'al-tri fa.
Komm tan - ze Freund Ma-set-to!
Eh bal - la, a-mi - co mi-o!
Masetto
M.
Nein, nein, ich mag nicht tanzen.
No, no, bal-lar non vo-glio.
Nein!
No!
443 Orchester III
Orchestra III
(Stimmend)
(Accordano)
pizz.
Orchester II
Orchestra II
443 Orchester I
Orchestra I
a 2
Donna Anna [zu Donna Elvira]
[a Donna Elvira]
D.A.
Ich kann mich nicht mehr fas - sen.
Re-si - ster non poss' i - o.
Donna Elvira
D.E.
Ver - stel - lung gilt es
Fin - ge - te, per pie
Don Ottavio
D.O.
Ver - stel - lung gilt es
Fin - ge - te, per pi
Leporello
Ja, lie-ber Ma-set-to, tan - ze, tan - ze!
Si, ca-ro Ma-set-to! Bal - la, bal - la!
Masetto
Nein, nein, ich mag nicht, nein, nein, ich
No, no, non vo - glio, no, no, no

449
Orchester III
Orchestra III
arco
pizz.
arco
(Gibt das Zeichen)
(Dà il segno)
(Leporello - Masetto)
Viol.
Vc. e Cb.
Orchester II
Orchestra II
Orchester I
Orchestra I
Ob.
Cor. in G
a 2
Viola
D. E.
hier.
tà!
D. O.
hier.
tà!
D. G.
Don Giovanni
Komm nur mit
Vie - ni con
L.
Leporello
(Tanzt mit Masetto den Deutschen)
(Balla la Teitsch con Masetto)
Komm tan - ze, Freund Ma - set - to, so wie's die an - dern tun.
Eh bal - la, a - mi - co mi - o, fac - ciam quel ch'al - tri fa.
M.
mag nicht.
vo - glio.
455
Z.
Zerlina
Ich Ar - me bin ver-
Oh Nu - mi, son tra-
(Zieht die sich Sträubende mit sich fort)
(Conducendola via quasi per forza)
mir, Ge - lieb - te, komm, o folg mir!
me, mia vi - ta, vie - ni, vie - ni!
Masetto
(Entwindet sich Leporellos Händen und folgt Zerlina)
(Si cava dalle mani di Leporello e seguita la Zerlina)
Laß mich los, hin - weg, Zer - li - na!
La - scia - mi, ah no, Zer - li - na!

Orchester III
Orchestra III
Viol.
Vc. e Cb.
Orchester II
Orchestra II
Viol.
Vc. e Cb.
459
Orchester I
Orchestra I
Ob.
Cor. in G
a 2
Viol. I II
Viola
Vc. e Cb.
459
D. A.
D. E.
Z.
D. O.
L.
Donna Anna
Im eig- - nen Ne-tze
L'i- ni- - quo da se
Donna Elvira
Im eig- - nen Ne-tze
L'i- ni- - quo da se
lo- - ren!
di- - ta!
Don Ottavio
Im eig- - nen Ne-tze
L'i- ni- - quo da se
Leporello
Ein Unglück wird es ge-ben!
Qui nasce u-na ru-i-na!
(Geht eilig ab)
(Sorte in fretta)
Orchester III
Orchestra III
Orchester II
Orchestra II
463
Orchester I
Orchestra I
463
fängt nun der Schänd - li-che sich hier!
stes - so nel lac- - cio se ne và.
fängt nun der Schänd - li-che sich hier!
stes - so nel lac- - cio se ne và.
Zerlina (hinter der Szen
(di dentro [ad al
Ach, zu
Gen - te a -
fängt nun der Schänd - li-che sich hier!
stes - so nel lac- - cio se ne và.

Allegro assai
[Im Orchester]
[Nell' Orchestra]
468
Fl.
Ob.
Clar. in B
Fag.
a 2
Allegro assai
[Im Orchester]
[Nell' Orchestra]
468
I
Viol.
II
Viola
D. A.
Auf, ent-reißt sie sei - nen Ar-men, auf, ent - reißt sie sei - nen
Soc-cor - ria-mo l'in - no - cen - te, soc-cor - ria-mo l'in - no -
D. E.
Auf, ent-reißt sie sei - nen Ar-men, auf, ent - reißt sie sei - nen
Soc-cor - ria-mo l'in - no - cen - te, soc-cor - ria-mo l'in - no -
[mit lauter Stimme; Geräusch von Fußtritten zur Rechten])
voce; strepito di piedi a destra])
Z.
Hil - fe, habt Er - barmen!
ju - to, a - ju - to gen-te!
D. O.
Auf, ent-reißt sie sei - nen Ar-men, auf, ent - reißt sie sei - nen
Soc-cor - ria-mo l'in - no - cen - te, soc-cor - ria-mo l'in - no -
Vc.
Cb.

474
Fl.
Ob.
Clar. in B
Fag.
Cor. in C
in C
a 2
p cresc. f
Viol. I II
Viola
[Die Musikanten und die andern entfernen sich verstört]
[I Suonatori e gli altri partono confusi]
D.A.
Armen! Ha, sie rief auf je - ner Sei - te, _ je - ner
cen - te! O - ra gri - da _ da _ quel la - to, _ da _ que
D.E.
Armen! Ha, sie rief auf je - ner Sei - te, _ je - ner
cen - te! O - ra gri - da _ da _ quel la - to, _ da _ que
Zerlina [Hinter der Szene; man hört den Schrei und den Lärm von der entgegengesetzten Seit
[Di dentro; si sente il grido e lo strepito dalla parte opposta]
Z.
Helft mir Ar - - - men!
Scel - le - ra - - - to!
D.O.
Armen! Ha, sie rief auf je - ner Sei - te, _ je - ner
cen - te! O - ra gri - da _ da _ quel la - to, _ da _ qu
Masetto
M.
Ach, Zer - li - na, ach, Zer - li - na!
Ah Zer - li - na, ah Zer - li - na!
Vc.
Cb.

481
a 2
Fl.
p cresc.
f
Ob.
[p] cresc.
Clar. in B
[p]
cresc.
Fag.
Cor. in C
Viol.
I
II
Viola
[Sie sprengen die Tür]
[Gittano giù la porta]
D.A.
Sei-te! Sprengt die Tü - re, sprengt die Tü-re, laßt uns ei - len!
la-to! Ah git - tia-mo giù_ la_ por-ta, giù la_ por - ta!
D.E.
Sei-te! Sprengt die Tü - re, sprengt die Tü-re, laßt uns ei - len!
la-to! Ah git - tia - mo giù_ la_ por-ta, giù la_ por - ta!
Zerlina
Z.
Helft mir Ar - - men! Kommt zu Hil - fe mir,
Scel - le - ra - - to! Soc - cor - re - te-mi,
D.O.
Sei-te! Sprengt die Tü - re, sprengt die Tü-re, laßt uns ei - len!
la-to! Ah git - tia - mo giù_ la_ por-ta, giù la_ por - ta!
Vc.
Cb.

488
Fl.
Ob.
Clar. in B
Fag.
Cor. in C
Viol. I
Viol. II
Viola
D.A.
D.E.
Z.
D.O.
M.
Vc.
Cb.
mf cresc.
cresc.
p cresc.
f
Donna Anna
Wir sind hier zu dei-ner Hil-fe, wir sind hier zu dei-ner
Siam qui noi per tua di - fe - sa, siam qui noi per tua di
Donna Elvira
Wir sind hier zu dei-ner Hil-fe, wir sind hier zu dei-ner
Siam qui noi per tua di - fe - sa, siam qui noi per tua di
Zerlina
ach, kommt zu Hil - fe mir, ich ster - - be!
ah soc - cor - re - te-mi, o son mor - - ta!
[Kommt von einer anderen Seite herein]
[Esce da un' altra parte]
Don Ottavio
Wir sind hier zu dei-ner Hil-fe, wir sind hier zu dei-ner
Siam qui noi per tua di - fe - sa, siam qui noi per tua di
Masetto
Wir sind hier zu dei-ner Hil-fe, wir sind hier zu dei-ner
Siam qui noi per tua di - fe - sa, siam qui noi per tua di -

495
Andante maestoso
Fl.
Ob.
Clar. in B
Fag.
a 2
in C
[f]
Viol. I
Viol. II
Viola
p
Donna Anna
D.A.
Hil-fe, zu dei-ner Hil-fe, zu dei-ner Hil-fe!
fe-sa, per tua di - fe-sa, per tua di - fe-sa!
Donna Elvira
D.E.
Hil-fe, zu dei-ner Hil-fe, zu dei-ner Hil-fe!
fe-sa, per tua di - fe-sa, per tua di - fe-sa!
Don Ottavio
D.O.
Hil-fe, zu dei-ner Hil-fe, zu dei-ner Hil-fe!
fe-sa, per tua di - fe-sa, per tua di - fe-sa!
Don Giovanni
[führt mit dem Degen in der Hand an einem Arme Leporello herein und tut, als wollte er ihn erstechen, aber der Degen geht nicht aus der Scheide]
[esce con spada in mano, conduce seco per un braccio Leporello, e finge di voler ferirlo, ma la spada non esce dal fodero]
D.G.
Frecher Bube, sie be-leid'gen; doch be-
Ec-co il birbo, che t'ha of-fe-sa; ma da
Masetto
M.
Hil-fe, zu dei-ner Hil-fe, zu dei-ner Hil-fe!
fe-sa, per tua di - fe-sa, per tua di - fe-sa!
Vc.
Cb.

502
Fl.
Ob.
Fag.
Cor. in C
Viol. I II
Viola
D.G.
strafen will ich ihn, be-stra-fen ihn! Stirb, Ver-weg-ner, du mußt sterben, du mußt sterben!
me_la_ pe-na a-vrà, la pe-na a-vrà! Mo-ri, i-ni-quo, mo-ri, i-ni-quo, mo-ri, di-co!
Leporello
L.
Ach, habt Er-barmen, ach, habt Er-bar-men, ach, habt Er
Ah co-sa fa-te, ah co-sa fa-te, ah co-sa
Vc.
Cb.
507
D.A.
D.E.
D.O.
Donna Anna (nimmt die Maske a
(si cava la maschera
Hof - fe nimmer, uns zu
L'em - pio cre-de con tal
Donna Elvira (nimmt die Maske ab)
(si cava la maschera)
Hof - fe nimmer, uns zu täu - schen, uns zu
L'em - pio cre-de con tal fro - de, con tal
Don Ottavio (mit der Pistole in der Hand)
(pistola in mano)
(Nimmt die Maske ab)
(Si cava la maschera)
Dei - ne Possen sind ver - gebens! Hof - fe nimmer, uns zu täu - schen, uns zu täu - schen, uns zu
Nol spe-ra-te, nol spe-ra-te! L'em - pio cre-de con tal fro - de, con tal fro - de, con tal
barmen!
fa - te!

512
Fl.
Ob.
Fag.
Cor. in C
Viol. I II
Viola
D.A.
täu-schen durch dein eit - les Gau - kel-spiel, durch dein Spiel!
fro - de di na-scon - der l'em - pie - tà, l'em - pie - tà!
D.E.
täu-schen durch dein eit - les Gau - kel-spiel, durch dein Spiel! Ja, Ver-rä-ter!
fro - de di na-scon - der l'em - pie - tà, l'em - pie - tà! Sì, mal-vaggio!
D.O.
täu-schen durch dein eit - les Gau - kel-spiel, durch dein Spiel! Ja, ich
fro - de di na-scon - der l'em - pie - tà, l'em - pie - tà! Sì, Si-
Don Giovanni
D.G.
Wie, El - vi-ra! Don Ottavio!
Don-na El-vi-ra! Don Ottavio!
Vc.
Cb.
516
a 2
Donna Anna
Ehr - ver-geßner, Ehr vergeß - ner, schweig und zittre! Al-les, al-les wis-sen
Tra - di - to - re, tra-di-to - re, tra - di-to-re! Tut-to, tut-to già si
Donna Elvira
Ehr vergeß - ner, schweig und zittre! Al-les, al-les wis-sen
Tra-di - to - re, tra - di-to-re! Tut-to, tut-to già si
Zerlina
Z.
Ehr vergeß - ner, schweig und zittre! Al-les, al-les wis-sen wir, al-les,
Tra-di - to - re, tra - di-to-re! Tut-to, tut-to già si sà, tut-to,
bin es! Ehr vergeß - ner, schweig und zittre! Al-les, al-les wis-sen
gnore! Tra-di - to - re, tra - di-to-re! Tut-to, tut-to già si
Don Giovanni (zu Donna Anna)
(a Donna Anna)
Könnt Ihr glauben!
Ah cre-de - te!
Masetto
M.
Ehr-vergeß - ner, schweig und zittre! Al-les, al-les wis - sen
Tra-di-to - re, tra - di-to-re! Tut-to, tut-to già si

521
Fl.
Ob.
Clar. in C
in C
Fag.
Cor. in C
Viol. I
Viol. II
Viola
D.A.
D.E.
Z.
D.O.
M.
Vc.
Cb.
p
cresc.
f
wir, al-les, al-les wis-sen wir, al-les, al-les wis-sen wir, al-les, al-les, al-les,
sà, tut-to, tut-to già si sà, tut-to, tut-to già si sà, tut-to, tut-to, tut-to,
al-les wis-sen wir, al-les, al-les wis-sen wir, wis-sen wir, al-les, al-les, al-les,
tut-to già si sà, tut-to, tut-to già si sà, già si sà, tut-to, tut-to, tut-to,
wir, al-les, al-les wis-sen wir, al-les, al-les wis-sen wir, al-les
sà, tut-to, tut-to già si sà, tut-to, tut-to già si sà, tut-to,
wir, al-les, al-les wis-sen wir, al-les, al-les wis-sen
sà, tut-to, tut-to già si sà, tut-to, tut-to già si

527
Fl.
Ob.
Clar. in C
Fag.
Cor. in C
Tr. in C
Timp.
Viol. I
II
Viola
D.A.
al - les wis - sen wir, al-les, al-les, al - - les!
tut - to già si sà, tut-to, tut-to, tut - - to!
D.E.
al - les wis - sen wir, al-les, al-les, al - - les!
tut - to già si sà, tut-to, tut-to, tut - - to!
Z.
al - les wis - sen wir, al-les, al-les, al - - les!
tut - to già si sà, tut-to, tut-to, tut - - to!
D.O.
al - les wis - sen wir, al-les, al-les, al - - les!
tut - to già si sà, tut-to, tut-to, tut - - to!
M.
wir, al-les, al-les wis-sen wir, al-les, al-les, al - - les!
sà, tut-to, tut-to già si sà, tut-to, tut-to, tut - - to!
Vc.
Cb.

*) See Editors' Commentary.

540
Fl.
Ob.
Clar. in C
Fag.
Cor. in C
Tr. in C
Timp.
Viol. I
Viol. II
Viola
D. A.
D. E.
Z.
D. O.
D. G.
L.
M.
Vc.
Cb.
a 2
cresc.
sotto voce
Mis - se - tä - ter, be - - - be, be - be,
scel - le - ra - to, tre - - - ma, tre - ma, o
Don Giovanni
Mir ver - wir - ren sich die Sin - ne,
È con - fu - sa la mia te - sta,
Leporello
Ihm ver - wir - ren sich die Sin - ne,
È con - fu - sa la sua te - sta,

546
a 2
Fl.
Ob.
Clar. in C
Fag.
Cor. in C
Tr. in C
Timp.
546
I
Viol.
II
Viola
D.A.
Mis - se - tä-ter! Bald soll al - le_ Welt mit Grau-en dein ver - ruch-tes_ Herz durch -
scel - le - ra-to! Sa-prà to - sto il mon-do in - te - ro il mis - fat - to or - ren - do e_
D.E.
Mis - se - tä-ter! Bald soll al - le_ Welt mit Grau-en dein ver - ruch-tes_ Herz durch -
scel - le - ra-to! Sa-prà to - sto il mon-do in - te - ro il mis - fat - to or - ren - do e_
Z.
Mis - se - tä-ter! Bald soll al - le_ Welt mit Grau-en dein ver - ruch-tes_ Herz durch -
scel - le ra-to! Sa-prà to - sto il mon-do in - te - ro il mis - fat - to or - ren - do e_
D.O.
Mis - se - tä-ter! Bald soll al - le_ Welt mit Grau-en dein ver - ruch-tes_ Herz durch -
scel - le - ra-to! Sa-prà to - sto il mon-do in - te - ro il mis - fat - to or - ren - do e_
D.G.
kaum vermag ich mich zu fas - sen, wild er-reg - te Stür-me ra - sen, drohn von
non so più quel ch'io mi fac - cia, e un or - ri - bi - le tem - pe - sta mi - nac-
L.
kaum vermag er sich zu fas - sen, wild er-reg - te Stür-me ra - sen, drohn von
non sa più quel ch'ei si fac - cia, e un or - ri - bi - le tem - pe - sta mi - nac-
M.
Mis - se - tä-ter! Bald soll al - le_ Welt mit Grau-en dein ver - ruch-tes_ Herz durch -
scel - le - ra-to! Sa-prà to - sto il mon-do in - te - ro il mis - fat - to or - ren - do e_
Vc.
Cb.

552
Fl.
a 2
Ob.
a 2
Clar. in C
a 2
Fag.
a 2
Cor. in C
Tr. in C
tr
Timp.
552
I
Viol.
II
Viola
D.A.
schau-en, deine grausam wil-de_ Gier, dei - ne grau - sam wil - de Gier!
ne - ro, la tua fie - ra_ cru-del - tà, la tua fie - ra cru - del - tà!
D.E.
schau-en, deine grausam wil-de_ Gier, dei - ne grau - sam wil - de Gier!
ne - ro, la tua fie - ra_ cru-del - tà, la tua fie - ra cru - del - tà!
Z.
schau-en, deine grausam wil-de_ Gier, dei - ne grau - sam wil - de Gier!
ne - ro, la tua fie - ra_ cru-del - tà, la tua fie - ra cru - del - tà!
D.O.
schau-en, deine grausam wil-de_ Gier, dei - ne grau - sam wil - de Gier!
ne - ro, la tua fie - ra_ cru-del - tà, la tua fie - ra cru - del - tà!
D.G.
al - len Sei - ten mir! Mir verwir - ren
cian-do oh Dio mi va! È con-fu - sa
L.
al - len Sei - ten hier! Ihm ver-
cian-do oh Dio lo va! È con-
M.
schau-en, deine grausam wil-de_ Gier, dei - ne grau - sam wil - de Gier!
ne - ro, la tua fie - ra_ cru-del - tà, la tua fie - ra cru - del - tà!
Vc.
Cb.
p

558
Fl.
Ob.
Clar. in C
Fag.
Cor. in C
a 2
cresc.
p
f
558
I
Viol.
II
Viola
D. A.
Be - be, be - be!
Tre - ma, tre - ma!
D. E.
Be - be, be - be!
Tre - ma, tre - ma!
Z.
Be - be, be - be!
Tre - ma, tre - ma!
D. O.
Be - be, be - be!
Tre - ma, tre - ma!
D. G.
sich die Sin - ne, kaum ver-mag ich mich zu fas - sen, wild er - reg - te Stür - me
la mia te - sta, non so più quel ch'io mi fac - cia, e un or - ri - bi - le tem-
L.
wir - ren sich die Sin - ne, kaum ver-mag er sich zu fas - sen, wild er-reg - te Stür - me
fu - sa la sua te - sta, non sa più quel ch'ei si fac - cia, e un or-ri - bi - le tem-
M.
Be - be, be - be!
Tre - ma, tre - ma!
Vc.
Cb.

563
Fl.
Ob.
Clar. in C
Fag.
Cor. in C
Tr. in C
Timp.
563
I
Viol.
II
sopra una corda
sopra una corda
Viola
D.A.
Be - be, be - - be,
Tre - ma, tre - - ma, o
D.E.
Be - be, be - - be,
Tre - ma, tre - - ma, o
Z.
Be - be, be - be, Mis - se - tä - ter, du
Tre - ma, tre - ma, tre - ma, tre - ma, o
D.O.
Be - be, be - be, Mis - se - tä - ter, du
Tre - ma, tre - ma, tre - ma, tre - ma, o
D.G.
ra - sen, drohn von al - len Sei - ten mir!
pe - sta mi - nac - cian-do oh Dio mi va!
L.
ra - sen, drohn von al - len Sei - ten hier!
pe - sta mi - nac - cian-do oh Dio lo va!
M.
Be - be, be - be, Mis - se - tä - ter, du
Tre - ma, tre - ma, tre - ma, tre - ma, o
Vc.
Cb.

568
Fl.
Ob.
a 2
Clar. in C
Fag.
Cor. in C
Tr. in C
Timp.
Viol. I
Viol. II
Viola
D. A.
Mis - se - tä - ter! Hör des Don - ners Ra - che -
scel - le - ra - to! O - di il tuon del - la ven -
D. E.
Mis - se - tä - ter! Hör des Don - ners Ra - che -
scel - le - ra - to! O - di il tuon del - la ven -
Z.
Mis - se - tä - ter! Hör des Don - ners Ra - che -
scel - le - ra - to! O - di il tuon del - la ven -
D. O.
Mis - se - tä - ter! Hör des Don - ners Ra - che -
scel - le - ra - to! O - di il tuon del - la ven -
D. G.
Mir verwir-ren sich die Sin-ne, kaum vermag ich mich zu fas-sen,
È con-fu-sa la mia te-sta, non so più quel ch'io mi fac-cia,
L.
Ihm verwir-ren sich die Sin-ne, kaum vermag er sich zu fas-sen,
È con-fu-sa la sua te-sta, non sa più quel ch'ei si fac-cia,
M.
Mis - se - tä - ter! Hör des Don - ners Ra - che -
scel - le - ra - to! O - di il tuon del - la ven -
Vc.
Cb.

573
Fl.
Ob.
Clar. in C
Fag.
Cor. in C
Tr. in C
Timp.
573
I
Viol.
II
Viola
D.A.
D.E.
Z.
D.O.
D.G.
L.
M.
Vc.
Cb.
a 2
tr
stim-me, hör des Don - ners Ra - che - stim-me, sieh den
det - ta, o - di il tuon del - la ven - det - ta, che ti
wild er-reg-te Stürme ra-sen, drohn von al-len Sei-ten mir!
e un or-ri-bi-le tem-pe-sta mi-nacciando oh Dio mi va!
wild er-reg-te Stürme ra-sen, drohn von al-len Sei-ten hier!
e un or-ri-bi-le tem-pe-sta mi-nacciando oh Dio lo va!

578
a 2
Fl.
a 2
Ob.
a 2
Clar. in C
Fag.
Cor. in C
Tr. in C
Timp.
578
I
Viol.
II
Viola
D. A.
Blitz und za - ge, za - ge, weh dir, noch an die - sem Ta - ge tref - fe dich sein Feu - er -
fi - schia in - tor - no, in - tor - no; sul tuo ca - po in que - sto gior - no il suo ful - mi - ne ca -
D. E.
Blitz und za - ge, za - ge, weh dir, noch an die - sem Ta - ge tref - fe dich sein Feu - er -
fi - schia in - tor - no, in - tor - no; sul tuo ca - po in que - sto gior - no il suo ful - mi - ne ca -
Z.
Blitz und za - ge, za - ge, weh dir, noch an die - sem Ta - ge tref - fe dich sein Feu - er -
fi - schia in - tor - no, in - tor - no; sul tuo ca - po in que - sto gior - no il suo ful - mi - ne ca -
D. O.
Blitz und za - ge, za - ge, weh dir, noch an die - sem Ta - ge tref - fe dich sein Feu - er -
fi - schia in - tor - no, in - tor - no; sul tuo ca - po in que - sto gior - no il suo ful - mi - ne ca -
M.
Blitz und za - ge, za - ge, weh dir, noch an die - sem Ta - ge tref - fe dich sein Feu - er -
fi - schia in - tor - no, in - tor - no; sul tuo ca - po in que - sto gior - no il suo ful - mi - ne ca -
Vc.
Cb.

583
Fl.
Ob.
Clar. in C
Fag.
Cor. in C
Tr. in C
Timp.
Viol. I
Viol. II
Viola
D. A.
strahl, tref - fe dich sein Feu - er - strahl!
drà, il suo ful - mi - ne ca - drà!
D. E.
strahl, tref - fe dich sein Feu - er - strahl!
drà, il suo ful - mi - ne ca - drà!
Z.
strahl, tref - fe dich sein Feu - er - strahl!
drà, il suo ful - mi - ne ca - drà!
D. O.
strahl, tref - fe dich sein Feu - er - strahl!
drà, il suo ful - mi - ne ca - drà!
Don Giovanni
D. G.
Mir verwir - ren sich die Sin - ne,
È con-fu - sa la mia te - sta,
Leporello
L.
Ihm ver-wir - ren sich die
È con - fu - sa la sua
M.
strahl, tref - fe dich sein Feu - er - strahl!
drà, il suo ful - mi - ne ca - drà!
Vc.
Cb.

588
Fl.
Ob.
Clar. in C
Fag.
Cor. in C
a 2
Viol. I
Viol. II
Viola
D.A.
Be - be, be - be!
Tre - ma, tre - ma!
D.E.
Be - be, be - be!
Tre - ma, tre - ma!
Z.
Be - be, be - be!
Tre - ma, tre - ma!
D.O.
Be - be, be - be!
Tre - ma, tre - ma!
D.G.
kaum vermag ich mich zu fas - sen, wild er - reg - te Stür - me ra - sen, drohn von
non so più quel ch'io mi fac - cia, e un or - ri - bi - le tem - pe - sta mi - nac -
L.
Sin - ne, kaum ver - mag er sich zu fas - sen, wild er - reg - te Stür - me ra - sen, drohn von
te - sta, non sa più quel ch'ei si fac - cia, e un or - ri - bi - le tem - pe - sta mi - nac -
M.
Be - be, be - be!
Tre - ma, tre - ma!
Vc.
Cb.
cresc.

593
Fl.
Ob.
Clar. in C
Fag.
Cor. in C
Tr. in C
f
Timp.
f
593
[sopra] una corda
Viol. I
[sopra] una corda
Viol. II
Viola
D. A.
Be - be, be - - - - - - - - - be, Mis - se -
Tre - ma, tre - - - - - - - - - ma, o scel - le -
D. E.
Be - be, be - - - - - - - - - be, Mis - se -
Tre - ma, tre - - - - - - - - - ma, o scel - le -
Z.
Be - be, be - be, Mis - se - tä - ter, du Mis - se -
Tre - ma, tre - ma, tre - ma, tre - ma, o scel - le -
D. O.
Be - be, be - be, Mis - se - tä - ter, du Mis - se -
Tre - ma, tre - ma, tre - ma, tre - ma, o scel - le -
D. G.
al - len Sei - ten mir!
ciando oh Dio mi va!
L.
al - len Sei - ten hier!
ciando oh Dio lo va!
M.
Be - be, be - be, Mis - se - tä - ter, du Mis - se -
Tre - ma, tre - ma, tre - ma, tre - ma, o scel - le -
Vc.
Cb.

598
Fl.
Ob.
Clar. in C
Fag.
Cor. in C
Tr. in C
Timp.
a 2
598
Viol. I
Viol. II
Viola
tr
D.A.
tä-ter! Hör des Don-ners Ra-che-stimme,
ra-to! O di il tuon del-la ven-det-ta,
D.E.
tä-ter! Hör des Don-ners Ra-che-stimme,
ra-to! O di il tuon del-la ven-det-ta,
Z.
tä-ter! Hör des Don-ners Ra-che-stimme,
ra-to! O di il tuon del-la ven-det-ta,
D.O.
tä-ter! Hör des Don-ners Ra-che-stimme,
ra-to! O di il tuon del-la ven-det-ta,
D.G.
Mir ver-wir-ren sich die Sin-ne, kaum ver-mag ich mich zu fassen, wild er-reg-te Stürme
È con-fu-sa la mia te-sta, non so più quel ch'io mi fac-cia, e un or-ri-bi-le ten
L.
Ihm ver-wir-ren sich die Sin-ne, kaum ver-mag er sich zu fassen, wild er-reg-te Stürme
È con-fu-sa la sua te-sta, non sa più quel ch'ei si fac-cia, e un or-ri-bi-le ten
M.
tä-ter! Hör des Don-ners Ra-che-stimme,
ra-to! O di il tuon del-la ven-det-ta,
Vc.
Cb.

603
Fl.
Ob.
Clar. in C
Fag.
Cor. in C
Tr. in C
Timp.
Viol. I
Viol. II
Viola
D.A.
D.E.
Z.
D.O.
D.G.
L.
M.
a 2
tr
hör des Don - ners Ra - che - stimme, sieh den Blitz und za - ge,
o - di il tuon del - la ven - det - ta, che ti fi - schia in - tor - no, in -
rasen, drohn von al - len Seiten mir!
pe - sta mi - nacciando oh Dio mi va!
rasen, drohn von al - len Seiten hier!
pe - sta mi - nacciando oh Dio lo va!

608
a 2
Fl.
Ob.
Clar. in C
Fag.
Cor. in C
Tr. in C
Timp.
608
I
Viol.
II
Viola
D.A.
D.E.
Z.
D.O.
M.
za - ge, weh dir, noch an die - sem Ta - ge tref - fe dich sein Feu - er - strahl, tref -
tor - no; sul tuo ca - po in que - sto gior - no il suo ful - mi - ne ca - drà, sì
Vc.
Cb.

613
Fl.
Ob.
Clar. in C
Fag.
a 2
Cor. in C
Tr. in C
Timp.
613
I
Viol.
II
Viola
D.A.
dich, tref - fe dich sein Feu - er-strahl!
drà, il suo ful - mi-ne ca - drà!
D.E.
dich, tref - fe dich sein Feu - er-strahl!
drà, il suo ful - mi-ne ca - drà!
Z.
dich, tref - fe dich sein Feu - er-strahl!
drà, il suo ful - mi-ne ca - drà!
D.O.
dich, tref - fe dich sein Feu - er-strahl!
drà, il suo ful - mi-ne ca - drà!
Don Giovanni
D.G.
Mut - los soll mich nie - mand se - hen,
Ma non man - ca in me co - rag - gio,
Leporello
L.
Mutlos wird ihn niemand
Ma non manca in lui co -
M.
dich, tref - fe dich sein Feu - er-strahl!
drà, il suo ful - mi-ne ca - drà!
Vc.
Cb.

618
Fl.
Ob.
Clar. in C
Fag.
Cor. in C
Tr. in C
Timp.
618
I
Viol.
II
Viola
D.A.
Hör den Sturm!
O - di il tuon!
Hör den
O - di il
D.E.
Hör den Sturm!
O - di il tuon!
Hör den
O - di il
Z.
Hör den Sturm!
O - di il tuon!
Hör den
O - di il
D.O.
Hör den Sturm!
O - di il tuon!
Hör den
O - di il
D.G.
mag die Welt in Trüm - mer ge - hen,
non mi per - doo mi con - fon - do
L.
se - hen,
rag - gio,
mag die Welt in Trümmer ge - hen,
non si per-deo si con-fon - de,
M.
Hör den Sturm!
O - di il tuon!
Hör den
O - di il
Vc.
Cb.

623 Più stretto
a 2
Fl.
Ob.
Clar. in C
Fag.
Cor. in C
Tr. in C
Timp
ff
f
623 Più stretto
I
Viol.
II
Viola
D.A.
Sturm; weh dir, noch an die-sem Ta-ge treffe dich der Ra-che
tuon; sul tuo ca-po in que-sto gior-no il suo ful-mi-ne ca-
E.
Sturm; weh dir, noch an die-sem Ta-ge treffe dich der Ra-che
tuon; sul tuo ca-po in que-sto gior-no il suo ful-mi-ne ca-
Z.
Sturm; weh dir, noch an die-sem Ta-ge treffe dich der Ra-che
tuon; sul tuo ca-po in que-sto gior-no il suo ful-mi-ne ca-
O.
Sturm; weh, noch heu-te, weh dir, noch heu-te
tuon; sul tuo ca-po in que-sto gior-no
G.
mag die Welt in Trüm-mer gehn, nie-mand soll mich za-gen sehn, nein,
se ca-des-se an-co-ra il mon-do, ca-des-se an-co-ra il mon-do,
mag die Welt in Trüm-mer gehn, nie-mand wird ihn za-gen sehn, nein,
se ca-des-se an-co-ra il mon-do, ca-des-se an-co-ra il mon-do,
Sturm; weh, noch heu-te, weh dir, noch heu-te
tuon; sul tuo ca-po in que-sto gior-no

628
Fl.
Ob.
Clar. in C
Fag.
Cor. in C
Tr. in C
Timp
a 2
628
I
Viol
II
Viola
D.A.
Strahl, tref - fe dich der Ra - che Strahl, weh dir,
drà, il suo ful - mi - ne ca - drà, sul tuo
D.E.
Strahl, tref - fe dich der Ra - che Strahl, weh dir,
drà, il suo ful - mi - ne ca - drà, sul tuo
Z.
Strahl, tref - fe dich der Ra - che Strahl, weh dir,
drà, il suo ful - mi - ne ca - drà, sul tuo
D.O
tref - fe dich der Ra - che Strahl, weh,
il suo ful - mi - ne ca - drà, sul
D.G.
ich bleib fest, ja fest und trotz dem All, mag die Welt in Trüm-
nul - la mai te - mer, te - mer mi fa, se ca - des - se an - co - ra
L.
er bleibt fest, ja fest und trotzt dem All, mag die Welt in Trüm-
nul - la mai te - mer, te - mer lo fa, se ca - des - se an - co - ra
M.
tref - fe dich der Ra - che Strahl, weh,
il suo ful - mi - ne ca - drà, sul
Vc.
Cb.

633
a 2
Fl.
Ob.
lar.in C
Fag.
or.in C
r.in C
imp.
633
I
iol.
II
ola
noch an die - sem Ta - ge treffe dich der Ra - che Strahl, tref - fe dich der
ca - po in que - sto gior - no il suo ful - mi - ne ca - drà, il suo ful - mi -
noch an die - sem Ta - ge treffe dich der Ra - che Strahl, tref - fe dich der
ca - po in que - sto gior - no il suo ful - mi - ne ca - drà, il suo ful - mi -
noch an die - sem Ta - ge treffe dich der Ra - che Strahl, tref - fe dich der
ca - po in que - sto gior - no il suo ful - mi - ne ca - drà, il suo ful - mi -
heu - te, weh dir, noch heu - te tref - fe dich der
ca - po in que - sto gior - no il suo ful - mi -
gehn, nie - mand soll mich za - gen sehn, nein, ich bleib fest, ja fest und
mon - do, ca - des - se an - co - ra il mon - do, nul - la mai te - mer, te -
gehn, nie - mand wird ihn za - gen sehn, nein, er bleibt fest, ja fest und
mon - do, ca - des - se an - co - ra il mon - do, nul - la mai te - mer, te -
heu - te, weh dir, noch heu - te tref - fe dich der
ca - po in que - sto gior - no il suo ful - mi -

688
Fl
Ob.
Clar. in C
a 2
Fag.
Cor. in C
Tr. in C
Timp.
638
I
Viol.
II
Viola
D. A
Ra - che Strahl, tref - fe dich der Ra - che Strahl, tref - fe dich der Ra - che Strahl, tref - fe dich der Ra-
ne ca - drà, il suo ful - mi - ne ca - drà, il suo ful - mi - ne ca - drà, il suo ful - mi - ne
D. E
Ra - che Strahl, tref - fe dich der Ra - che Strahl, tref - fe dich der Ra - che Strahl, tref - fe dich der Ra-
ne ca - drà, il suo ful - mi - ne ca - drà, il suo ful - mi - ne ca - drà, il suo ful - mi - ne
Z.
Ra - che Strahl, tref - fe dich der Ra - che Strahl, tref - fe dich der Ra - che Strahl, tref - fe dich der Ra-
ne ca - drà, il suo ful - mi - ne ca - drà, il suo ful - mi - ne ca - drà, il suo ful - mi - ne
D. O.
Ra - che Strahl, tref - fe dich der Ra - che Strahl, tref - fe dich der Ra - che Strahl, tref - fe dich der Ra-
ne ca - drà, il suo ful - mi - ne ca - drà, il suo ful - mi - ne ca - drà, il suo ful - mi - ne
D. G.
trotz dem All, ich bleib fest und trotz dem All, ich bleib fest und trotz dem All, ich bleib fest und trotz
mer mi fa, nul - la mai te - mer mi fa, nul - la mai te - mer mi fa, nul - la mai te - mer
L.
trotzt dem All, er bleibt fest und trotzt dem All, er bleibt fest und trotz dem All, er bleibt fest und trotzt
mer lo fa, nul - la mai te - mer lo fa, nul - la mai te - mer lo fa, nul - la mai te - mer
M.
Ra - che Strahl, tref - fe dich der Ra - che Strahl, tref - fe dich der Ra - che Strahl, tref - fe dich der Ra-
ne ca - drà, il suo ful - mi - ne ca - drà, il suo ful - mi - ne ca - drà, il suo ful - mi - ne
Vc.
Cb.

Ende des ersten Aktes
Fine dell' Atto primo

ZWEITER AKT

Straße

Erste Szene

Don Giovanni. Leporello.

ATTO SECONDO

Strada

Scena I

Don Giovanni, e Leporello.

Nº 14. Duetto

18
Ob.
Cor. in G
Viol. I
Viol. II
Viola
D. G.
fie - le?
sciar-mi?
Es wa-ren Pos-sen, es wa-ren Possen, Possen, Possen, wer-de doch
Va, che sei mat-to, va, che sei mat-to, mat-to, mat-to; fu per bur -
L.
Nichts, nur mein Le-ben stand auf dem Spie-le!
Oh nien-te af-fat-to, qua-si am-maz-zar-mi!
Vc.
Cb.
cresc.
26
klug!
lar.
Gib dich zu - frie - den, laß dich be -
Eh via buf - fo - ne, sen - ti - mi, a -
Von sol-chen Pos-sen, von sol-chen Possen, Possen, Possen hab ich ge - nug!
Ed io non bur-lo, ed io non bur-lo, bur-lo, bur-lo; ma vo-glio an-dar.
Wir sind ge - schie - den,
No, no, pa - dro - ne,

33
Ob.
Cor. in G
Viol.
I
II
Viola
D. G.
lehren, es waren Possen, es waren Possen, es waren Possen, es waren Possen, Possen, Possen,
mi-co, va, che sei matto, va, che sei matto, va, che sei matto, va, che sei matto, matto, matto,
L.
mag nichts mehr hören; nein, nein, nein, nein,
vo'andar, vi dico; no, no, no, no,
Vc.
Cb.
39
Possen,
matto,
es waren Possen, es ware
va, che sei matto, va, che se
nein, nein, nein, nein, nein, nein, nein, nein, nein, nein, nein, mag nichts mehr hören, ich hab genug, ja,
no, no, no, no, no, no, no, no, no, no, no, non vo' restar, no, non vo' restar, sì,
cresc.
tr

Ob.
Cor. in G
Viol.
Viola
D. G.
L.
Vc.
Cb.
cresc.
Pos-sen, es wa-ren Pos-sen, es wa-ren Pos-sen, Pos-sen, Pos-sen, Pos-sen.
mat-to, va, che sei mat-to, va, che sei mat-to, mat-to, mat-to, mat-to.
ja, ja, ja, ja, ja, ja, ja, ja, ja, ja, ja, ja, ja, ja, mag nichts mehr
sì, sì, sì, sì, sì, sì, sì, sì, sì, sì, sì, sì, sì, sì, vo-glio an-
Gib dich zu-frie-den, zu-frie-den, wer-de doch
Eh via buf-fo-ne, buf-fo-ne, non mi sec-
hö-ren, ich hab ge-nug, wir sind ge-schie-den, wir sind ge-schie-den, ich hab ge-
dar, sì, sì, vo-glio an-dar, no, no, pa-dro-ne, no, no, pa-dro-ne, non vo' re-

57
Ob.
Cor. in G
crésc.
cresc.
p
sf
57
Viol.
I
II
Viola
D. G.
L.
Vc.
Cb.
klug, gib dich zu-frie-den, gib dich zu-frie-den, wer-de doch klug, o wer-de klug, o wer-de
car. Va, che sei mat-to, va, che sei mat-to; fu per bur-lar, fu per bur-lar, fu per bur-
nug, wir sind ge-schie-den, wir sind ge-schie-den, ich hab ge-nug, ich hab ge-nug, ich hab ge-
star. Ed io non bur-lo, ed io non bur-lo, ma vo-glio an-dar, ma vo-glio an-dar, ma vo-glio an-
63
a 2
f
[f]
klug, o wer-de klug!
lar, fu per bur-lar.
[Will gehen, Don Giovanni ruft ihn zurück]
[Va per partire; Don Giovanni lo richiama]
nug, ich hab ge-nug.
dar, ma vo-glio an-dar.

Recitativo

[Gibt ihm Geld]
[Gli dà del danaro]
Don Giov. Leporello Don Giovanni Leporello Don Giovanni Leporello
D. G.
L.
Le-po-rel-lo! Eu'r Gnaden! Komm her, wir schließen Frieden: Nimm da! Was denn? Vier Du-blo-nen. Gut, doch hört mich: Für diesmal
Le-po-rel-lo. Si-gno-re. Vien quì, fac-cia-mo pa-ce: pren-di! Co-sa? Quattro dop-pie. Oh sen-ti-te, per que-sta
Cembalo e Basso continuo
5
L.
will ich zum Frieden mich be-que-men, al-lein, Ihr dürft nicht glau-ben, daß Ihr mich und meines-gleichen ver-füh-ren könnt wie die
vol-ta la ce-ri-monia ac-cet-to: ma non vi ci av-vez-za-te; non cre-de-ste di se-dur-re i miei pa-ri co-me le
Cemb. e Basso cont.
8
L.
D.G.
Don Giovanni
Lep.
Wei-ber durch Geld und gu-te Wor-te. Jetzt kein Wort mehr da-von; hast du noch Mut ge-nug, zu tun, was ich dir sa-ge? Ge-
don-ne, a for-za di da-na-ri. Non par-liam più di ciò; ti ba-sta l'a-ni-mo di far quel ch'io ti di-co? Pur-
Cemb. e Basso cont.
12
L.
D.G.
Don Giovanni
wiß, nur laßt die Frau-en. Die Wei-ber las-sen, Dumm-kopf, die Wei-ber las-sen! So hö-re, die Frau-en sind mir
chè la-sciam le don-ne. La-sciar le don-ne, paz-zo, la-sciar le don-ne! Sai ch'el-le per me son ne-ces-
Cemb. e Basso cont.
15
D.G.
L.
Leporello
nöt'-ger, als das Brot zum Es-sen und die Luft, die ich at-me! Und den-noch könnt Ihr sie al-le be-
sa-rie più del pan che man-gio, più dell' a-ria che spi-ro! E a-ve-te co-re d'in-gan-nar-le poi
Cemb. e Basso cont.
18
L.
D.G.
Don Giovanni
trü-gen? O, nur aus Lie-be. Wer nur ei-ne wollt lie-ben, muß die an-dern be-trü-gen; in mei-nem
tut-te? È tut-to a-mo-re. Chi a u-na so-la è fe-de-le ver-so l'al-tre è cru-de-le; io che in me
Cemb. e Basso cont.

21
D. G.
Her-zen, das Na-tur so groß ge-schaf-fen, ist Raum ge-nug für al-le, und nur die Frau-en, die das nicht be-grei-fen, sie
sen-to si e-ste-so sen-ti-men-to, vo' be-ne a tut-te quan-te: le don-ne poi che cal-co-lar non san-no, il
Cemb. e Basso cont.
24
D. G.
L.
Leporello
hal-ten mei-ne Lie-be gleich für Un-treu. Noch nie sah ich im Le-ben solch ein Herz vol-ler Lie-be und sol-cher Gü-te.
mio buon na-tu-ral chia-ma-no in-gan-no. Non ho ve-du-to ma-i na-tu-ra-le più va-sto e più be-ni-gno.
Cemb. e Basso cont.
28
L.
D. G.
Don Giovanni
Nun wohl, was steht zu Dien-sten? Hö-re, sahst du ein-mal die Kam-mer-zo-fe von Don-na El-
Or-sù, co-sa vor-re-ste? O-di, ve-de-sti tu la ca-me-rie-ra di Don-na El
Cemb. e Basso cont.
31
D. G.
L.
Leporello
Don Giovanni
vi-ra? Ich, nein! Dann hast du nie-mals et-was Schö-nes ge-se-hen, mein gu-ter Le-po-rel-lo: Bei ihr nun
vi-ra? Io no. Non hai ve-du-to qual-che co-sa di bel-lo, ca-ro il mio Le-po-rel-lo: o-ra io con
Cemb. e Basso cont.
34
D. G.
will ich heut mein Glück noch ver-su-chen; mein Plan ist fer-tig, so-bald der A-bend an-bricht, will ich im
le-i vo' ten-tar la mia sor-te; ed ho pen-sa-to, già che siam ver-so se-ra, per a-guz
Cemb. e Basso cont.
37
D. G.
L.
Leporello
Dun-kel, um sie zu ge-win-nen, in dei-nem al-ten Man-tel vor ihr er-schei-nen. A-ber wär es nicht bes-ser
zar-le me-glio l'ap-pe-ti-to, di pre-sen-tar-mi a lei col tuo ve-sti-to. E per-chè non po-tre-ste
Cemb. e Basso cont.

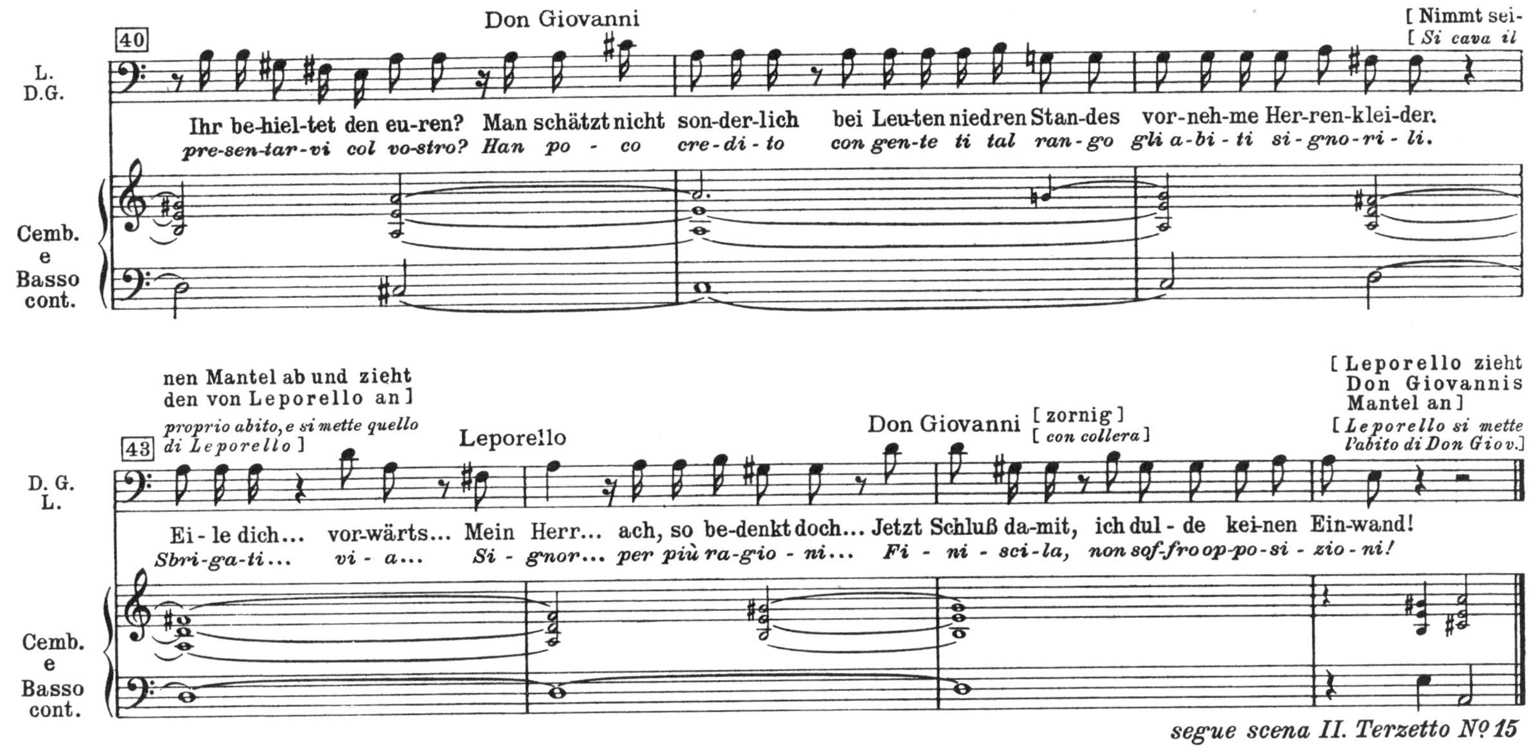

Zweite Szene

[Don Giovanni. Leporello. Donna Elvira (am Fenster).]

[Es wird allmählich dunkel]

Scena II

[Don Giovanni, Leporello; Donna Elvira (alla finestra)]

[Si fa notte a poco a poco]

Nº 15. Terzetto

7
Fl.
Clar. in A
Fag.
Cor. in A
Viol. I II
Viola
D. E.
auf, für ihn zu- schla- gen; der Fal-sche hat mich ver- ra-ten, nicht
pal- pi- tar- mi in se- no; è un em-pio, è un tra-di- to- re, è
Vc.
Cb.
11
a 2
p cresc.
D. E.
darf ich ihm ver- zeihn, nicht darf ich ihm ver-zeihn.
col- pa a-ver pie- tà, è col- pa a-ver pie- tà.
Leporello
L.
Das ist El- vi- ras Stimme, wohl hab ich sie ver-
Zit- to, di Donna El- vi- ra, Si- gnor, la vo-ce io

16
a 2
Fl.
Clar. in A
Fag.
Cor. in A
Viol. I II
Viola
[Stellt sich hinter Leporello und
[Si mette dietro Leporello e parla a
Don Giovanni
D. G.
Das ist mir sehr will-kommen, nimm mei-ne Stel-le ein, nimm mei-ne Stel-le ein.
Co-glie-rei o vo'il mo-men-to; tu fer-ma-ti un po' là, tu fer-ma-ti un po' là.
El-
El-
L.
nom-men.
sen-to.
Vc.
Cb.
21
sf
[div.]
spricht zu Donna Elvira]
Donna Elvira]
vi-ra, du mein Le-ben,
vi-ra, i-do-lo mi-o,
El-vi-ra, du mein Le-ben.
El-vi-ra, i-do-lo mi-o.

27
Fl.
Clar. in A
Fag.
Cor. in A
mf
[p]
Viol. I
Viol. II
Viola
D. E.
D. G.
Vc.
Cb.
p
Donna Elvira
Ist das nicht sei-ne Stim-me?
Non è co-stui l'in-gra-to?
Don Giovanni
Ich bin's, o mei-ne Ge-lieb-te, fleh
Sì, vi-ta mi-a son i-o, e
31
L.
I
Ban-gend in ra-schen Schlä-gen
Nu-mi, che stra-no af-fet-to
fühl ich mein Herz sich re-gen,
mi si ri-sveglia in pet-to,
dich um Mit-leid an!
chie-do ca-ri-tà!
Leporello
Merk schon, die gu-te När-rin
Sta-tea ve-der la paz-za
ver-zeiht ihm noch ein-
che an-cor gli cre-de-

34
Fl.
Clar. in A
Fag.
Viol. I
Viol. II
Viola
D.E.
fühl ich mein Herz_ sich re-gen.
mi si ri-sve-glia in pet-to.
D.G.
O komm her-ab, mein Lieb-chen, o
Dis-cen-di,o gio-ja bel-la, o
L.
mal,_ ja sie ver-zeiht_ihm noch ein-mal.
rà,_gli cre-de-rà,_gli cre-de-rà.
Vc.
Cb.
cresc.
38
komm,___ mein Lieb-chen: Ich schwö-re dir aufs neu-e für Tod und Le-ben
gio- ja bel-la: ve-drai che tu sei quel-la, che a-do-ra l'al-ma

43
Fl.
Clar. in A
Fag.
Viol. I
Viol. II
Viola
D.E.
D.G.
Vc.
Cb.
fp
[div.]
Donna Elvira
Dir glaub ich nun und nim-mer-mehr,
No, non ti cre-do, o bar-ba-ro,
Treu-e, sieh mich vol-ler Reu-e nahn. Ach,
mi-a; pen-ti-to io so-no già. Ah
47
Cor. in A
cresc.
p cresc.
dir glaub ich nun und nim-mer-mehr, dir glaub ich nun und nimmermehr, nun und nimmer!
no, non ti cre-do, o bar-ba-ro, no, non ti cre-do, o bar-ba-ro, non ti cre-do.
glau-be mir, ach, glau-be mir, ach, glau-be mir, sonst ver-
cre-di-mi, ah cre-di-mi, ah cre-di-mi, o m'uc-

50
Fl.
Clar. in A
Fag.
Cor. in A
Viol. I
Viol. II
Viola
D.G.
L.
Vc.
Cb.
cresc.
un poco cresc.
[un poco cresc.]
(Überschwänglich, wie weinend)
(Con trasporto e quasi piangendo)
zweifl ich, sonst ver-zweifl ich, sonst ver-zweifl ich!
ci - do, io m'uc - ci - do, ah m'uc - ci - do!
Leporello (leise zu Don Giovanni)
(piano a Don Giovanni)
Ich kann nicht mehr vor Lachen, ich kann nicht mehr vor Lachen, ich kann nicht mehr, ich la-che, la-che, la-che,
Se se - gui - ta - te io ri - do, se se - gui - ta - te io ri - do, se se - gui - ta - te, io ri - do, ri - do, ri - do,
53
[div.]
Donna Elvira [beiseite] [a parte]
D.E.
Gott schen - ke jetzt mir
Dei, che ci - men - to è
En - gel, o komm her - ab.
I - do - lo mio, vien quà.
[Beiseite] [A parte]
Dank dir, o Se - re-
Spo ro cho ca da
la - che, la - che, la - che, la - che, la - che, la - che, la - che.
ri - do, ri - do, ri - do, ri - do, ri - do, ri - do, ri - do.
Sie glaubt der Mas - ke -
Già quel men - da - ce

57
Fl.
Clar. in A
Fag.
Cor. in A
Viol. I
Viol. II
Viola
D.E.
Gnade, er lenke meine Pfade; wie rührt mich,
que-sto, non so s'io va-do, o re-sto; ah, pro-teg-
D.G.
na-de, hilf du nun, Maske-ra-de; wie ich es recht ver-
pre-sto, che bel col-pet-to è que-sto; più fer-ti-le ta-
L.
ra-de, nun schenke Gott ihr Gna-de; schützt er sie
lab-bro, tor-na a se-dur co-ste-i; deh pro-teg-
Vc.
Cb.
63
ach, sein Fle-hen, kaum kann ich wi-der-stehn, kaum wi-der-
ge-te vo-i la mia cre-du-li-tà, cre-du-li-
ste-he, das kann ein je-der sehn, wie ich es recht ver-ste-he, ja, das kann ein je-der
len-to del mio, no, non si dà, più fer-ti-le ta-len-to, no, del mio, no, non si
nicht vor dem Un-heil, dann ist's um sie ge-schehn, um sie ge-
ge-te, oh De-i, la sua cre-du-li-tà, cre-du-li-

67
Fl.
Clar. in A
Fag.
Cor. in A
Viol. I II
Viola
D.E.
stehn! Gott schen-ke jetzt mir Gna-de, er_ len-ke mei-ne Pfa-de, er schenk mir
tà! Dei,_ che ci-men-to è que-sto, Dei, che ci-men-to è que-sto, non so s'io
D.G.
sehn! Dank dir, o Se-re-na-de, hilf du nun, Mas-ke-
dà! Spe-ro che ca-da pre-sto, che_ bel col-pet-to è
L.
schehn! Sie glaubt der Mas-ke-
tà! Già quel men-da-ce
Vc.
Cb.
70
cresc.
Gna-de, lenk mei- ne Pfa-de, Gott schen-ke jetzt mir Gna-de, er_ len-ke mei-ne
va-do, non so s'io re-sto, Dei, che ci-men-to è que-sto, non so s'io va-do, o
ra-de, o Mas- ke-ra-de, Dank dir, o Se-re-na-de, hilf du nun, Mas-ke-
que-sto, che bel___ col-pet-to, spe-ro che ca-da pre-sto, che_ bel col-pet-to è
ra-de, nun schen-ke Gott ihr Gna-de, sie glaubt der Mas-ke-ra-de, nun schen-ke Gott ihr
lab-bro, tor-na a se-dur co-ste-i, già quel men-da-ce lab-bro tor-na a se-dur co-

73
Fl.
Clar. in A
Fag.
Cor. in A
Viol. I
Viol. II
Viola
D.E.
Pfa - de; wie rührt mich, ach, sein
re - sto; ah, pro - teg - ge - te
D.G.
ra - de; wie ich es recht ver - ste - he, das kann ein je - der
que - sto; più fer - ti - le ta - len - to del mio, no, non si
L.
Gna - de; schützt er sie nicht vor dem
ste - i; deh pro - teg - ge - te, oh
Vc.
Cb.
76
a 2
Fle - hen, kaum kann ich wi - der - stehn, kaum wi - der - stehn, kau
vo - i la mia cre - du - li - tà, cre - du - li - tà, la
sehn, wie ich es recht ver - ste - he, ja, das kann ein je - der sehn,
dà, più fer - ti - le ta - len - to, no, del mio, no, non si dà,
Un - heil, dann ist's um sie ge - schehn, um sie ge - schehn,
De - i, la sua cre - du - li - tà, cre - du - li - tà,
sf p mf sfp p cresc.

80
a 2
Fl.
Clar. in A
Fag.
Cor. in A
80
I
Viol.
II
Viola
D.E.
D.G.
L.
Vc.
Cb.
p cresc.
pp
[p]
[cresc.]
(Verläßt das Fenster)
(Parte dalla finestra)
kann ich wi - der - stehn, kaum kann ich wi - der - stehn!
mia cre - du - li - tà, la mia cre - du - li - tà!
ein je - der sehn, ein je - der sehn!
no, non si dà, no, non si dà!
um sie ge - schehn, um sie ge - schehn!
cre - du - li - tà, cre - du - li - tà!

Recitativo

Don Giovanni [sehr heiter] [allegrissimo]
Leporello
Don Giovanni
D.G.
L.
Nun Freund, was sagst du jetzt? Ich kann nur sa-gen: Ihr habt ein Herz von Ei - sen. Geh, geh, sei nicht so albern! Nun gib wohl
A - mi - co, che ti par? Mi par che abbia-te un' a - ni - ma di bron-zo. Va là, che sei il grangonzo! A-scol-ta
Cembalo e Basso continuo
5
D.G.
acht; siehst du die Tür sie öff-nen, so eilst du ihr ent-ge-gen, schließt sie in dei-ne Ar-me, ahmst mei-ne Stim-me
be - ne; quan - do co-stei qui vie - ne, tu cor-ri ad abbrac-ciar-la, fal - le quat-tro ca-rez-ze, fin - gi la vo - ce
Cemb. e Basso cont.

Dritte Szene

Die Vorigen. Donna Elvira.

Scena III

I suddetti. Donna Elvira.

segue Canzonetta di Don Giovanni Nº 16

№ 16. Canzonetta

16
Viol. I
II
Viola
Mand.
D.G.
flehn, so macht ein ra - scher Tod, du Fal - sche, sollst es sehn, ein
dar qual - - che ri - sto - - ro, da - van - ti a-gli oc-chi tuoi mo - -
Vc.
Cb.
21
En - de mei - ner Not. Mir lacht dein sü - ßes
rir vogl' i - - o. Tu ch'hai la boc - ca
26
Münd - chen vol - - ler Won - ne, und dein lieb - li - ches Au - ge strahlt
dol - ce più che il me - le, tu che il zuc - che - ro por - ti in

31
Viol. I
Viol. II
Viola
Mand.
D.G.
wie die Son - - ne; magst
mez - zo il co - - re, non
Vc.
Cb.
35
du auch grau - sam sein, was gilt's, du hast mich lieb: las - se mich nicht al -
es - ser, gio - ja mia, con me cru - de - - le: la - scia - ti al - men ve -
40
lein, du lo - ser Her - zens-dieb.
der, mio bell' a - mo - - re.

Vierte Szene

Der Vorige. Masetto (mit Gewehr und Pistole bewaffnet). Bauern.

Scena IV

Masetto (armato d'archibuso e pistola), contadini, e suddetto.

Recitativo

segue Aria di Don Giovanni Nº 17

Nº 17. Aria

5
Cor. in F
5
I
Viol.
II
Viola
D.G.
klug und still, dann fangt ihr ihn, er ist nicht weit von hier, ja, ja,
pian pia-nin lo cer-chi-no, lon-tan non fia di quà, no, lon-
Vc.
Cb.
9
Fl.
a 2
[p]
Ob.
[p]
I
Fag.
[p]
9
I
Viol.
II
Viola
D.G.
ja, er ist nicht weit von hier. Zeigt sich auf je-nem Platze ein Mann mit sei-nem
tan, lon-tan non fia di quà. Se un uom e u-na ra-gaz-za pas-seg-gian per la
Vc.
Cb.

13
Ob.
Fag.
Cor. in F
Viol. I II
Viola
D.G.
Schatze, hört un-ter ei-nem Fenster ihr Lie-bes-lie-der sin-gen, dann haltet ihn und faßt ihn, dann packt ihn und er-
piazza, se sotto a u-na fi-ne-stra fa-re all' a-mor sen-ti-te, fe-ri-te pur, fe-ri-te, fe-ri-te pur, fe
Vc.
Cb.
17
Fl.
a 2
[div.]
schlagt ihn,
ri-te,
den sau-bren Ka-va-lier.
il mio pa-dron sa-rà.
Noch mer-ke sich ein
In te-sta egli ha un cap

21
Fl.
Ob.
Fag.
Cor. in F
Viol. I
Viol. II
Viola
D.G.
Vc.
Cb.
a 2
cresc.
tr
je - der, am Hut die wei - ße Fe - der, den Man - tel um - ge -
pel - lo con can - di - di pen - nac - chi, ad - dos - so un gran man -
25
schla - gen, am De - gen gleich die Hand, am De - gen gleich die
tel - lo, e spa - da al fian - co e - gli ha, e spa - da al fian - co e -

29
Fl.
Ob.
Fag.
Cor. in F
Viol. I II
Viola
D.G.
Vc.
Cb.
a 2
cresc.
Hand, am Degen gleich die Hand, das ist er, glaubet mir, der saubre Kava-
gli ha, e spada al fianco e-gli ha, e spa-da al fianco e-gli ha, e spada al fianco e-
33
lier.
gli ha.
Zeigt sich auf jenem Platze ein Mann mit seinem Schatze,
Se un uom e una ragazza passeggian per la piazza,

37
Cor. in F
p
cresc.
37
I
Viol.
II
tr
cresc.
[div.]
Viola
cresc.
D.G.
hört un-ter ei-nem Fen - ster ihr Liebeslie - der singen, dann faßt ihn, dann faßt ihn, dann packt ihn und er-
se sotto a una fi - ne - stra fare all'a-mor sen - ti - te, fe - ri - te, fe - ri - te, fe - ri - te pur, fe-
Vc.
Cb.
cresc.
42
Fl.
Ob.
Cor. in F
f
decresc.
p
42
I
Viol.
II
Viola
D.G.
schlagt ihn, dann packt ihn und er-schlagt ihn, erschlagt ihn! Ihr geht nach je ner Sei te hin, durch
ri - te, fe - ri - te pur, fe - ri - te, fe - ri - te! Me - tà di voi quà va - da-no, e
Vc.
Cb.

46
Fl.
Ob.
Fag.
Cor. in F
Viol. I II
Viola
D. G.
Vc.
Cb.
die - se Gas-se ihr,
gli al-tri va-dan là,
nur klug und still, dann fangt ihr ihn,
e pian pia-nin lo cer-chi-no,
er
lon
50
I
a 2
tr
ist nicht weit von hier, ja, ja, ja, er ist nicht weit von hier.
tan non fia di quà no, lon - tan, lon-tan non fia di quà.
Nur hur-tig oh-
An - da - te, fa-

54
Fl.
Ob.
Fag.
Cor. in F
Viol. I II
Viola
D.G.
Vc.
Cb.
a 2
cresc.
[Die Bauern gehen ab] [Zu Masetto]
[I contadini partono] [A Masetto]
Weilen, nur hurtig ohne Weilen, ohne Weilen, ohne Weilen, oh-ne Weilen, oh-ne Weilen! Nur du, du bleibst bei
presto, an-da-te, fa-te presto, fa-te presto, fa-te presto, presto, presto, presto, presto! Tu sol ver-rai con
58
mir, nur du, du bleibst bei mir, du bleibst bei mir, du bleibst bei mir. Glaub_mir, o Freund Ma-set-to, den
me, tu sol ver-rai con me, ver-rai con me, ver-rai con me. Noi__far dob-bia-mo il re-sto, e

63
Fl.
Ob.
Fag.
Cor. in F
Viol. I
Viol. II
Viola
D. G.
Rest be-sor-gen wir, ja, ja, ja, ja, glaub ___ mir, o Freund Ma-set-to, den Rest be-sor-gen
già ve-drai cos' è, cos' è, cos' è, noi ___ far dob-bia-mo il re-sto, e già ve-drai cos'
Vc.
Cb.
69
wir, ja, ja, ja, ja, den Rest be-sor-gen wir, ja, ja, ja, ja, den Rest be-sor-gen wir, den Rest be-sor-gen
è, cos' è, cos' è, e già vedrai cos' è, cos' è, cos' è, e già vedrai cos' è, e già ve-drai cos

74
Fl.
Ob.
Fag.
Cor. in F
Viol. I
Viol. II
Viola
(Nimmt Masetto mit sich [und geht ab])
(Prende seco Masetto [e parte])
D. G.
wir, den Rest be-sor-gen wir, den Rest be-sor-gen wir.
è, e già ve-drai cos' è, e già ve-drai cos' è.
Vc.
Cb.
79
I
a 2
f

Fünfte Szene

Don Giovanni. Masetto.

[Don Giovanni kommt, Masetto an der Hand führend, zurück]

Scena V

Don Giovanni, e Masetto.

[Ritorna in scena Don Giovanni, conducendo seco per la mano Masetto]

Recitativo

Sechste Szene

Masetto. Dann **Zerlina** (mit einer Laterne).

Scena VI

Masetto, poi **Zerlina** (con lanterna).

41
Zerlina
M.
Z.
Hän-den. Je nun, das tut nicht viel, wenn du sonst nur heil bist. Komm nur mit mir nach Hau-se, und
ma-no. Via, via, non è gran mal, se il re-sto è sa-no. Vien-te-ne me-co a ca-sa, pur-
Cemb. e Basso cont.
44
Z.
wenn du mir versprichst, die Ei-fer-sucht auf-zu-ge-ben, dann will ich dich schon hei-len, mein Ma-set-to.
chè tu mi pro-met-ta d'es-se-re men ge-lo-so, io, io ti gua-ri-rò, ca-ro il mio spo-so.
Cemb. e Basso cont.
segue Aria di Zerlina Nº 18

Nº 18. Aria

Grazioso
2 Flauti
2 Clarinetti in C
2 Fagotti
2 Corni in C
mezza voce
p
Grazioso
Violino I
Violino II
mezza voce
[mezza voce]
tr
Viola
Zerlina
Wenn du fein ar-tig bist, will ich dir
Ve-drai, ca-ri-no, se sei buo
Violoncello
Contrabasso

12
Fl.
Clar. in C
Fag.
Cor. in C
p
12
Viol. I
Viol. II
Viola
Z.
hel - fen, ich weiß ein Mit - tel, das hel-fen kann. 's ist so na - tür - lich,
ni - no, che bel ri - me - dio ti vo - glio dar. È na - tu - ra - le,
Vc.
Cb.
23
Fl.
Fag.
23
Viol. I
Viol. II
Viola
Z.
es schmeckt so lieb - lich, kein A - po - the - ker kennt sei - ne Kraft, nein, kein A - po - the - ker kennt sei - ne Kraft.
non dà dis - gu - sto, e lo spe - cia - le non lo sa far, no, non lo sa far, no, non lo sa far.
Vc.
Cb.

34
Fl.
Clar. in C
Fag.
Cor. in C
Viol. I II
Viola
Z.
Ja, die-ser Bal-sam wirk-te schon Wun-der, willst du ihn pro-ben, ich bin be-reit.
E un cer-to bal-sa-mo che por-to ad-dos-so; da-re te'l pos-so, se'l vuoi pro-var.
Vc.
Cb.
44
a 2
Willst du auch wis-sen, wo ich ihn ber-ge, wo ich ihn heimlich ver-ber-ge?
Sa-per vor-re-sti do-ve mi sta, do-ve, do-ve, do-ve mi sta?

54
Fl.
Clar. in C
Fag.
Cor. in C
Viol. I II
Viola
[div.]
Z.
(Führt seine Hand an ihr Herz)
(Facendogli toccar il core)
Fühlst du es klo - pfen hier, das heilt dein Leid, fühlst du es
Sen - ti - lo bat - te - re, toc - ca - mi quà, sen - ti - lo
Vc.
Cb.
mf
62
p
tr
klo - pfen hier, fühlst du es klo - pfen hier, das heilt dein Leid, fühlst du es klopfen hier, fühlst du es
bat - te - re, sen - ti - lo bat - te - re, toc - ca - mi quà, sen - ti - lo bat - te - re, sen - ti - lo

69
Fl.
Clar. in C
Fag.
Cor. in C
Viol. I
Viol. II
Viola
Z.
Vc.
Cb.
p
tr
klopfen hier, füh-le dies Klopfen hier, das heilt dein Leid, dein Leid, Fühlst du es-
bat-te-re, sen-ti-lo bat-te-re, toc-ca-mi quà, quà, quà, sen-ti-lo
77
klo-pfen hier, füh-le dies Klo-pfen, füh-le dies Klo-pfen, füh-le dies Klo-pfen, das heilt dein
bat-te-re, toc-ca-mi quà, quà, toc-ca-mi quà, quà, toc-ca-mi quà, quà, toc-ca-mi
cresc.

85
Fl.
Clar. in C
Fag.
a 2
Cor. in C
85
I
Viol.
II
Viola
(Geht mit Masetto ab)
(Parte con Masetto)
Z.
Leid.
quà.
Vc.
Cb.
95
Fl.
Clar. in C
Fag.
Cor. in C
95
(Vorhang zu)
I
Viol.
II
Viola
Vc.
Cb.

Verwandlung

Dunkle [im Erdgeschoß gelegene] Vorhalle mit drei Türen [im Haus von Donna Anna].

Siebente Szene

Leporello. Donna Elvira. Dann Donna Anna, Don Ottavio [und Diener (mit Fackeln)].

Mutazione

Atrio [terreno] oscuro con tre porte [in casa di Donna Anna].

Scena VII

Leporello, Donna Elvira, poi Donna Anna, Don Ottavio [con servi e lumi].

Recitativo

segue Sestetto Nº 19

Nº 19. Sestetto

Fl.
Ob.
Clar. in B
Fag.
Cor. in Es
Viol. I
Viol. II
Viola
D.E.
Vc.
Cb.
Seele, sie bebt befangen, neuer Jammer ahnet mir,_ neuer Jam - - - mer ahnet
sale un tal spavento, che mi sembra di morir,_ che mi sem - - - bra di mo-
cresc.
mir!
rir.
Leporello [geht tastend umher]
[andando a tentone]
L.
Ach, vergebens, wo ich suche, keine Türe, keine Türe ist zu finden.
Più che cerco, men ritrovo questa porta, questa porta sciagurata.
a 2

18
Fl.
Clar. in B
Fag.
Cor. in Es
a 2
[p]
Viol. I II
Viola
Leporello
[Verfehlt die Tür]
[Sbaglia la porta]
L.
Sach-te, sachte, ja, da ist sie, ja, da ist sie, jetzt ver-schwinde ich von hier, jetzt ve
Pia-no, pia-no, l'ho tro-va-ta, l'ho tro-va-ta, ec-co il tem-po di fug-gir, ec-co
Vc.
Cb.
24
Fl.
Ob.
Clar. in B
Fag.
Cor. in Es
Tr. in D
Timp.
p
Viol. I II
Viola
[Donna Anna und Don Ottavio tr
[Donna Anna e Don Ottavio entran
L.
schwin-de ich von hier, jetzt verschwinde, jetzt verschwinde, jetzt verschwinde ich von hier.
tem-po di fug-gir, ec-co il tem-po, ec-co il tem-po, ec-co il tem-po di fug-gir.
Vc.
Cb.

30
Fl.
Ob.
Fag.
Tr. in D
Timp.
30
Viol. I
Viol. II
Viola
in Trauerkleidung ein]
stiti a lutto]
Don Ottavio
D.O.
Blick em - por, ge - lieb - tes We - sen, und laß ab von_ dei - - nem
Ter-gi il ci - glio, o vi - ta mi - a, e dà cal - - - - ma al tuo do -
Vc.
Cb.
35
Ob.
Fag.
Tr. in D
Timp.
35
Viol. I
Viol. II
Viola
D.O.
Kum - - mer; ach, dei - - nes Va - ters_ ew' - gen
lo - re; l'om - - - - - - bra o - mai del_ ge - ni -
Vc.
Cb.

39
Fl.
Ob.
Fag.
Tr. in D
Timp.
Viol. I
Viol. II
Viola
D.O.
Schlum - mer stört dein schmerz - lich kla - gend
to - re pe - na a - vrà de' tuoi mar -
Vc.
Cb.
48
Donna Anna
D.A.
Laß mich kla - gen, laß mich
La - scia, la - scia al - la mia
Herz, dein kla - gend Herz.
tir, de' tuoi mar - tir.

47
Fl.
Ob.
Fag.
Cor. in D
in Es
Timp.
in Es und B
Viol. I II
Viola
D.A.
wei - nen, gön-ne mir den Trost der Trä - nen; erst im
pe - na que-sto pic - cio - lo ri - sto - ro; so - la
Vc.
Cb.
51
Fl.
Ob.
Cl. in B
Fag.
Cor. in Es
Viol. I II
Viola
D.A.
Gra - be, erst im Gra - be wird all mein Seh - nen,
mor - te, so - la mor - te, o mio te - so - ro,
Vc.
Cb.

55
Fl.
Ob.
Clar. in B
Fag.
Cor. in Es
Viol. I II
Viola
D. A.
wird mein Schmerz er - lo - schen sein, wird mein Schmerz
il mio pian - to può fi - nir, il mio pian
Vc.
Cb.
59
er - lo - schen sein!
to può fi - nir!
Donna Elvira [ohne gesehen
[senza esser vi
D. E.
Ach, wo mag der Gat-
Ah dov' è lo spo-

63
Viol. I
II
Viola
D.E.
werden]
wei - len?
mi - o?
Leporello [von der Tür aus, ungesehen]
[dalla porta, senza esser visto]
Hier die Tür, nun will ich ei-len, sach-te, sach-te fort von
U - na por - ta là vegg' i - o, che - ta, che - ta vo' par-
L.
Trifft sie mich, bin ich ver - lo-ren!
Se mi tro - va son per - du - to!
Hier die Tür, nun will ich
U - na por - ta là vegg'
Vc.
Cb.
67
Clar. in B
Fag.
67
Viol. I
II
[div.]
Viola
[Beim Fortgehen stoßen sie auf Zerlina und Masetto]
[Nel sortire s'incontrano in Zerlina e Masetto]
D.E.
hier, sach - te, sach - te fort von hier!
tir, che - ta, che - ta vo' par - tir!
L.
ei - len, sach - te, sach - te fort von hier, hier die Tür, nun will ich ei - len, sach - te, sach - te fort von
i - o, che - to, che - to vo' par - tir, che - to, che - to, che - to, che - to, che - to, che - to vo' par-
Vc.
Cb.

Achte Szene

[Die Vorigen. Zerlina. Masetto]

Scena VIII

[I suddetti. Zerlina. Masetto]

74
Fl.
Ob.
Clar. in B
Fag.
a 2
Cor. in Es
a 2
74
I
Viol.
II
p
p
Viola
p
D.A.
Schänd - lichen, der mich ver - ra - ten, der mich ver - ra - ten!
per - fi-do, che m'ha tra - di - to, che m'ha tra - di - to!
Z.
Schänd - lichen, der mich ver - ra - ten, der mich ver - ra - ten!
per - fi-do, che m'ha tra - di - to, che m'ha tra - di - to!
Donna Elvira
D.E.
Schont mei - nes
È mio ma -
D.O.
Schänd - lichen, der mich ver - ra - ten, der mich ver - ra - ten!
per - fi-do, che m'ha tra - di - to, che m'ha tra - di - to!
M.
Schänd - lichen, der mich ver - ra - ten, der mich ver - ra - ten!
per - fi-do, che m'ha tra - di - to, che m'ha tra - di - to!
Vc.
p
Cb.
p

78
I
Viol.
II
Viola
D.A.
Z.
D.E.
D.O.
M.
Vc.
Cb.
sotto voce
Was muß ich se-hen, was muß ich
È Don-na El-vi-ra, è Don - na E
sotto voce
Was muß ich se-hen, was muß ich
È Don-na El-vi-ra, è Don-na E
Gat - ten, er - barmt, er-barmt euch mein!
ri - to, pie - tà, pie-tà, pie - tà!
sotto voce
Was muß ich sehn,was muß ich
È Don-na El-vi - ra,Don-na E
sotto voce
Was muß ich
È Don-na E
82
se - hen, Don - na El - vi - ra, kaum kann ich's ve
vi - ra, quel - la ch'io ve - do, ap - pe - na i
se - hen, Don - na El - vi-ra, kaum kann ich's ver- ste - hen, kaum kann ich's v
vi - ra, quel - la ch'io ve-do, ap - pe - na il cre - do, ap - pe - na i
se - hen, Don-na El - vi - ra, kaum kann ich's ver
vi - ra, quel - la ch'io ve - do, ap - pe - na il
se - hen, Don - na El - vi - ra, kaum kann ich's ver
vi - ra, quel - la ch'io ve - do, ap - pe - na il

86
Fl.
Ob.
lar.in B
a 2
Fag.
r.in Es
86
I
Viol.
II
Viola
D.A.
ste - hen! Nein, nein, nein, nein, er stirbt!
cre - do! No, no, no, no, mor - rà!
Z.
ste - hen! Nein, nein, nein, nein, er stirbt!
cre - do! No, no, no, no, mor - rà!
Donna Elvira
D.E.
Er - barmt euch mein! Er -
Pie - tà, pie - tà! Pie -
D.O.
ste - hen! Nein, nein, nein, nein, er stirbt!
cre - do! No, no, no, no, mor - rà!
M.
ste - hen! Nein, nein, nein, nein, er stirbt!
cre - do! No, no, no, no, mor - rà!
Vc.
Cb.

91
a 2
Fl.
Ob.
Clar. in B
Fag.
Cor. in Es
Viol. I
Viol. II
Viola
D.A.
Nein, nein, nein, nein, nein
No, no, no, no, no
Z.
Nein, nein, nein, nein, nei
No, no, no, no, no
D.E.
barmt, er - barmt, er - barmt euch mein!
tà, pie - tà, pie - tà, pie - tà!
D.O.
Nein, nein, nein, nein, nei
No, no, no, no, nc
M.
Nein, nein, nein, nein, nei
No, no, no, no, nc
Vc.
Cb.

96
Fl.
Ob.
Clar. in B
Fag.
Cor. in Es
I
a 2
p
cresc.
96
Viol. I
Viol. II
Viola
[div.]
fp
D.A.
nein,
no,
er stirbt!
mor - rà!
Z.
nein,
no,
er stirbt!
mor - rà!
D.O.
[Will ihn töten]
[In atto di ucciderlo]
nein,
no,
er stirbt!
mor - rà!
Leporello (zeigt sein Gesicht und wirft sich vor den andern auf die Knie; weinerlich)
([si scopre e si mette in ginocchio;] quasi piangendo)
L.
Ach, habt Er - bar - men und schont mich Ar - men,
Per-don, per - do - no, Si - gno - ri mie - i,
M.
nein,
no,
er stirbt!
mor - rà!
Vc.
Cb.

102
Fl.
Clar. in B
Fag.
Cor. in Es
Viol. I
Viol. II
Viola
L.
das hier sind lei - der nur sei-ne Klei - der; o tut mir nur kein Lei
quel-lo io non so - no, sba-glia co - ste - i; vi-ver la-scia-te-mi
Vc.
Cb.
108
Fl.
Ob.
Clar. in B
Fag.
Cor. in Es
Viol. I
Viol. II
Viola
L.
Barmher - zig - keit, o tut mir nur kein Leid, Barmher - zig - keit, Barmherzig - keit, Barmherzi
per ca - ri - tà, vi-ver la-scia-te-mi per ca - ri - tà, per ca-ri - tà, per ca -
Vc.
Cb.

114
Fl.
Ob.
Clar. in B
Fag.
Cor. in Es
a 2
Viol. I
II
Viola
Donna Anna
sotto voce
D.A.
Wie, Le-po - rel - lo, welch neu - e Täu-schung, Le - - po-
Dei, Le-po - rel - lo, che in-gan-no è que - sto, Le - - po-
Zerlina
Z.
Wie, Le-po - rel - lo, welch neu - e Täu-schung, Le - - po-
Dei, Le-po - rel - lo, che in-gan-no è que - sto, Le - - po-
Donna Elvira
D.E.
Wie, Le-po - rel - lo, welch neu - e Täu-schung, Le - - po-
Dei, Le-po - rel - lo, che in-gan-no è que - sto, Le - - po-
Don Ottavio
D.O.
Wie, Le-po - rel - lo, welch neu - e Täu-schung, Le - - po-
Dei, Le-po - rel - lo, che in-gan-no è que - sto, Le - - po-
L.
keit!
tà!
Masetto
M.
Wie, Le-po - rel - lo, welch neu - e Täu-schung, Le - - po-
Dei, Le-po - rel - lo, che in-gan-no è que - sto, Le - - po-
Vc.
Cb.

119
Fl.
Ob.
Clar. in B
Fag.
Cor. in Es
a 2
Viol. I
II
Viola
D.A.
Z.
D.E.
D.O.
M.
Vc.
Cb.
sotto voce
rel - lo, welch neu - e Täu-schung! Stau-nen er-faßt mich,
rel - lo, che in-gan-no è que - sto! Stu - pi - da re - sto,

124
Fl.
Ob.
Clar. in B
Fag.
Cor. in Es
a 2
p
124
I
Viol.
II
Viola
D.A.
was ist zu tun, o Gott, was ist, o Gott, was ist hier nun zu tun!
che mai sa-rà, che mai sa-rà, che mai sa-rà, che mai sa-rà!
Z.
was ist zu tun, o Gott, was ist hier nun zu tun, o Gott, was ist hier nun zu tun!
che mai sa-rà, che mai sa-rà, che mai sa-rà, che mai sa-rà, che mai sa-rà!
D.E.
was ist zu tun, o Gott, was ist hier nun zu tun, o Gott, was ist hier nun zu tun!
che mai sa-rà, che mai sa-rà, che mai sa-rà, che mai sa-rà, che mai sa-rà!
D.O.
was ist zu tun, o Gott, was ist hier nun zu tun, o Gott, was ist hier nun zu tun!
che mai sa-rà, che mai sa-rà, che mai sa-rà, che mai sa-rà, che mai sa-rà!
M.
was ist zu tun, hier nun zu tun, o Gott, was ist hier nun zu tun!
che mai sa-rà, che mai sa-rà, che mai sa-rà, che mai sa-rà!
Vc.
Cb.

131 Molto Allegro
Fl.
Ob.
Clar. in B
Fag.
Cor. in Es
Tr. in Es
in Es und B
Timp.
131 Molto Allegro
Viol. I
II
Viola
Donna Anna
D. A.
Tau - send schreck-li - che Ge
Mil - le tor - bi - di pe
Zerlina
Z.
Tau - send schreck-li - che Ge
Mil - le tor - bi - di pe
Donna Elvira
D. E.
Tau - send schreck-li-che
Mil - le tor - bi-di
Don Ottavio
D. O.
Tau - send schreck-li - che Ge
Mil - le tor - bi - di pe
Leporello
L.
Tau - send schreck - li - che Ge - dan-ken
Mil - le tor - bi - di pen - sie-ri
Masetto
M.
Tau - send schreck-li-che Ge
Mil - le tor - bi-di pe
Vc.
Cb.

139
Fl.
a 2
Ob.
Clar. in B
Fag.
Cor. in Es
Tr. in Es
Timp.
139
Viol. I
Viol. II
Viola
D. A.
dan-ken
sie-ri
ja - gen wild durch mei-ne
mi s'ag - gi - ran per la
Z.
dan-ken
sie-ri
ja - gen wild durch mei-ne
mi s'ag - gi - ran per la
D. E.
dan-ken
sie-ri
ja - gen wild durch mei - ne
mi s'ag - gi - ran per la
D. O.
dan-ken
sie-ri
ja - gen wild durch mei - ne
mi s'ag - gi - ran per la
L.
ja - gen wild durch mei - ne Sin-ne,
mi s'ag - gi - ran per la te-sta,
M.
dan-ken
sie-ri
ja - gen wild durch mei-ne
mi s'ag - gi - ran per la
Vc.
Cb.

147
Fl.
Ob.
Clar. in B
Fag.
Cor. in Es
Tr. in Es
Timp.
147
Viol. I
Viol. II
Viola
D.A.
Sin - ne!
te - sta!
Z.
Sin - ne!
te - sta!
D.E.
Sin - ne!
te - sta!
D.O.
Sin - ne!
te - sta!
L.
tausend schreckliche Ge-danken jagen wild durch meine Sin-ne, wenn ich heut dem Sturm ent-rin-ne, hat's ein Wun-der nur vo
mil-le tor - bi-di pen-sie-ri mi s'ag-gi-ran per la te-sta; se mi sal-vo in tal tem-pe-sta, è un pro-di-gio in ve-r
M.
Sin - ne!
te - sta!
Vc.
Cb.
a 2
p
cresc.
f

151
Fl.
Ob.
Clar. in B
Fag.
Cor. in Es
Tr. in Es
Timp.
Viol. I
Viol. II
Viola
D. A.
Neu - e Fre - vel an je - dem Ta - ge, an je - dem Ta - ge!
Che gior - na - ta, o stel - le, è que - sta, o stel - le, è que - sta!
Z.
Neu - e Fre - vel an je - dem Ta - ge, an je - dem Ta - ge!
Che gior - na - ta, o stel - le, è que - sta, o stel - le, è que - sta!
D. E.
Neu - e Fre - vel an je - dem Ta - ge, an je - dem Ta - ge!
Che gior - na - ta, o stel - le, è que - sta, o stel - le, è que - sta!
D. O.
Neu - e Fre - vel an je - dem Ta - ge, an je - dem Ta - ge!
Che gior - na - ta, o stel - le, è que - sta, o stel - le, è que - sta!
L.
bracht, hat ein Wun - der es nur voll - bracht, wenn ich
tà, è un pro - di - gio in ve - ri - tà, se mi
M.
Neu - e Fre - vel an je - dem Ta - ge, an je - dem Ta - ge!
Che gior - na - ta, o stel - le, è que - sta, o stel - le, è que - sta!
Vc.
Cb.

158
Fl.
Ob.
Clar. in B
Fag.
158
Viol. I
II
Viola
L.
heu - te dem Sturm ent - rin - ne, hat ein Wun - der es nur voll - bracht, wenn ich heut dem Sturm ent -
sal - vo in tal tem - pe - sta, è un pro - di - gio in ve - ri - tà, è un pro - di - gio in ve - ri -
Vc.
Cb.
162
Fl.
Ob.
Clar. in B
Fag.
162
Viol. I
II
Viola
L.
rin - ne, hat's ein Wun - der nur voll - bracht, hat's ein Wun - der nur voll - -
tà, in ve - ri - tà, in ve - ri - tà, è un pro - di - gio in ve - - - ri - - -
Vc.
Cb.
sf
fp

166
Fl.
Ob.
Clar. in B
Fag.
Cor. in Es
Viol. I
Viol. II
Viola
Donna Anna
sotto voce
D.A.
Neu - es Un - heil je - de Nacht,
Che im - pen - sa - ta no - vi - tà,
Zerlina
sotto voce
Z.
Neu - es Un - heil je - de Nacht,
Che im - pen - sa - ta no - vi - tà,
Donna Elvira
sotto voce
D.E.
Neu - es Un - heil je - de Nacht,
Che im - pen - sa - ta no - vi - tà,
Don Ottavio
sotto voce
D.O.
Neu - es Un - heil je - de Nacht,
Che im - pen - sa - ta no - vi - tà,
L.
bracht! Tausend schreck-li-che Ge - dan-ken ja-gen wild durch mei-ne
tà! Mil-le tor - bi-di pen - sie-ri mi s'ag - gi - ran per la
Masetto
sotto voce
M.
Neu - es Un - heil je - de Nacht,
Che im - pen - sa - ta no - vi - tà,
Vc.
Cb.

174
Fl.
Ob.
Clar. in B
Fag.
Cor. in Es
a 2
Tr. in Es
Timp.
174
Viol. I
Viol. II
Viola
[p]
D.A.
neu - es Un - heil, neu - es Un - heil je - de Nacht,
che im - pen-sa - ta, che im - pen-sa - ta no - vi - tà,
Z.
neu - es Un - heil, neu - es Un - heil je - de Nacht,
che im - pen-sa - ta, che im - pen-sa - ta no - vi - tà,
D.E.
neu - es Un - heil, neu - es Un - heil je - de Nacht,
che im - pen-sa - ta, che im - pen-sa - ta no - vi - tà,
D.O.
neu - es Un - heil, neu - es Un - heil je - de Nacht,
che im - pen-sa - ta, che im - pen-sa - ta no - vi - tà,
L.
Sin - ne, wenn ich heu - te dem Sturm ent-rin - ne hat ein Wun-der es nur voll - bracht,
te - sta; se mi sal - vo in tal tem-pe - sta, è un pro - di - gio in ve - ri - tà,
M.
neu - es Un - heil, neu - es Un - heil je - de Nacht,
che im - pen-sa - ta, che im - pen-sa - ta no - vi - tà,
Vc.
Cb.

180
Fl.
Ob.
lar. in B
Fag.
a 2
or. in Es
r. in Es
Timp.
180
Viol. I II
[div.]
Viola
D. A.
je - de Nacht! Tau - send schreck-li - che Ge -
no - vi - tà! Mil - le tor - bi - di pen -
Z.
neu - es Un - heil je - de Nacht!
che im - pen - sa - ta no - vi - tà!
D.E.
neu - es Un - heil je - de Nacht! Tau - send, tau - send
che im - pen - sa - ta no - vi - tà! Mil - le, mil - le
D.O.
neu - es Un - heil je - de Nacht! Tau - send schreck-li - che Ge -
che im - pen - sa - ta no - vi - tà! Mil - le tor - bi - di pen -
L.
hat's ein Wun - der nur voll-bracht!
è un pro - di - gio in ve - ri - tà!
M.
neu - es Un - heil je - de Nacht!
che im - pen - sa - ta no - vi - tà!
Vc.
Cb.

186
Fl.
Ob.
Clar. in B
Fag.
a 2
Cor. in Es
Tr. in Es
Timp.
186
Viol. I
Viol. II
Viola
D. A.
dan-ken ja - gen wild durch mei-ne Sin-ne!
sie-ri mi s'ag - gi-ran per la te-sta!
Zerlina
Z.
f
Tau - send schreck-li - che Ge - dan-ken ja - gen wild durch mei-ne
Mil - le tor - bi - di pen - sie-ri mi s'ag - gi-ran per la
D. E.
schreck - li - che Ge - dan - ken ja - gen wild durch mei - ne
tor - bi - di pen - sie - ri mi s'ag - gi - ran per la
D. O.
dan-ken ja - gen wild durch mei-ne Sin-ne!
sie-ri mi s'ag - gi-ran per la te-sta!
Masetto
M.
f
Tau - send schreck-li - che Ge - dan-ken ja - gen wild durch mei-ne
Mil - le tor - bi - di pen - sie-ri mi s'ag - gi-ran per la
Vc.
Cb.

192
Fl.
a 2
p
cresc.
f
Ob.
a 2
p
cresc.
f
Clar. in B
a 2
p
cresc.
f
Fag.
a 2
p
cresc.
f
Cor. in Es
Cor. in Es
Timp.
192
I
Viol.
II
p
cresc.
f
Viola
p
cresc.
f
Z.
Sin-ne!
te-sta!
D.E.
Sin-ne!
te-sta!
Leporello
p
cresc.
f
L.
Tausend schreckliche Ge-dan-ken ja-gen wild durch mei-ne Sin-ne, wenn ich heut dem Sturm ent-rin-ne, hat's ein Wun-der nur voll-
Mil-le tor-bi-di pen-sie-ri mi s'ag-gi-ran per la te-sta; se mi sal-vo in tal tem-pe-sta, è un pro-di-gio in ve-ri-
M.
Sin-ne!
te-sta!
Vc.
p
cresc.
f
Cb.
p
cresc.
f

196
Fl.
Ob.
Clar. in B
Fag.
Cor. in Es
Tr. in Es
Timp.
a 2
I
[f]
196
Viol. I
Viol. II
Viola
sf
[sf]
f
D.A.
Donna Anna
Neu - e Fre - vel an je - dem Ta - ge, an je - dem Ta - ge!
Che gior - na - ta, o stel - le, è que - sta, o stel - le, è que - sta!
Z.
Zerlina
Neu - e Fre - vel an je - dem Ta - ge, an je - dem Ta - ge!
Che gior - na - ta, o stel - le, è que - sta, o stel - le, è que - sta!
D.E.
Donna Elvira
Neu - e Fre - vel an je - dem Ta - ge, an je - dem Ta - ge!
Che gior - na - ta, o stel - le, è que - sta, o stel - le, è que - sta!
D.O.
Don Ottavio
Neu - e Fre - vel an je - dem Ta - ge, an je - dem Ta - ge!
Che gior - na - ta, o stel - le, è que - sta, o stel - le, è que - sta!
L.
bracht, hat ein Wun - der es nur voll - bracht, wenn
tà, è un pro - di - gio in ve - ri - tà, se
M.
Masetto
Neu - e Fre - vel an je - dem Ta - ge, an je - dem Ta - ge!
Che gior - na - ta, o stel - le, è que - sta, o stel - le, è que - sta!
Vc.
Cb.

203
Fl.
Ob.
Clar. in B
Fag.
Viol. I
Viol. II
Viola
L.
heu - te dem Sturm ent - rin - ne, hat ein Wun - der es nur voll - bracht, wenn ich heut dem Sturm ent -
sal - vo in tal tem - pe - sta, è un pro - di - gio in ve - ri - tà, è un pro - di - gio in ve - ri -
Vc.
Cb.
207
sf
fp
rin - ne, hat's ein Wun - der nur voll - bracht, hat's ein Wun - der nur voll -
tà, in ve - ri - tà, in ve - ri - tà, è un pro - di - gio in ve - ri -

211
Fl.
Ob.
Clar. in B
Fag.
Cor. in Es
Tr. in Es
Timp.
Viol. I II
Viola
Donna Anna sotto voce
D. A.
Neu - es Un - heil je - de Nacht, neu -
Che im - pen - sa - ta no - vi - tà, che im -
Zerlina sotto voce
Z.
Neu - es Un - heil je - de Nacht, neu -
Che im - pen - sa - ta no - vi - tà, che im -
Donna Elvira sotto voce
D. E.
Neu - es Un - heil je - de Nacht, neu -
Che im - pen - sa - ta no - vi - tà, che im -
Don Ottavio sotto voce
D. O.
Neu - es Un - heil je - de Nacht, neu -
Che im - pen - sa - ta no - vi - tà, che im -
L.
bracht! Tausend schreckli-che Ge - danken ja-gen wild durch mei-ne Sin-ne, wenn ich
tà! Mil-le tor - bi-di pen - sie-ri mi s'ag-gi - ran per la te - sta; se m
Masetto sotto voce
M.
Neu - es Un - heil je - de Nacht, neu -
Che im - pen - sa - ta no - vi - tà, che im -
Vc.
Cb.

220
Fl.
Ob.
Clar. in B
Fag.
Cor. in Es
a 2
Tr. in Es
Timp.
220
Viol. I
II
Viola
D. A.
es Un - heil, neu - es Un - heil je - de Nacht,
pen - sa - ta, che im - pen - sa - ta no - vi - tà,
Z.
es Un - heil, neu - es Un - heil je - de Nacht,
pen - sa - ta, che im - pen - sa - ta no - vi - tà,
D. E.
es Un - heil, neu - es Un - heil je - de Nacht, neu - es
pen - sa - ta, che im - pen - sa - ta no - vi - tà, che im - pen -
D. O.
es Un - heil, neu - es Un - heil je - de Nacht, neu - es
pen - sa - ta, che im - pen - sa - ta no - vi - tà, che im - pen -
L.
heu - te dem Sturm ent - rin - ne, hat ein Wun - der es nur voll - bracht,
sal - vo in tal tem - pe - sta, è un pro - di - gio in ve - ri - tà,
M.
es Un - heil, neu - es Un - heil je - de Nacht, neu - es
pen - sa - ta, che im - pen - sa - ta no - vi - tà, che im - pen -
Vc.
Cb.

226
Fl.
Ob.
Clar. in B
Fag.
Cor. in Es
Viol. I
Viol. II
Viola
[div.]
D. A.
je - de Nacht, neu - es Un - heil je - de Nacht,
no - vi - tà, che im - pen - sa - ta no - vi - tà,
Z.
neu - es Un-heil je - de Nacht, neu - es Un - heil je - de Nacht, neu - es
che im-pen - sa - ta no - vi - tà, che im - pen - sa - ta no - vi - tà, che im - pen -
D. E.
Un - heil je - de Nacht, neu - es Un - heil je -
sa - ta no - vi - tà, che im - pen - sa - ta no -
D. O.
Un - heil je - de Nacht, neu - es Un - heil je -
sa - ta no - vi - tà, che im - pen - sa - ta no -
L.
hat's ein Wun-der nur voll-bracht, hat's ein Wun - der, ein Wun -
è un pro - di-gio in ve - ri - tà, è un pro - di - gio in ve -
M.
Un - heil je - de Nacht, neu - es Un - heil je -
sa - ta no - vi - tà, che im - pen - sa - ta no -
Vc.
Cb.

234
Ob.
Fag.
Cor. in Es
Viol. I
II
Viola
D.A.
neu - es Un - heil je - de Nacht, neu - es Un - heil
che im - pen - sa - ta no - vi - tà, che im - pen - sa - ta
Z.
Un - heil je - de Nacht, neu - es Un - heil
sa - ta no - vi - tà, che im - pen - sa - ta
D.E.
de Nacht, je - de Nacht, neu - es Un - heil
vi - tà, no - vi - tà, che im - pen - sa - ta
D.O.
- de Nacht, je - de Nacht, neu - es Un - heil
- vi - tà, no - vi - tà, che im - pen - sa - ta
L.
der voll - bracht, es nur voll - bracht, hat's ein Wun - der
ri - tà, in ve - ri - tà, è un pro - di - gio in
M.
de Nacht, je - de Nacht, neu - es Un - heil
vi - tà, no - vi - tà, che im - pen - sa - ta
Vc.
Cb.

242
Fl.
Ob.
Clar. in B
Fag.
Cor. in Es
Tr. in Es
Timp.
242
Viol. I
Viol. II
Viola
D.A.
je - de Nacht, neu - es Un - heil je - de Nacht, neu - es Un - heil,
no - vi - tà, che im - pen - sa - ta no - vi - tà, che im - pen - sa - ta,
Z.
je - de Nacht,_ neu - es Un - heil je - de Nacht,_ neu - es Un - heil,
no - vi - tà,_ che im - pen - sa - ta no - vi - tà,_ che im - pen - sa - ta,
D.E.
je - de Nacht,_ neu - es Un - heil je - de Nacht,_ neu - es Un - heil,
no - vi - tà,_ che im - pen - sa - ta no - vi - tà,_ che im - pen - sa - ta,
D.O.
je - de Nacht,_ neu - es Un - heil je - de Nacht,_ neu - es Un - heil,
no - vi - tà,_ che im - pen - sa - ta no - vi - tà,_ che im - pen - sa - ta,
L.
nur voll - bracht,_ hat's ein Wun - der nur voll - bracht,_ hat's ein Wun - der,
ve - ri - tà,_ è un pro - di - gio in ve - ri - tà,_ è un pro - di - gio,
M.
je - de Nacht,_ neu - es Un - heil je - de Nacht,_ neu - es Un - heil,
no - vi - tà,_ che im - pen - sa - ta no - vi - tà,_ che im - pen - sa - ta,
Vc.
Cb.

251
Fl.
Ob
lar in B
Fag.
or. in Es
r. in Es
Timp.
Viol. I II
Viola
D.A.
neu - es Un - - - - heil je - de Nacht, neu - es Un - heil
che im - pen - sa - - - - ta no - - vi - tà, che im - pen - sa - ta
Z.
neu - es Un - - heil je - - - - de Nacht, neu - es Un - heil
che im-pen - sa - - - ta no - - - - vi - tà, che im - pen - sa - ta
D.E.
neu - es Un - - - - - - heil je - de Nacht, neu - es Un - heil
che im - pen - sa - - - - - - ta no - vi - tà, che im - pen - sa - ta
D.O.
neu - es Un - heil je - de Nacht, neu - es Un - heil
che im - pen - sa - ta no - vi - tà, che im - pen - sa - ta
L.
hat's ein Wun - - der
è un pro - di - - - gio in
M.
neu - es Un - heil je - de Nacht, neu - es Un heil
che im - pen - sa - ta no - vi - tà, che im - pen - sa - ta
Vc.
Cb.

262
Fl.
Ob.
Clar. in B
a 2
Fag.
Cor. in Es
Tr. in Es
Timp.
262
I
Viol.
II
Viola
D. A.
je - de Nacht, neu - es Un - heil je - de Nacht, neu - es
no - vi - tà, che im - pen - sa - ta no - vi - tà, che im - pen -
Z.
je - de Nacht, neu - es Un - heil je - de Nacht, neu - es
no - vi - tà, che im - pen - sa - ta no - vi - tà, che im - pen -
D. E.
je - de Nacht, neu - es Un - heil je - de Nacht, neu - es
no - vi - tà, che im - pen - sa - ta no - vi - tà, che im - pen -
D. O.
je - de Nacht, neu - es Un - heil je - de Nacht, neu - es
no - vi - tà, che im - pen - sa - ta no - vi - tà, che im - pen -
L.
nur voll - bracht, hat's ein Wun - - der nur voll - bracht, hat's ein Wun -
ve - ri - tà, è un pro - di - - gio in ve - ri - tà, è un pro - di -
M.
je - de Nacht, neu - es Un - heil je - de Nacht, neu - es
no - vi - tà, che im - pen - sa - ta no - vi - tà, che im - pen -
Vc.
Cb.

269
Fl.
Ob.
Clar. in B
Fag.
Cor. in Es
Tr. in Es
Timp.
a 2
Viol. I
Viol. II
Viola
D.A.
Z.
D.E.
D.O.
L.
M.
Vc.
Cb.
[Geht mit den Dienern ab]
[Parte coi servi]
Un - heil je - de Nacht!
sa - ta no - vi - tà!
- der__ nur voll - bracht!
- gio in ve - ri - tà!

Neunte Szene

Donna Elvira. Don Ottavio. Leporello. Zerlina Masetto.

Scena IX

Donna Elvira, Don Ottavio, Leporello, Zerlina e Masetto.

Recitativo

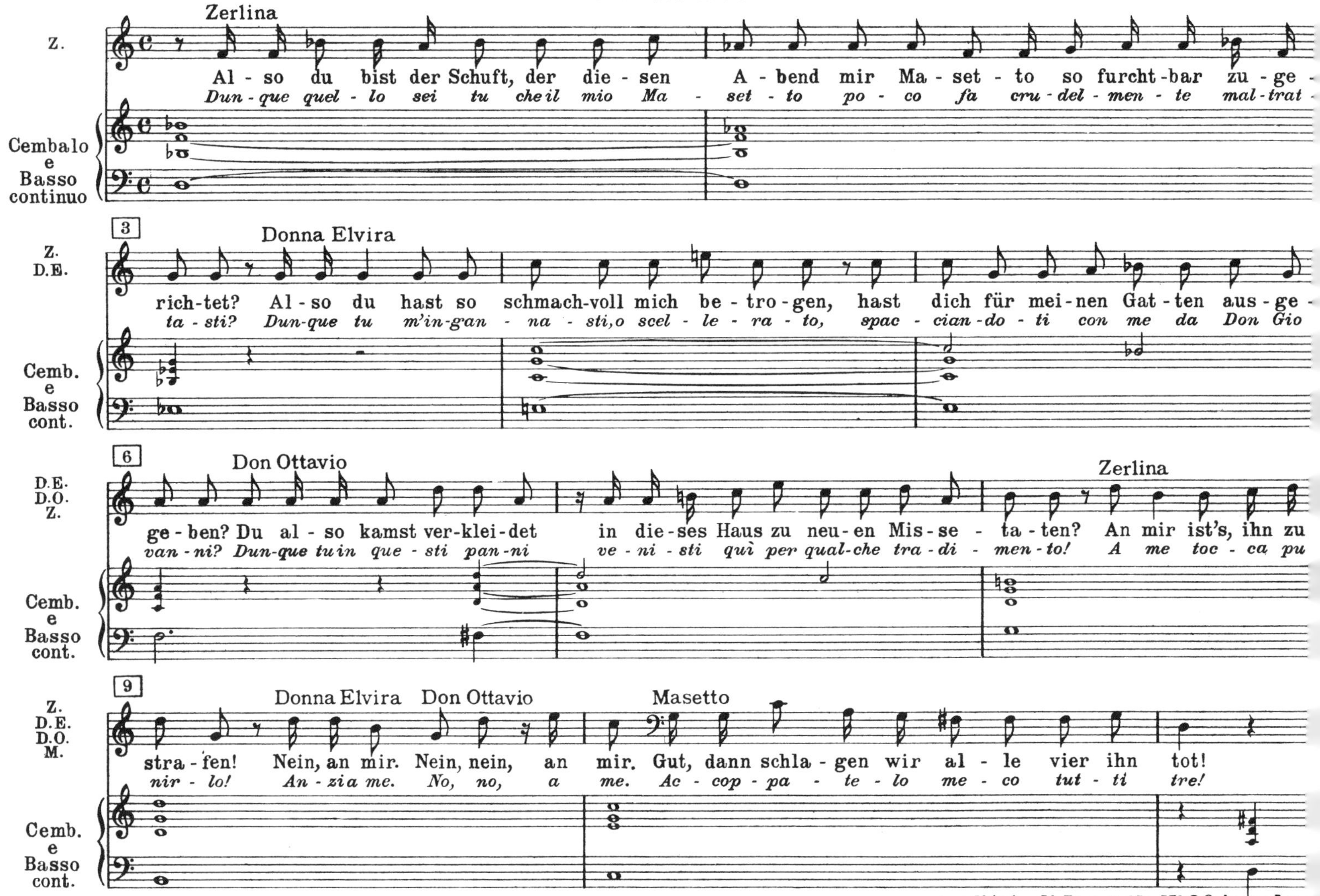

segue l'Aria di Leporello N.º 20. in caden[za]

N.º 20. Aria

9
Fl.
Fag.
Cor. in G
Viol. I
Viol. II
Viola
L.
recht, ja, und recht hat sie, ja, und recht hat sie, ja, doch, doch, doch der Schuld'ge, doch der Schuld'ge bin ich nicht,
gio - ne a voi e le - i, a voi e le - i, ma, ma, il de - lit - to, il de - lit - to mio non è,
Vc.
Cb.
20
a 2
bin ich nicht. Er ist Herr, und er ge bot mir, mei - ne Un-schuld ist ganz klar, mei - ne Un - schuld
mio non è. Il Pa - dron con pre - po - ten - za l'in - no - cen - za mi ru - bò, l'in - no - cen - za

32
Fl.
Fag.
Cor. in G
a 2
Viol. I II
Viola
L.
Vc.
Cb.
(Leise zu Donna Elvira)
(Piano a Donna Elvira)
ist ganz klar. Don-na El - vi - ra, ach, so helft mir,
mi ru - bò. Don-na El - vi - ra, com-pa - ti - te,
38
[div.]
helft, o Don-na! Wißt ja sel-ber, wie es war, wißt ja sel-ber, wißt
com-pa - ti - te! Già ca - pi - te co-me an-dò, già ca - pi - te, già

44
Fl.
Fag.
r. in G
a 2
Viol. I
Viol. II
Viola
[Zu Zerlina]
[A Zerlina]
L.
selber, wißt ja selber, wie es war. Von Masetto weiß ich gar nichts, von Masetto weiß ich gar nichts, weiß ich
pite, già capite come andò! Di Masetto non so nulla, non so nulla, nulla, nulla, nulla,
Vc.
Cb.
49
Fl.
Fag.
in G
Viol. I
Viol. II
Viola
(Auf Donna Elvira deutend)
(Accennando Donna Elvira)
L.
gar nichts, diese Dame, diese Dame wird dir bekunden, daß wir beide
nulla, vel dirà questa fanciulla, questa fanciulla; è un' oretta
Vc.
Cb.

55
Fl.
Fag.
Cor. in G
Viol. I
Viol. II
Viola
L.
schon seit Stun - den ganz al - lein und un - ge - sehn, still - ver -
cir - cum - cir - ca, che con lei gi - ran - do vo, che con
Vc.
Cb.
62
gnügt spa - zie - ren gehn. Für Eu-er Gna-den ge-nügt ein Wörtlein...
lei gi - ran - do vo. A voi, Si-gno-re, non di - co nien-te...
(Verlegen zu Don Ottavio)
(A Don Ottavio con confusione)

69
Fl.
a 2
Fag.
r. in G
Viol. I II
Viola
L.
ich sah durch Zu-fall... hier die-ses Pfört-lein, da drau-ßen Licht-schein, doch hier kein Licht-lein,
cer-to ti-mo-re... cer-to ac-ci-den-te, di fuo-ri chia-ro, di den-tro scu-ro,
Vc.
Cb.
77
(Auf die Tür zeigend, die er irrtümlich geschlossen glaubte)
(Additando la porta dov'erasi chiuso per errore)
ich fühl-te Schauer, die Pfor-te, die Mauer, der... das... die... schien ein Ver-steck mir...
non c'è ri-pa-ro... la por-ta... il mu-ro... lo... il... la... vo da quel la-to...

85
Cor. in G
Viol. I II
Viola
L.
so wi - der Wil - len... bald da, bald dort...
poi quì ce - la - to... l'af - far si sa...
Vc.
Cb.
89
Fl.
Fag.
Cor. in G
Viol. I II
Viola
L.
(Nähert sich geschickt der Tür)
(S'avvicina con destrezza alla porta)
da, bald dort... dacht ich im stil - len,
oh si sa... ma s'io sa - pe - va,
Vc.
Cb.

Zehnte Szene

Donna Elvira. Don Ottavio. Zerlina. Masetto.

Scena X

Donna Elvira, Don Ottavio, Zerlina e Masetto.

Recitativo

segue l'Aria di Don Ottavio № 21

Nº 21. Aria

Andante grazioso
2 Clarinetti in B
2 Fagotti
2 Corni [in B]
Andante grazioso
con sord.
Violino I
Violino II
Viola
Don Ottavio
pizz.
Violoncello
Contrabasso
7
Clar. in B
Fag.
Viol. I
Viol. II
Viola
D.O.
Don Ottavio
Fol-get der Heiß-ge - lieb - ten und sagt_ ihr, was Trost_ ihr_bring-
Il mio te - so - ro in - tan - to an - da - te, an - da - - te a_con-s
Vc.
Cb.

14
Clar. in B
Fag.
Cor. in B
Viol. I
II
Viola
D.O.
kann, trock-net ihr Aug von Trä - nen und nehmt euch ih - rer an, o trö - stet die
lar, e del bel ci-glio il pian - to cer-ca - te dia-sciu - gar, cer-ca - te, cer-
Vc.
Cb.
20
Teu - re und nehmt euch ih - rer an, und sagt,
ca - te, cer-ca - te dia - sciu - gar, cer-ca -
tr

27
Clar. in B
Fag.
Cor. in B
a 2
27
senza sord.
Viol. I
Viol. II
senza sord.
Viola
senza sord.
D. O.
was Trost bringen kann! Sagt, daß ich dem Ver - bre - cher
- te dia - sciu - gar! Di - te - le, che i suoi tor - ti
arco
Vc.
arco
Cb.
32
Clar. in B
cresc.
Fag.
a 2
cresc.
Cor. in B
a 2
32
Viol. I
cresc.
Viol. II
cresc.
Viola
[cresc.]
D. O.
blu - ti - gen Lohn werd ge - ben, blu - ti - gen Lohn werd ge - ben,
a ven - di - car io va - do, a ven - di - car io va - do:
Vc.
cresc.
Cb.
cresc.

36
ar. in B
Fag.
r. in B
a 2
Viol. I II
iola
o. O.
Vc.
Cb.
Kampf auf Tod und Le - ben
sol di stra - gi e mor - ti
eil ich zu_ra - scher Tat, eil
nun - zio vogl'io tor - nar, nun -
cresc.
40
ich zu ra - scher_ Tat, ja, eil ich zu ra - scher_ Tat.
- zio vogl' io tor - nar, sì, nun - zio vogl'io tor - nar.

44
Clar. in B
Fag.
Cor. in B
Viol. I II
Viola
D. O.
Vc.
Cb.
p
49
con sord.
pizz.
I
Folget der Heißgeliebten und sagt ihr, was Trost ihr bringen kann,
Il mio tesoro intanto andate, andate a consolar,

56
lar. in B
Fag.
or. in B
Viol. I II
Viola
D.O.
trocknet ihr Aug von Trä - nen und nehmt euch ih - rer an, o trö - stet die Teu - re und nehmt euch
e del bel ci-glio il pian - to cer-ca - te_di a-sciu-gar, cer-ca - te, cer-ca - te, cer-ca - te
Vc.
Cb.
63
ih - rer an, und sagt, was Trost bringen
di a - sciu - gar, cer - ca - te dia - sciu-

70
Clar. in B
Fag.
Cor. in B
Viol. I
Viol. II
senza sord.
Viola
D. O.
kann! Sagt, daß ich dem Ver-bre-cher blu-ti-gen Lohn werd ge-ben,
gar! Di-te-le, che i suoi tor-ti a ven-di-car io va-do,
arco
Vc.
Cb.
cresc.
75
a 2
blu-ti-gen Lohn werd ge- - - - - - - ben, im Kampf auf Tod u
a ven-di-car io va- - - - - - - do: che sol di stra-g

80
Clar. in B
a 2
Fag.
Cor. in B
80
Viol. I II
Viola
D. O.
Leben eil ich zu rascher Tat,
morti nunzio vogl'io tornar,
Vc.
Cb.
84
Clar. in B
Fag.
Cor. in B
a 2
84
Viol. I II
Viola
D. O.
ja, eil ich zu rascher Tat, im Kampf auf Tod und Leben
nunzio, nunzio vogl'io tornar, che sol di stragi e morti
Vc.
Cb.

90
Clar. in B
Fag.
Cor. in B
a 2
Viol.
I
II
Viola
D. O.
[Sie gehen ab]
[Partono]
eil ich zu ra-scher Tat, ja, eil ich zu ra-scher Tat.
nun-zio vogl'io tor-nar, sì nun-zio vogl'io tor-nar.
Vc.
Cb.
95
tr

The following scenes, Xa–Xd, were composed for the first performance in Vienna. Originally the Aria No. 21 was followed immediately by Scene XI.

Zehnte Szene (a)

[Zerlina. Leporello. Später ein Bauer.]

[Zerlina, mit einem Messer in der Hand, zerrt Leporello an den Haaren herein]

Scena X (a)

[Zerlina e Leporello, poi un Contadino.]

[Zerlina, con coltello alla mano, conduce fuori Leporello per i capelli]

24
Z.
L.
Leporello
Teu-fel, wo steckt er nur? He - da, Leu-te! Nie-mand kommt, kei-ner hört mich... So schrei doch nicht so
dia-vo-lo è i - to? Ser-vi, gen-te! Nes-sun vien, nes-sun sen-te... Fa pia-no per pie-
Cemb. e Basso cont.
[Ein Bauer tritt auf]
[Entra un contadino]
27
Zerlina
laut, hör end-lich auf, mich wie ein Pferd zu schinden! Ei, wart nur, wart, bald wird sich al-les fin-den! Bring mir schnell je-nen
tà, non stra-sci-nar-mi a co-da di ca-val-lo! Ve-drai, ve-drai co-me fi-ni-sce il bal-lo! Pre-sto quà quel-la
30
Leporello Zerlina Leporello Zerlina
Sessel! Hier ist er! Setz dich! Bin gar nicht müd. Setz dich, o-der ich zer-reiß dir das Herz im Leib und werf es vor die
se-dia! Ec-co-la! Sie-di! Stan-co non son. Sie-di, o con que-ste ma-ni ti strap-po il cor, e poi lo get-to a
33
Leporello [setzt sich] [siede]
Zerlina
Hun-de. Si-tze schon; doch sei so gut jetzt und leg weg die-ses Mes-ser, o-der bist du ein Bar-bier? Ja, fre-cher
ca-ni. Sie-do; ma tu, di gra-zia, met-ti giù quel ra-so-jo: mi vuoi for-se sbar-bar? Sì, ma-scal
36
Leporello Zerlina Leporello
Schur-ke, und ich werd dich bar-bie-ren oh-ne Sei-fe. Barm-herz'ger Him-mel! Her dei-ne Hand! Da ist sie.
zo-ne, io sbar-ba-re ti vo' sen-za sa-po-ne. E-ter-ni De-i! Dam-mi la man! La ma-no.
39
Zerlina Leporello Zerlina
[bindet Leporello die Hände mit dem Taschentuch; der Bauer hilft ihr]
[lega le mani a Leporello col fazzoletto; il contadino l'ajuta]
Bei-de! Was willst du ma-chen? Was ich ma-che mit dir? Nun, du wirst se-hen.
L'al-tra! Ma che vuoi far-mi? Vo-glio far, vo-glio far quel-lo che par-mi.

Nº 21a. Duetto

11
Fl.
Ob.
Fag.
Cor. in C
Viol. I II
Viola
Zerlina
Z.
Für sol-che Räu-ber-ban-de wär Nachsicht ei-ne Schan-de: O hätt ich Ti-ger-kral-len, dich grimmig an-zu-
Non v'è pie-tà, bric-co-ne, non v'è pie-tà, bric-co-ne: son u-na ti-gre i-ra-ta, un a-spi-de, un le-
L.
an!
me!
Vc.
Cb.
15
fal-len; nein, Mit-leid kenn ich nicht, das kenn ich nicht, nein, Mit-leid kenn ich nicht,
o-ne, no, no, pie-tà non v'è, pie-tà non v'è, no, no, pie-tà non v'è,
cresc.

19
Fl.
Ob.
Cor. in C
Viol. I
Viol. II
Viola
Z.
L.
Vc.
Cb.
I
p
cresc.
nein, Mit-leid kenn ich nicht!
no, no, pie-tà non v'è!
Es ko - stet dir das
Sei mor - to se ti
Leporello
Ach, könnt ich nur ent - wi-schen, ach, könnt ich nur ent - wi-schen!
Ah di fug-gir si pro-vi, ah di fug-gir si pro-vi!
23
Fag.
a 2
tr
f
Le-ben, wenn du dich noch be - wegst, ja, ja, es ko-stet dir das Le-ben!
mo-vi, sei mor-to se ti mo-vi, se ti mo-vi, se ti mo-vi!
Schänd -
Bar -
Schänd - lich werd ich be -
Bar - ba-ri, in-giu-sti

27
Fl.
Ob.
Viol. I
II
Viola
Z.
- lich hast du ge - han - delt, schänd-lich hast du ge - han - delt, o hätt ich dei - nen
- ba - ro tra - di - to - re, bar - ba - ro tra - di - to - re, del tuo pa - dro - ne il
L.
han - delt, schänd-lich werd ich be - han - delt, mich
De - i, bar - ba - ri, in - giu - sti De - i, in
Vc.
Cb.
31
Fag.
[p]
[Bindet ihn auf den Stuhl fest]
[Lo lega sulla sedia]
Her - ren wie dich in mei - ner Macht, o hätt ich dei - nen Her - ren wie dich in mei - ner
co - re a - ves - si qui con te, del tuo pa - dro - ne il co - re a - ves - si quì con
wirk - lich ein - zu - sper - ren, der Dra - che hat's voll - bracht, der Dra - che hat's voll
ma - no di co - ste - i chi ca - pi - tar mi fe', chi ca - pi - tar mi

34
Fl.
Fag.
Cor. in C
Viol. I II
Viola
Z.
L.
Vc.
Cb.
sfp
[p]
Macht!
te!
Laß
Sen
bracht! Ach, schnü - re nicht so fe - ste, mir geht der A - tem aus!
fe'! Deh non mi strin - ger tan - to, l'a - ni - ma mia sen va!
39
Ob.
gehn ihn o - der blei - ben, wenn du nur bleibst an dei-nem Ort!
va da, oon va - da, o re - sti: in - tan - to non par - ti - rai di quà!
Wie
Che

43
Fl.
Ob.
Fag.
Viol. I II
Viola
Z.
Wie gut ist's, ein Ver-
Di gio-ja e di di-
L.
en - ge, welch har-te Pla - ge, ist's Nacht, ist es am Ta - ge?
stret - te, oh Dei, che bot - te, è gior - no ov-ve - - ro è not - te?
Vc.
Cb.
47
bre - chen gleich nach der Tat zu_rä-chen, wie gut ist's, ein Ver - bre - chen gleich nach der Tat zu_rä-chen; ging's je-dem Bö-se-
let - to sen-to bril-lar-mi il pet-to, di gio-ja e di di - let - to sen-to bril-lar-mi il pet-to. Co - sì, co-sì cogl
Welch Sto - - ßen, bebt die Er-de, die
Che scos - - se di tre-muo-to, che

51
Fl.
Viol. I II
Viola
Z.
wich - te nur so, nur so, nur so, ging's je-dem Bö-se - wich - te nur so, nur so, nur so!
uo - mi-ni, co - sì, co - sì si fa, co - sì, co - sì cogl' uo - mi-ni, co - sì, co - sì si fa!
L.
Welt ver - sinkt in Nacht, die Welt ver - sinkt in Nacht! Ach, könnt ich nur ent-
bu - ja o - scu - ri - tà, che bu - ja o - scu - ri - tà! Ah di fug-gir si
Vc.
Cb.
55
Fl.
Ob.
Fag.
Cor. in C
a 2
Viol. I II
Viola
cresc.
Z.
Wenn du dich regst, bist du des To-des, ja, des To-des, ja, des To - des!
Sei mor-to, mor - to, mor - to, mor-to, se ti mo-vi, se ti mo - vi!
L.
wischen, ach, könnt ich nur ent-wi-schen! Ach,
pro-vi, ah di fug-gir si pro - vi! Deh
Vc.
Cb.

59
Fl.
Ob.
Fag.
Viol. I
Viol. II
Viola
Z.
L.
Vc.
Cb.
Laß
Sen
schnü - re — nicht — so — fe - ste,
non — mi — strin - ger — tan - to,
mir geht der A - tem aus!
l'a - ni - ma mia sen va!
63
Fl.
Ob.
Fag.
a 2
Cor. in C
Viol. I
Viol. II
Viola
Z.
Vc.
Cb.
gehn — ihn — o - der — blei - ben,
va - da, sen va - da, o re - sti:
wenn du nur bleibst an dei-nem Ort, wenn du nur bleibst an dei-nem
in - tan - to non par-ti - rai di quà, non par-ti - rai, non par-ti -

67
Fl.
Ob.
Fag.
Cor. in C
Viol. I
Viol. II
Viola
Z.
L.
Vc.
Cb.
a 2
cresc.
f
p
sf
Ort, wenn du nur bleibst am Ort.
rai, non par-ti-rai di quà!
Leporello
Wie en-ge, welch har-te Pla-ge, ist's
Che stret-te, oh Dei, che bot-te, è
71
fp
tr
Nacht, ist es am Ta-ge?
gior-no ov-ve-ro è not-te?
Wie gut ist's, ein Ver-bre-chen gleich nach der Tat zu-rä-chen, wie gut ist's, ein Ver-
Di gio-ja e di di-let-to sen-to bril-lar-mi il pet-to, di gio-ja e di di-
Welch Sto-ßen,
Che scos-se

75
Fl.
[p]
Ob.
Fag.
Cor. in C
75
I
Viol.
II
Viola
Z.
bre - chen gleich nach der Tat zu_ rä - chen; ging's je - dem Bö - se - wich - te nur so, nur so, nur
let - to sen - to bril - lar - mi il pet - to. Co - sì, co - sì cogl' uo - mi - ni, co - sì, co - sì si
L.
bebt die Er - de, die Welt ver - sinkt in
di tre - muo - to, che bu - ja o - scu - ri -
Vc.
Cb.
78
Fl.
Ob.
Fag.
78
I
Viol.
II
Viola
Z.
so, ging's je - dem Bö - se - wich - te nur so, nur so, nur so, nur so, nur so, nur so, nur so,
fa, co - sì, co - sì cogl' uo - mi - ni, co - sì, co - sì si fa, co - sì, co - sì, co - sì si fa,
L.
Nacht, die Welt ver - sinkt in Nacht! O Him - mel, wel - che har - te
tà, che bu - ja o - scu - ri - tà! Oh Dei, che strette, oh Dei, che
Vc.
Cb.

82
Fl.
Ob.
Fag.
Cor. in C
Viol. I
Viol. II
Viola
Z.
nur so, nur so, nur so, nur so, nur so,ging's ihm nur
co - sì, co - sì, co - sì si fa, co - sì, co-sì, co-sì, co-sì, co-sì, co - sì si
L.
Pla - ge, ist's Nacht um mich, ist es am Ta - ge? Welch
bot - te, è not - te o gior-no, è gior-no o not - te? Che
Vc.
Cb.
85
so,nur so,nur so,nur so,nur so,ging's ihm nur so,nur so,nur so,nur so,nur so,ging's ihm nur so, nur so, nur so,
fa, co-sì, co-sì, co-sì, co-sì, co - sì si fa, co-sì, co-sì, co-sì, co-sì, co - sì si fa, co - sì, co - sì,
Sto - - - - - ßen, bebt die Er - de, die
scos - - - - - se di tre - muo - to, che
p
sf
tr
I

88
Fl.
Ob.
Fag.
Viol. I
II
Viola
Z.
L.
Vc.
Cb.
cresc.
tr
f
— nur so, ging's ihm nur so, nur so, nur so, — nur so, ging's ihm nur so, nur so, nur so, —
— co - sì, co - sì si fa, co - sì, co - sì, — co - sì, co - sì si fa, co - sì, co - sì, —
Welt ver - sinkt in Nacht, die Welt ver - sinkt in Nacht, die gan - ze
bu - ja o - scu - ri - tà, che bu - ja o - scu - ri - tà, che bu - ja,
92
Cor. in C
a 2
[Geht ab]
[Parte]
— ging's ihm nur — so!
— co - sì si — fa!
Welt ver - sinkt in Nacht!
bu - ja o - scu - ri - tà!

Zehnte Szene (b)

Leporello. Ein Bauer.

Scena X (b)

Leporello e un Contadino.

Recitativo

Zehnte Szene (c)

[Zerlina. Donna Elvira. Dann Masetto mit zwei Bauern.]

Scena X (c)

[Zerlina, Donna Elvira, poi Masetto con due Contadini]

segue Recitativo Istromentato di Donna Elvira ed Aria Nº 21 b

ozart composed the following recitative and aria on April 30, 1788, for the soprano aterina Cavalieri, who sang the role of Elvira at the Vienna première of the opera.

Zehnte Szene (d) — Scena X (d)

Donna Elvira (allein). — Donna Elvira (sola).

Nr. 21 b. Rezitativo ed Aria

Recitativo

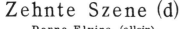

7
Viol. I
II
Viola
D.E.
Vc.
Cb.
Him-mel, in wel-chen Höl-len-pfuhl gräß-li-cher Ver-bre-chen ver-sank der Un-glück-sel'-ge!
Nu-mi, in quai mis-fat-ti or-ri-bi-li, tre-men-di è av-vol-to il scia-gu-ra-to!
11
Nein, nein, nicht län-ger wird Got-tes Zorn ihn ver-schonen, die Ge-rech-tig-keit wacht!
Ah no, non puo-te tar-dar l'i-ra del cie-lo, la giu-sti-zia tar-dar!
16
Schon seh ich flammen den ver-nich-ten-den Blitzstrahl, der das Haupt ihm zer-schmet-tert
Sen-tir già par-mi la fa-ta-le sa-et-ta, che gli piom-ba sul ca-po,

r Mozart's alteration for transposing the aria to D Major, see Supplement II, page 460.

Aria
Allegretto
Clar. in B
Fag.
Allegretto
Viol. I
Viol. II
Viola
D.E.
Mich ver-riet der Un - dank - ba - re, der Un - dank - ba-re, gab dem Jam - mer, der
Mi tra - dì quell' al - ma in - gra - ta, quell' al - ma in - gra-ta, in - fe - li - ce o
Vc.
Cb.
43
Clar. in B
Fag.
Cor. in Es
a 2
Viol. I
Viol. II
Viola
D.E.
Schmach mich hin, gab der Schmach, dem Jam - mer mich hin, gab der Schmach, dem Jam-mer, der
Dio mi fa, in - fe - li - ce o Di - o mi fa, in - fe - li - ce o Di - o, o-
Vc.
Cb.

50
Fl.
[p]
Clar. in B
Fag.
50
I
Viol.
II
Viola
D.E.
Schmach mich hin.
Dio mi fa.
Doch ver - ra - ten,
Ma tra - di - ta,
Vc.
Cb.
57
Fl.
Clar. in B
Fag.
57
I
Viol.
II
Viola
D.E.
von ihm ver - las - sen, fühl ich Mit - leid noch für ihn,
e ab - ban - do - na - ta, pro - vo an - cor per lui pie - tà,
Vc.
Cb.

64
Fag.
Viol.
I
II
Viola
D.E.
fühl ich Mit - leid noch für ihn, fühl ich Mit - lei
pro - - vo an - cor per lui, pie - tà, pro - - - - vo an - cor pe
Vc.
Cb.
mfp
71
Clar. in B
Fag.
Cor. in Es
Viol.
I
II
Viola
D.E.
fühl ich Mit - leid für ihn! Mich ver - riet der Un - dank - ba - re,
lui, per lu - - i pie - tà! Mi tra - dì quell'al - ma in - gra - ta,
Vc.
Cb.
mfp

78
ar. in B
Fag.
or. in Es
Viol. I II
Viola
O.E.
Vc.
Cb.
cresc.
p cresc.
a 2
p
mfp
sfp
Un - dank - ba - re, gab — dem — Jam - mer, der Schmach mich — hin, gab — der Schmach, dem
al - ma in-gra-ta, in - fe - li - ce o Dio — mi — fa, in - fe - li - ce o
85
Jam - mer mich hin, gab — der Schmach, dem Jam-mer, der Schmach mich hin. Wenn ich
Di - o mi fa, in - fe - li - ce o Di - o, o — Dio mi fa. Quan - do

92
Fl.
Clar. in B
Fag.
Cor. in Es
a 2
Viol. I
II
Viola
D. E.
den-ke_ all_ des Leids, das ich_er - fah-ren, dann verlangt mein Herz nach Ra-che,
sen-to il mio tor - men - to, il mio tor - men - to, di ven-det - ta il cor fa - vel - la;
Vc.
Cb.
99
doch er - blick_ ich_ ihn in Ge - fah - ren, ach, dann zagt dies schwa - ch
ma se guar - do_ il suo ci - men - to, pal - pi - tan - do il cor m

106
Fl.
. in B
ag.
I
iol.
II
ola
. E.
Herz, ach, dann zagt dies
va, pal - pi - tan - do il
Vc.
Cb.
113
Fl.
. in B
ag.
I
ol.
II
ola
E.
schwa - che Herz, es zagt mein Herz! Mich ver-riet der Un-dank-ba-re, der
cor mi va, pal - pi - tan - do! Mi tra-dì quell' al-ma ingra-ta, quell'
Vc.
Cb.

120
Clar. in B
Fag.
Cor. in Es
a 2
cresc.
Viol. I
Viol. II
Viola
D. E.
Un- dank- ba-re, gab dem Jam-mer, der Schmach mich hin, gab der Schmach, dem Jam - mer mi
al - ma in-grata, in - fe - li - ce o Dio mi fa, in - fe - li - ce o Di - o m
Vc.
Cb.
128
Fl.
Clar. in B
Fag.
Cor. in Es
Viol. I
Viol. II
Viola
D. E.
hin, gab der Schmach, dem Jammer, der Schmach mich hin. Doch
fa, in - fe - li - ce o Di - o, o Dio mi fa. Ma
Vc.
Cb.

136
Fl.
Fag.
Viola
ra - ten, von ihm ver - las - sen, fühl ich Mit - leid, Mit - leid, ach,
di - ta, ab - ban - do - na - ta, pro - vo an - cor per lui pie - tà,
Vc.
Cb.
143
a 2
für ihn, für ihn, fühl ich Mit - leid
per lui pie - tà, provo an - cor per

151
Fl.
Clar. in B
Fag.
Cor. in Es
151
Viol. I
Viol. II
Viola
D. E.
noch für ihn, fühl ich Mit - leid noch für ihn, fühl Mit - lei
lui pie - tà, provo an - cor per lui pie - tà, per lui pi
Vc.
Cb.
sf
p
158
Fl.
Clar. in B
Fag.
Cor. in Es
cresc.
f
158
(Vorhang zu)
Viol. I
Viol. II
Viola
D. E.
[Geht ab]
[Parte]
Mit - leid noch für ihn!
tà, per lui pie - tà!
Vc.
Cb.

Verwandlung

Umfriedeter Kirchhofsplatz.
[Verschiedene Reiterstatuen; das Standbild des Komturs.]

Mutazione

Loco chiuso [in forma di sepolcreto.
Diverse statue equestri; statua del Commendatore.]

Elfte Szene

Don Giovanni (steigt lachend über die Mauer).
Dann Leporello. [Später der Komtur.]

Scena XI

Don Giovanni (entra pel muretto ridendo),
indi Leporello. [Poi il Commendatore.]

Recitativo

*) e two wind passages are generally played on stage, although there is no indication of
s in the early manuscripts.

13
Lep. (von der Mauer) (dal muretto)
Don Giovanni
Leporello
Don Giovanni
Leporello
L.
D. G.
Wer ruft mich? Kennst du nicht deinen Herrn? Ich wollt, ich kennt ihn nicht mehr! Wie, du Schur-ke? Ach, seid Ihr's selbst,
Chi mi chia-ma? Non co-no-sci il pa-dron? Co-sì nol co-no-sces-si! Co-me, bir-bo? Ah, sie-te voi,
Cemb. e Basso cont.
16
Don Giovanni
Leporello
Don Giovanni
L.
D.G.
zeiht mir! Nun, wie ging es? An eu-rer Statt wurd ich bei-nah erschla-gen. Je nun, wär das nicht wirklich ei-ne Eh-re
sa-te! Co-sa è sta-to? Per ca-gion vo-stra io fui quasi ac-cop-pa-to. Eb-ben, non e-ra que-sto un o-no-re
Cemb. e Basso cont.
19
Leporello
Don Giovanni
Leporello
D. G.
L.
dich? Nein, Herr, ich dan-ke. Schon gut, komm jetzt, hör zu! Die schönsten Sachen erzähl ich dir! Doch was macht Ihr denn hier?
te? Si-gnor, vel do-no. Via, via, vien quà, vien quà! Che bel-le co-se ti deg-gio dir! Ma co-sa fa-te quì?
Cemb. e Basso cont.
23
D. G.
her, dann sollst du's wis-sen. Ver-schiedne A-ben-teu-er, die ich glücklich be-stan-den, seit du fort-gingst, sollst du spä-ter
den-tro, e lo sa-prai. Di-ver-se i-sto-riel-le, che ac-ca-du-te mi son da che par-ti-sti, ti di-rò un' al-
Cemb. e Basso cont.
26
Leporello
Don Giovanni
D. G.
L.
fah-ren, a-ber das schön-ste, das er-zähl ich dir gleich. Si-cher mit Frau-en? Na-tür-lich! Ein jun-ges Mäd-che
vol-ta; or la più bel-la ti vo' so-lo nar-rar. Don-ne-sca al cer-to? C'è dub-bio! U-na fan-ciul-la
Cemb. e Basso cont.
29
D. G.
al-ler-liebst, hübsch und fein, begegnet mir auf der Stra-ße; ich folg ihr ei-lig und fas-se ih-re Hand, sie will ent-flie-
bel-la, gio-vin, ga-lan-te, per la stra-da in-con-tra-i; le va-do appresso, la prendo per la man, fug-gir mi vuo-
Cemb. e Basso cont.

32
D. G.
L.
Leporello
Don Giovanni
Lep.
ein paar Wor - te nur sag ich, und sie, sie hält mich, nun für wen? Weiß es nicht. Für Le-po-rel - lo. Für
di - co po - che pa-ro - le, el - la mi pi - glia, sai per chi? Non lo so. Per Le-po-rel - lo. Per
Cemb. e Basso cont.
35
L.
D. G.
D. Giov.
Leporello
Don Giovanni
Leporello
D. Giov.
mich? Für dich. Nicht ü - bel. Bei der Hand nimmt sie mich nun ganz zärt-lich. Ei, im-mer bes-ser. Sie um-
me? Per te. Va be - ne. Per la ma - no es - sa al - lo - ra mi pren-de. An-co-ra me-glio. M'ac-ca-
38
D. G.
armt mich, sie küßt mich: Mein lie-ber Le - po - rel - lo, Le - po - rel - lo, mein Teu-rer! Nun erst bemerk ich,
rez - za, mi ab-brac-cia: ca - ro il mio Le - po - rel - lo, Le-po - rel - lo, mio ca - ro! Al - lor m'ac-cor - si,
41
D. G.
L.
Leporello
Don Giovanni
es war eins dei-ner Schätzchen. Oh, al - le Teu-fel! Ich be-nu - tze den Irr-tum, doch plötz - lich, als sie mich er -
ch'e-ra qual-che tua bel - la. Oh ma-le - det - to! Dell' in-ganno ap-pro-fit - to: Non so co - me mi ri - co -
44
D. G.
kannt hat, schreit sie; es kommen Leu-te, ich verschwinde nun ei-lig ü-ber die Mau-er und komm hierher an die-sen Ort der
no - sce; gri - da; sen-to gen-te, a fug - gi - re mi met-to, e pronto, pron-to per quel mu-ret-to in que-sto lo-co io
47
D. G.
L.
Leporello
Don Giovanni
Leporello
Trau-er. Und das sagt Ihr mir al - les mit sol-cher See-len - ru - he? War-um nicht? Doch ge-setzt, mei-ne Frau wär es ge-
mon-to. E mi di - te la co - sa con ta - le in-dif-fe - ren-za? Per-chè no? Ma se fos - se co-stei sta - ta mia

50
Adagio
a 2
Ob.
Clar. in B
Fag.
I. II
Trb.
III
Vc. e Cb.
Don Giovanni (lacht laut auf) (ride molto forte)
Komtur
Il Commendatore
Don Giovanni
Leporello (furchtsam) (con atti di paura
L. D. G. K.
we-sen? De- sto bes-ser! Dein La-chen wird ver-gehn, e - he der Tag graut. Wer sprach hier? Ach, ge-wiß war es ein
mo-glie? Me-glio an-co-ra! Di ri-der fi - ni - rai pria dell' au - ro - ra. Chi ha par - la - to? Ah qual-che a - ni-ma sa -
Cemb. e Basso cont.
Don Giovanni [legt die Hand an den Degen, sucht hier und dort auf dem Kirchhof und klopft mehrmals an die Standbilder]
[mette mano alla spada, cerca quà e là pel sepolcreto, dando diverse percosse alle statue]
56
L. D. G.
Geist aus an-dern Wel-ten, der euch wohl gut ge - kannt hat. Schweig, du Dummkopf! Wer ist da, wer ist da?
rà dell' al-tro mon-do, che vi co - no-sce a fon - do. Ta - ci, scioc - co! Chi va là, chi va là?
58 Adagio
Komtur
Il Commendatore
Leporello
Don Giovanni
K. L. D. G.
Ver-wegner, ent-wei-che, gön-ne Ru-he den To - ten. Nun, was sagt ich? Mir scheint, ein Tollkopf macht sich draußen ü-ber u
Ri-bal-do, au - da-ce, la-scia a' mor-ti la pa - ce. Ve l'ho det-to! Sa - rà qual-cun di fuo-ri che si burla a

[Mit Gleichgültigkeit und Geringschätzung]
[Con indifferenza e sprezzo]
65
D. G.
L.
Leporello
lu-stig. Ei, ist das nicht das Standbild un-sers wackern Kom-tu-ren? Ge - he hin und lies mir die In-schrift! Ent-schul-digt, so
no - i. Ehi, del Com-men-da - to - re non è que-sta la sta-tua? Leg-gi un po-co quel-la i-scri-zion! Scu - sa - te, non
Cemb. e Basso cont.
69
L.
D. G.
Don Giovanni
Leporello [liest] [legge]
weit hab ich's noch nicht gebracht, bei Mondenschein zu le-sen. Wirst du le-sen! „Den Frev-ler, der das Le-ben grausam mir
ho im-pa - ra - to a leg - ge - re a' rag - gi del - la lu - na. Leg - gi di - co! „Dell' em - pio, che mi tras - se al pas - so e -
73
Don Giovanni
raub-te, er - war - tet hier die Stra - fe!" Ver-nahmt Ihr's? Ich be - be! Der när - ri - sche
stre - mo, qui at - ten - do la ven - det - ta!" U - di - ste? Io tre - mo! O vec-chio buf - fo -
76
Leporello
Al-te! Sag ihm, daß ich noch heu-te zum Nachtmahl ihn er - war-te. Seid Ihr toll? Doch mir scheint... o Himmel, seht nur, wie
nis-si-mo! Di - gli, che que-sta se - ra l'at - ten - do a ce - na me - co. Che paz-zia! Ma mi par... oh Dei, mi - ra - te, che ter-
80
Don Giovanni
dro-hend er auf uns bei-de blickt! Er hat Le - ben, scheint zu füh - len, er will mit uns spre-chen! Wohl-an, mach
ri - bi - li oc-chia-te e - gli ci dà! Par vi - vo, par che sen - ta e che vo-glia par-lar! Or - sù va
83
Leporello
schnell, sonst bring ich dich um und be-gra-be dich da - ne-ben! Nur ge-mach, gnäd'ger Herr, ich will ge-hor-chen!
là, o quà t'am-maz-zo, e poi ti sep-pel - li - sco! Pia-no, pia - no, Si - gno-re; o - ra ub-bi - di - sco!

Nº 22. Duetto

Allegro
2 Flauti
2 Fagotti
a 2
2 Corni in E
Allegro
Violino I
Violino II
Viola
Don Giovanni
Komtur
La Statua
Leporello
Leporello
O hoch-ver-ehr-te Sta-tu-e des gro-ßen Herrn Kom-tu-ren. Ach
O sta-tua gen-ti-lis-si-ma del gran Com-men-da-to-re... Pa
Violoncello
Contrabasso
7
Fl.
Fag.
a 2
Cor. in E
7
Viol. I
II
[div.]
Viola
D. G.
Don Giovanni
Nun wird es bald, rasch v
Fi-ni-sci-la, o n
L.
Herr, ich zag und zitt-re, ich kann nicht, o Herr, verschonet mich.
dron... mi tre-ma il co-re; non pos-so, non pos-so ter-mi-nar.
Vc.
Cb.

12
Fl.
Fag.
Cor. in E
Viol. I
Viol. II
Viola
D. G.
L.
Vc.
Cb.
a 2
cresc.
f
fp
p
fp[div.]
en-de, sonst lehrt's mein De-gen dich, sonst lehrt's mein De-gen dich.
pet-to ti met-to questo ac-ciar, ti met-to questo ac-ciar.
Der Spaß kommt mir ge-
Che gu-sto, che spas-
Wie gott-los, wie ver-we-gen,
Che im-pic-cio, che ca-pric-cio,
16
le-gen,
set-to,
den Feig-ling kenn ich gut, den Feig-ling kenn ich gut.
lo vo-glio far tre-mar, lo vo-glio far tre-mar.
zu Eis er-starrt mein Blut, zu Eis er-starrt mein Blut. O
io sen-to-mi ge-lar, io sen-to-mi ge-lar. O

20
Fl.
Fag.
Cor. in E
a 2
Viol. I
Viol. II
Viola
L.
[Zu Don Giovanni]
[A Don Giovanni]
hoch - ver-ehr - te Sta - tu-e, wenn auch in Stein ge-hau-en... Gnäd'ger Herr, o Ent - se-tzen, o Grauen, ach,
sta - tua gen - ti - lis - si-ma, ben-chè di mar - mo sia-te... Ah Pa-dron... Pa-dron mi-o, mi-ra-te, mi-
Vc.
Cb.
26
[p] cresc.
[div.]
cresc.
D. G.
Don Giovanni
Stirb denn, stirb denn...
Mo - ri, mo - ri...
seht nur, wie fin-ster schaut er drein, wie fin-ster schaut er drein! Nein, nein, jetzt soll es
ra - te, che se-gui-ta a guardar, che se-gui-ta a guardar! No, no... no, no, at-te

31
Fl.
Fag.
Cor. in E
a 2
p
Viol. I II
Viola
L.
Vc.
Cb.
werden, war-tet, war-tet... Mein Herr, den dort Ihr
de-te... at-ten-de-te... Si-gnor, il Pa-dron
36
or. in E
se-het... nicht ich, daß Ihr's ver-ste-het,
mi-o... ba-da-te ben, non i-o,

41
Fl.
Fag.
a 2
Cor. in E
41
Viol. I
II
Viola
(Die Statue nickt)
(La statua china la testa)
L.
lädt euch zum Mah - le ein. Weh mir, weh, das ist ent
vor - ria con voi ce - nar. Ah, ah, ah, che sce-na è
Vc.
Cb.
46
Fl.
Fag.
Cor. in E
46
Viol. I
II
Viola
Don Giovanni
D. G.
Welch al-ber-nes Ge
Va là, che se'un buf
L.
setz-lich, weh mir, weh, das ist ent - setz - lich! O Gott, ich sah ihn ni - cken!
que-sta, ah, ah, ah, che sce-na è que - sta! O ciel, chi - nò la te - sta!
Vc.
Cb.

52
Fl.
Fag.
Cor. in E
Viol. I II
Viola
D. G.
ba-ren, du Narr, du bist von Sin-nen, bist von Sin-nen, bist von Sin-nen!
fo - ne, va là, che se'un buf-fo - ne, se'un buf-fo - ne, se'un buf - fo - ne!
L.
O seht nur, o seht nur, ich fleh euch an, o
Guar-da - te, guar-da - te, guar-da-te an-cor Pa-
Vc.
Cb.
cresc.
f
p
57
p cresc.
[div.]
mf
Was ist denn da zu se-hen, sprich, was ist denn da zu sehn?
E che degg' io guar-dar, degg' io guar-dar, degg' io guar-dar?
seht nur!
dro - ne!
Mit sei-nem Mar-mor-ko-pfe da
Col - la mar-mo-rea te-sta ei

63
Fl.
Fag.
Cor. in E
Viol. I
Viol. II
Viola
D.G.
L.
Vc.
Cb.
p
f
[div.]
(Die Statue nickt wieder)
(La statua china qui la testa)
(Sieht das Nicken)
(Vedendo il chino)
Mit sei-nem Mar - mor-kopfe da macht er so, ja so.
Col - la mar-mo - rea te-sta ei fa co - sì, co - sì.
(Macht der Statue nach)
(Imita la statua)
macht er so, ja so,
fa co - sì, co - sì,
mit sei-nem Mar - mor-kopfe da macht er so, ja so.
col - la mar-mo - rea te-sta ei fa co - sì, co - sì.
74
cresc.
Don Giovanni (zur Statue)
(alla statua)
Wohl - an denn, gib mir
Par - la - te, se po -

78
Fl.
Fag.
Cor. in E
Viol. I II
Viola
D.G.
K.
L.
Vc.
Cb.
a 2
sf[p]
fp
Antwort, kommst du zum Mahle, kommst du zum Mahle?
te - te, ver - re-te a ce - na, ver - re-te a ce - na?
Komtur
La Statua
Ja!
Sì!
Leporello
Kaum kann ich aufrecht
Mo - ver mi pos-so ap-
Wie
Bi -
87
selt-sam an - zu - se-hen, der gu-te Al - te kommt selbst zum Mah - le!
zarra è inver la sce - na; ver - rà il buon vecchio, il buon vec - chio a ce - na!
Daß wir es
A pre-pa-
ste-hen, die Luft will mir ver-ge-hen, das Standbild kommt zum Mah-le! Ach, lie-ber Gott... Er-
pe - na... mi man-ca, o Dei, la le - na, mi man-ca, o Dei, la le - na... Per ca - ri - tà... par-

93
Fl.
Fag.
Cor. in E
93
Viol. I
Viol. II
[div.]
Viola
D.G.
gut be - rei - ten, daß wir es gut be - rei - ten, laß uns nach Hau-se gehn; er
rar - - - la an - dia - mo, a pre-pa - rar-la an-dia - mo, par-tia - mo via di quì; biz -
L.
barmen, laßt uns nach Hause gehen, mir ist nicht recht ge - heu-er, o laßt uns nach Hau-se gehn, ach, lie-ber Gott, Er -
tia-mo, per ca - ri - tà, partiamo, an-dia-mo via di quì, an-dia-mo, an-dia - mo via di quì, per ca - ri - tà par
Vc.
Cb.
97
Fl.
Fag.
Cor. in E
97
Viol. I
Viol. II
Viola
D.G.
will zum Mah - le kom - men, ich sel - ber hab's ver - nom - men, daß
zar - ra è in - ver la sce - na; ver - rà il buon vec - chio a ce - na, a
L.
barmen, laßt uns nach Hause gehn, ach, lie-ber Gott, Er - bar-men, laßt uns nach Hause gehn, laßt uns nach Hause
tia-mo, an-dia-mo via di quì, per ca - ri - tà, par-tia - mo, an-dia-mo via di quì, an-dia-mo via di
Vc.
Cb.

101
Fl.
Fag.
Cor. in E
Viol. I
Viol. II
Viola
D.G.
wir es gut be-rei-ten, laß uns nach Hause gehn, laß uns nach Hau-se
pre-pa-rar-la an-dia-mo, par-tia-mo via di quì, par-tia-mo via di
L.
gehn, laßt uns nach Hause ge-hen, o laßt uns nach Hau-se ge-hen, o laßt uns nach Hause gehn, laßt uns gehn, laßt uns
quì, an-dia-mo via di quì, an-diamo, andiamo, andiamo, andiamo, andiamo, andia-mo via di quì, via di quì, via di
Vc.
Cb.
105
(Vorhang zu)
[div.]
pp
gehn.
quì.
[Sie gehen ab]
[Partono]
gehn, laßt uns nach Hau-se gehn.
quì, di quì, di quì, di quì.

Verwandlung

Düsteres Gemach

Zwölfte Szene

Donna Anna. Don Ottavio.

Mutazione

Camera tetra

Scena XII

Donna Anna e Don Ottavio.

Recitativo

attacca Recitativo Istromentato di Donna Ann
col Aria № 23

Nº 23. Recitativo ed Aria

8
Viol. I II
Viola
D.A.
ich fle-he... o Him - mel... Teu - - - rer,
mail mondo... oh Di - o... non se -
Vc.
Cb.
11
brich nicht die Trauer ei-nes lei-den-den Herzens, denn auf e - wig bleib ich dir nur er - ge-ben!
dur la co-stan-za del sen - si - bil mio co - re! Ab - bastan-za per te mi parla a - mo - re.
attacca Aria
Aria
16
Larghetto
Fl.
Clar. in C
Fag.
Cor. in F
dolce
[p]
sotto voce
[sotto voce]
Sag mir nicht, o
Non mi dir, bel

22
Fag.
Cor. in F
Viol. I
Viol. II
Viola
D.A.
mein Ge - lieb - ter, mein Ver - langen sei Grau - samkeit: Ja, du
i - dol mi - o, che son i - o crudel con te: tu ben
Vc.
Cb.
29
Clar. in C
Fag.
Viol. I
Viol. II
Viola
D.A.
weißt es, daß ich dich lie - be und mein Le - ben dir ge - weiht,
sa - i quant' io t'a - ma - i, tu co - no - sci la mia fè,
Vc.
Cb.

33
Fl.
Clar. in C
Fag.
Viol. I
Viol. II
Viola
D. A.
Vc.
Cb.
daß mein Le - ben dir ge-weiht.
tu co - no - sci la mia fè.
Laß, o
Cal - ma,
39
Cor. in F
laß dein zärtlich Drängen,
cal - mail tuo tor - mento,
daß vor Leid ich nicht ver - ge - he, daß vor
se di duol non vuoi ch'io mo - ra, se di

45
Fl.
Clar. in C
Fag.
Cor. in F
Viol. I II
Viola
D. A.
Leid ich nicht ver-ge-he, ich nicht ver-ge-he! Sag mir nicht, o mein Ge-
duol non vuoi ch'io mo-ra, non vuoi ch'io mo-ra! Non mi dir, bell' i - dol
Vc.
Cb.
51
Fl.
Fag.
Cor. in F
Viol. I II
Viola
D. A.
lieb-ter, mein Ver-langen sei Grau-samkeit. Laß, Ge-lieb-ter, dein zärtlich
mi-o, che son i-o cru-del con te. Cal-ma, cal-ma il tuo tor-
Vc.
Cb.

57
Fl.
Clar. in C
Fag.
Cor. in F
Viol. I II
Viola
D. A.
Vc.
Cb.
Drängen, daß vor Leid ich nicht ver - ge-he, vor Leid ver
men - to, se di duol non vuoi ch'io mo-ra, non vuoi ch'io
62
Allegretto moderato
ge - he!
mo - ra!

70
Fl.
lar. in C
Fag.
[p]
I
or. in F
a 2
70
tr tr tr tr
I
Viol.
II
D.A.
Laß, — o — laß mich hof-fen, daß — dem Stur - me fol - ge
For - se, for-se un gior-no il cie - lo an-co - ra sen - ti -
77
Fl.
ar. in C
Fag.
r. in F
77
I
Viol.
II
Viola
[p]
D.A.
kla-rer Son-nen - schein, ja, Son-nen - schein, — laß mich hof-fen, daß nach dem Stur-me fol-ge kla -
rà, — sen-ti - rà pie-tà — di - me, — forse un giorno il cie-lo an-co - ra sen-ti - rà —
Vc.
[p]
Cb.
[p]

83
Fl.
Clar. in C
Fag.
Viol. I
Viol. II
Viola
D. A.
Vc.
Cb.
88
Cor. in F
rer Son - nen-schein, daß de
pie - tà di - me, sen -

94
Fl.
Fag.
Viol.
Viola
D.A.
Sturm folge kla - - - - - - rer_ Son - nen - schein, kla - rer,
rà pie - tà, _____ pie - tà di me,_ sen - ti -
Vc.
Cb.
cresc.
100
kla - rer_ Sonnen - schein, laß mich hof-fen, daß fol - ge dem Sturme kla - rer,
rà_ pie - tà di me,_ for - se, for - se il cie - lo un gior - no sen - ti -

*) Often omitted.

segue Finale No. 2

Verwandlung

[Saal; ein gedeckter Tisch.]

Dreizehnte Szene

[Don Giovanni. Leporello. Einige Musikanten.]

Mutazione

[Sala; una mensa preparata per mangiare.]

Scena XIII

[Don Giovanni, Leporello, alcuni suonatori.]

Nº 24. Finale

e band generally plays the three pieces of music on stage, although there is no indication this in the autograph manuscript.

8
Fl.
Ob.
Clar. in A
Fag.
Cor. in D
Tr. in D
Timp.
Viol. I
Viol. II
Viola
Vc.
Cb.
a 2
cresc.
(Vorhang auf)
14
D. G.
Don Giovanni
Ha, das Mahl ist schon be-rei-tet;
Già la men-sa è pre-pa-ra-ta;
macht Mu-
voi suo-

22
Fl.
Ob.
ar. in A
Fag.
or. in D
r. in D
Timp.
a 2
[f]
f
p
cresc.
[cresc.]
22
I
Viol.
II
Viola
D.G.
[div.]
sik, ihr lie-ben Leu-te!
na-te,a-mi-ci_ ca-ri!
Fürst-lich will ich euch be-loh-nen, frohe
Già che spen-do i miei da-na-ri io mi
Vc.
Cb.
28
Fl.
Ob.
ar. in A
Fag.
r. in D
in D
Timp.
28
I
Viol.
II
iola
G.
3
Wei-sen spie-let mir!
vo-glio di-ver-tir!
Le-po-rel-lo,trag die Speisen auf!
Le-po-rel-lo,presto in ta-vo-la!
Leporello
L.
Ja,mein Herr, ich bin be-
Son pron-tis-si-mo a ser-
Vc.
Cb.

33
Fl.
Ob.
Clar. in A
Fag.
Cor. in D
Tr. in D
Timp.
I
Viol.
II
Viola
D. G.
L.
Vc.
Cb.
a 2
cresc.
[cresc.]
[div.]
[Die Diener tragen auf, während Leporello abgehen will]
[I servi portano in tavola, mentre Leporello vuol uscire]
Fürst - lich will ich euch be - loh - nen, fro - he
Già che spen - do i miei da - na - ri io m
reit, ja, mein Herr, ich bin be - reit.
vir, son pron - tis - si - mo a ser - vir.
38
in B
Wei - sen spie - let mir! Macht Mu - sik, ihr lie - ben Leu - te, fürstlich will ich euch be
vo - glio di - ver - tir! Voi suo - na - te, a - mi - ci ca - ri! Già che spen - do i miei da

[Auf der Bühne]
[Sopra il teatro]
Ob.
ar. in A
Fag.
or. in D
Vc.
Fl.
Ob.
Fag.
r. in D
. in D
imp.
I
iol.
II
iola
.G.
Vc.
Cb.
cresc.
in B
[Ißt; die Musikanten beginnen zu spielen]
[Mangia; i suonatori cominciano a suonare]
lohnen, frohe Weisen spielet mir, frohe Weisen spielet mir!
nari io mi voglio divertir, io mi voglio divertir!
Ob.
in A
ag.
c.
Leporello
Bravo! „Cosa rara!“
Bravi! „Cosa rara!“

59
Ob.
Clar. in A I II
Fag.
Cor. in D
Vc.
D.G.
L.
Don Giovanni
Wie be-hagt dir die-se Wei-se?
Che ti par del bel con-cer-to?
Leporello
Wie
E
64
Die-se Schüssel ist vortreff-lich, die-se Schüssel ist vortreff-lich, ganz
Ah che piat-to sa-po-ri-to, ah che piat-to sa-po-ri-to, sa-
macht, wie ge-macht zu eu-rem Prei-se.
for-me, è con-for-me al vo-stro mer-to.
71
treff-lich, ganz vor-treff-lich!
ri-to, sa-po-ri-to!
(Beiseite)
(A parte)
Er ist gut bei Ap-pe-ti-te,
Ah che bar-ba-ro ap-pe-ti-to,
was
che

79
Ob.
Clar. in A
Fag.
Cor. in D
Vc.
a 2
p
pp
[p]
[pp]
79
D. G.
L.
[Beiseite]
[A parte]
Wie er mich mit Neid be-
Nel ve-der i miei boc-
das für Rie-sen-bis-sen, und vor Hun-ger sterb ich hier, und vor Hun-ger sterb ich hier.
co-ni da gi-gan-te, mi par pro-prio di sve-nir, mi par pro-prio di sve-nir.
86
sf
fp
cresc.
f
[f]
trachtet, er ver-geht noch vor Be-gier, er ver-geht noch vor Be-gier.
co-ni gli par pro-prio di sve-nir, gli par pro-prio di sve-nir.
Er ist gut bei Ap-pe-ti-te, was sind
Ah che bar-ba-ro ap-pe-ti-to, che boc-
94
Wie er mich mit Neid be-trachtet, er vergeht noch, er vergeht noch vor Begier,
Nel ve-der i miei boc-co-ni gli par pro-prio, gli par pro-prio di sve-nir,
das für Rie-sen-bis-sen!
co-ni da gi-gan-te!
Er ist gut bei Ap-pe-
Ah che bar-ba-ro ap-pe-

102
Ob.
Clar. in A
Fag.
Cor. in D
Vc.
D. G.
ja, er schmauste gern mit mir, ja, er schmauste gern mit mir, er ver-geht noch vor
gli par pro-prio di sve-nir, gli par pro - prio di sve-nir, gli par pro-prio di
L.
ti - te, was sind das für Riesen-bis-sen, und vor Hun-ger sterb
ti - to, che boc-co-ni da gi-gan-te, mi par pro-prio di
110
in B
in F
I
Viol.
II
Viola
gier, er ver-geht noch vor Be-gier! Tel-ler!
nir, gli par pro-prio di sve-nir! Piat-to!
hier, und vor Hun-ger sterb ich hier! Zu die-nen!
nir, mi par pro-prio di sve-nir! Ser-vo!
Cb.

[Auf der Bühne]
[Sopra il teatro]
118
Ob.
Clar. in B
in B
Fag.
Cor. in F
in F
Vc.
118
I
Viol.
II
Viola
D. G.
Schenk den Wein ein!
Ver - sa il vi - no!
L.
Wie heißt doch die al-te O-per?
Ev - vi - va-no „i li - ti - gan-ti!“
Vc.
Cb.
128
Ob.
Clar. in B
Fag.
Cor. in F
Vc.
p
f
a 2
[p]
[f]
128
[Leporello schenkt Wein ein]
[Leporello versa il vino nel bicchiero]
Don Giovanni
[Leporello wechselt Don Giovanni die Teller und ißt in Eile]
[Leporello cangia il piatto a Don Giovanni e mangia in fretta]
D. G.
Ex-zel-len-ter Mar-zi-mi-no!
Ec-cel-len-te mar-zi-mi-no!
141
Ob.
Clar. in B
Fag.
a 2
Cor. in F
Vc.
p
141
D. G.
Don Giovanni
Ei, wie
Sta man-
Leporello [beiseite]
[a parte]
L.
Vom Fa-san hier die-sen Bissen bring ich sachte, sachte, sachte, sachte au-ßer Sicht.
Que-sto pez-zo di fa-gia-no pia-no, pia-no, pia-no, pia-no, pia-no, vo'in-ghiot-tir.

151
Ob.
Clar. in B
Fag.
Cor. in F
in B
Vc.
151
Viol. I
II
Viola
D. G.
schlingt er, wie ge-ris-sen, und er glaubt, ich seh_ es nicht.
gian-do quel mar-ra-no, fin-ge-rò, di non_ ca-pir.
Vc.
Cb.
Moderato
[Auf der Bühne]
[Sopra il teatro]
162
Ob.
Clar. in B I II
Fag.
a 2
Cor. in B
in B
Vc.
162
Moderato
Leporello
L.
Die Mu-sik kommt mir äußerst be-kannt vor!
Que-sta poi la co-no-sco pur trop-po!

168
Ob.
Clar. in B I II
Fag.
Cor. in B
Vc.
a 2
mfp
f
p
tr
D. G.
L.
Don Giovanni [ohne aufzusehen] [senza guardarlo]
Le - po - rel-lo!
Le - po - rel-lo!
Leporello (mit vollem Mund) (colla bocca piena)
Euch zu
Pa - - dron
174
II
[f]
[p]
Kerl, was steckt dir in der Keh-le, re-de lau-ter!
Par-la chiet-to, par-la chiet-to, ma-scal-zo-ne!
die - nen!
mi - o!
Ha-be Schnu-pfen, ha-be
Non mi la-scia u-na flus-
179
cresc.
Nun, so pfei-fe, kürz die
Men-tre io man-gio, fi-schia un
Husten, mit dem Spre-chen will's nicht gehn, mit dem Spre-chen will's nicht gehn.
sio-ne le pa-ro-le pro-fe-rir, le pa-ro-le pro-fe-rir.

185
Ob.
Clar. in B I II
Fag.
Cor. in B
Vc.
D. G.
L.
cresc.
(Bemerkt, daß er ißt)
(S'accorge che mangia)
Zeit mir.
po - co.
Warum?
Cos' è?
Kann es nicht.
Non so far.
Ver-zeiht mir, ver-zeiht mir, eu - er Koch sucht sei-nes -
Scu - sa - te, scu - sa - te, sì ec-cel - len-te è il vo-stro
190
glei - chen, eu - er Koch sucht sei-nes-glei-chen, sei-nes - glei - chen, der Ver-füh - rung mußt ich _ wei-chen, konn-te
cuo - co, sì ec-cel - len - te, sì ec-cel - len-te è il vo-stro cuo - co, che lo vol - li anch' io pro - var, _ che lo
a 2
mfp
195
Don Giovanni
Ja, mein Koch sucht sei-nes - glei-chen, ihm kann kei - ner wi - der-
Sì ec - cel - len - te è il cuo - co _ mi - o, che lo vol - le anch' ei pro -
nim - mer wi - der-stehn, konn-te nimmer, konn-te nim-mer wi-der-
vol - li anch' io pro - var, sì ec-cel - len - te, che lo vol-li anch' io pro -

Vierzehnte Szene / Scena XIV

[Die Vorigen. Donna Elvira (stürzt verzweifelt herein).]

[I suddetti, Donna Elvira (entra disperata).]

219
Fl.
Ob.
Clar. in B
Fag.
Cor. in B
Viol. I
Viol. II
Viola
D. E.
D. G.
L.
Vc.
Cb.
cresc.
f
fp
sf
p
Donna Elvira (kniet nieder) (s'inginocchia)
Nicht mehr ver-lan-get die Tief-ge-beug-te für ih-re Treu-e zärt-li-ch
Da te non chie-de quest' al-ma op-pres-sa del-la tua fe-de qual-che m
Don Giovanni (steht auf) (sorgendo)
Wes-halb, sag an?
Cos' è, cos' è?
Leporello
Wes-halb, sagt an?
Cos' è, cos' è?
230
a 2
[div.]
Lohn.
cè.
Don Giovanni
Stau-nen er-faßt mich, sag, was be-gehrst du, sag, was be-gehrst du? Doch wenn du kni-est,
Mi ma-ra-vi-glio, co-sa vo-le-te, co-sa vo-le-te? Se non sor-ge-te,

239
Fl.
Ob.
Clar. in B
Fag.
Cor. in B
Viol. I
Viol. II
Viola
D. E.
D. G.
L.
Vc.
Cb.
a 2
cresc.
[p] cresc.
[cresc.]
f
p
Donna Elvira
Ach, du ver-höhnst mich noch, lachst mei-ner Trä-nen,
Ah non de-ri-de-re gli af-fan-ni mie-i,
(Kniet nieder)
(S'inginocchia)
kni-e auch ich, kni-e auch ich!
non re-sto in piè, non re-sto in piè!
(Erhebt sich und
(Sorgendo fa sorgere
Wie,
Io
Leporello
Ach Gott, sie rüh-ret mich
Qua-si da pian-ge-re
[p]
249
tr
ach, du ver-höhnst mich noch,
ah non de-ri-de-re,
ach, du ver-höhnst mich noch!
ah non de-ri-de-re!
hilft Donna Elvira auf)
Donna Elvira)
(Mit übertriebener Zärtlichkeit)
(Con affettata tenerezza)
ich ver-höhn-te dich,
te de-ri-de-re,
wie, ich ver-höhn-te dich?
io te de-ri-de-re?
bei-nah zu Trä-nen,
mi fa co-ste-i,
ach Gott, sie rüh-ret mich bei-
qua-si da pian-ge-re mi

257
Fl.
Clar. in B
Fag.
Cor. in B
a 2
Viol. I II
Viola
D. E.
Ent - sag - dem La-ster!
Che vi - ta can-gi!
D. G.
Nein, wahr-lich nein!
Cie - li, per - chè?
Was soll ich, Teu-re?
Che vuoi, mio be - ne?
L.
nah zu Trä-nen!
fa co - ste - i!
Vc.
Cb.
cresc.
p
267
Ob.
fp
f
Ha, Schänd-li-cher,
Cor per - fi-do,
ha, Schänd-li-cher,
cor per - fi-do,
ha, Schänd -
cor per -
Bra-vo!
Bra-va!
Ha, Schänd -
Cor per -

278
Fl.
Ob.
Clar. in B
Fag.
a 2
Cor. in B
Viol. I II
Viola
D. E.
-li-cher!
-fi-do!
[Setzt sich wieder zum Essen]
[Torna a sedere a mangiare]
D. G.
Jetzt laß mich es-sen, jetzt laß mich es-sen;
La - scia ch'io man-gi, la - scia ch'io man-gi;
L.
-li-cher!
-fi-do!
Vc.
Cb.
289
Nun, so ver-sin-ke denn im Pfuhl der Höl-le,
Re-sta-ti, bar-ba-ro, nel lez-zo im-mon-do,
wenn's dir be-lie-bet, spei-se mit mir.
e se ti pia-ce, man-gia con me.
Wenn ih-re Kla-gen ihn nicht mehr
Se non si muo-ve nel suo do-

299
Fl.
Ob.
Clar. in B
Fag.
a 2
Cor. in B
Viol. I
Viol. II
Viola
D. E.
D. G.
L.
Vc.
Cb.
cresc.
p
f
[p]
als ew'- ge Mah-nung an Got-tes Ge-richt!
e-sem-pio or - ri-bi-le d'i-ni-qui-tà!
Mäd-chen und Re-ben-wein wür-zen das Le-ben, sie sind das
Vi-van le fem-mi-ne, vi-va il buon vi-no, so-ste-gno e
rüh-ren, dann ist sein Herz so hart wie Stein!
lo-re, di sas-so ha il co - re, o cor non ha!
308
[f]
fp
Nun, so ver-sin-ke denn
Re - sta - ti, bar-ba-ro,
Herr-lichste auf die-ser Welt, sie sind das Herr-lich-ste auf die-ser Welt, Mädchen und
glo-ri-a d'u-ma-ni - tà, so-ste-gno e glo-ri-a d'u-ma-ni - tà, vi-van le
Wenn ih - re
Se non si

318
Fl.
Ob.
Clar. in B
Fag.
Cor. in B
Viol. I II
Viola
D. E.
im Pfuhl der Höl-le, nun, so ver-sin-ke denn im Pfuhl der Höl-le, als
nel lez-zo im-mon-do, re-sta-ti, bar-ba-ro, nel lez-zo im-mon-do, e-
D. G.
Re-benwein, wür-zen das Le-ben, Mäd-chen und Re-benwein wür-zen das Le-ben, sie
fem-mi-ne, vi-va il buon vi-no, vi-van le fem-mi-ne, vi-va il buon vi-no, so-
L.
Kla-gen ihn nicht mehr rüh-ren, von Stein ist sein Herz dann, dann
muo-ve nel suo do-lo-re, di sas-so ha il co-re, di
Vc.
Cb.
327
cresc.
ew'-ge Mah-nung an Got-tes Ge-richt,
sem-pio or-ri-bi-le d'i-ni-qui-tà,
sind das Herr-lich-ste auf die-ser Welt, sie sind das Herr-lich-ste auf die-ser
ste-gno e glo-ri-a d'u-ma-ni-tà, so-ste-gno e glo-ri-a d'u-ma-ni-
ist sein Herz so hart wie Stein,
sas-so ha il co-re, o cor non ha,

336
Fl.
Ob.
Clar. in B
Fag.
Cor. in B
Viol. I II
Viola
D. E.
als ew'-ge Mah-nung an Got-tes Ge-richt, nun, so ver-sink im Höl-len-pfuhl, als ew'-ge
e-sempio or-ri-bi-le d'i-ni-qui-tà, d'i-ni-qui-tà, d'i-ni-qui-tà, e-sempio or-
D. G.
Welt, sie sind das Herr-lichste auf die-ser Welt, auf die-ser Welt, auf die-ser Welt, sie sind das
tà, so-ste-gno e glo-ri-a d'u-ma-ni-tà, d'u-ma-ni-tà, d'u-ma-ni-tà, so-ste-gno e
L.
dann hat ein Herz er hart wie von Stein, hart wie von Stein, hart wie von Stein, dann ist sein
di sas-so ha il co-re, o cor non ha, o cor non ha, o cor non ha, di sas-so ha il
Vc.
Cb.
346
a 2
in F
(Geht ab)
(Sorte)
(Kommt zurück und stürzt nach der anderen Seite ab)
(Rientra, e fugge dall' altra parte)
Mah-nung an Got-tes Ge-richt!
ri-bi-le d'i-ni-qui-tà!
Ach!
Ah!
Herr-lich-ste auf die-ser Welt!
glo-ri-a d'u-ma-ni-tà!
Was
Che
Herz so hart wie Stein!
co-re, o cor non ha!

355
Fl.
Ob.
Clar. in B
Fag.
a 2
Viol. I II
Viola
D. G.
L.
Vc.
Cb.
[cresc.]
cresc.
war das für ein Schreien, was war das, was war das für ein Schreien? Geh hin-aus und sieh nach, was es wohl
gri-do è que-sto ma-i, che gri-do, che gri-do è que-sto ma-i! Va a ve-der, va a ve-der che co-sa è
Leporello
Was war das für ein Schreien, was war das für ein Schreien?
Che gri-do è que-sto ma-i, che gri-do è que-sto ma-i!
362
sein mag!
sta-to!
(Leporello geht hinaus und stößt, ehe er zurückkommt, einen Schrei aus)
(Leporello sorte, e prima di tornare, mette un grido)
Zum Teu-fel die-ses Schreien, zum
Che gri-do in-dia-vo-la-to, che
Ach!
Ah!

371
Fl.
Ob.
Clar. in B
Fag.
a 2
Viol. I
Viol. II
Viola
(Leporello tritt entsetzt ein und schließt die Tür)
(Leporello entra spaventato e chiude l'uscio)
D. G.
Teu - fel die-ses Schreien! Le-po - rel - lo, sag, was gibt's, sag, was gibt's, sag, was gibt's?
gri - do in-dia-vo - la - to! Le-po - rel - lo, che cos' è, che cos' è, che cos' è?
Vc.
Cb.
379 Molto Allegro
Fl.
Fag.
Cor. in F
in F
Viol. I
Viol. II
Viola
Leporello
L.
Ach, mein Herr... o Schreck und Graus, ge-het ja nicht dort hin - aus, 's ist der
Ah Si - gnor... per ca - ri - tà, non an - da - te fuor di quà, l'uom di
Vc.
Cb.

386
Fl.
Fag.
Cor. in F
Viol. I
Viol. II
Viola
L.
wei-ße… Mann von Stei-ne… ach, wie schlot-tern mir Ar-me und Bei-ne… Hät-tet
sas-so… l'uo-mo bian-co… ah pa-dro-ne… io ge-lo… io man-co… se ve-
Vc.
Cb.
393
Fl.
Ob.
Clar. in B
Fag.
a 2
cresc.
Cor. in F
Don Giovanni
D. G.
Wer kann dies Gewäsch ver-ste-hen;
Non ca-pi-sco nien-te af-fat-to;
Ihr ihn nur ge-se-hen… seinen schweren Tritt ge-hört: Tap, tap, tap, tap, tap, tap, tap,
de-ste, che fi-gu-ra… se sen-ti-ste co-me fa: ta, ta, ta, ta, ta, ta, ta,

402
Fl.
Ob.
Clar. in B
Fag.
a 2
[p]
cresc.
f
Cor. in F
[cresc.]
[f]
sf
p
Viol. I
Viol. II
Viola
tr
(Man hört an die Tür klopfen)
(Si sente battere alla porta)
D.G.
Al - ter Narr, ich glaub der Wein hat dich be-rauscht, hat dich be-rauscht!
tu sei mat-to in ve - ri - tà, in ve - ri - tà, in ve - ri - tà!
L.
tap!
ta!
Hört Ihr's
Ah sen
Vc.
Cb.
409
Je-mand klopft da.
Qual-cun bat - te.
Öff-ne!
A - pri!
(Zitternd)
(Tremando)
Öff - ne, sag ich!
A - pri di - co!
klo-pfen!
ti - te!
Ich be - - be!
Io tre - - mo!

416
a 2
Fl.
Ob.
Fag.
Viol.
D.G.
Öff-ne! Feig-ling! Dies Gau-kel-spiel zu en-den, will ich selbst zu öff-nen gehn, ich
A-pri! Mat-to! Per to-glier-mi d'in-tri-co ad a-prir io stes-so an-drò, io
L.
Ach... Ach...
Ah... Ah...
Vc.
Cb.
cresc.
424
(Nimmt einen Leuchter und geht, um zu öffnen)
(Piglia lume e va per aprire)
(Öffnet)
(Apre)
selbst will gehn!
stes-so an-drò!
[Verkriecht sich unter den Tisch]
[S'asconde sotto la tavola]
Die-sen Gast will ich nicht se-hen, sach-te drum verberg ich mich, ver-berg ich mich.
Non vo' più ve-der l'a-mi-co; pian pia-nin m'a-scon-de-rò, m'a-scon-de-rò.

ünfzehnte Szene

[Die Vorigen. Der Komtur]

Scena XV

[I suddetti, il Commendatore]

442
a 2
Fl.
Ob.
Fag.
r. in F
r. in D
I.II
rb.
III
imp.
p
Viol.
Viola
Don Giovanni
D.G.
Nim-mer hätt ich euch er-war-tet; seid will-kom-men mir zu
Non l'a-vrei giammai cre-du-to; ma fa-rò quel che po-
K.
hab ich ver-nom-men.
e son ve-nu-to.
Vc.
Cb.

447
Fl.
Ob.
Clar. in B
Fag.
Cor. in F
a 2
Tr. in D
Timp.
447
I
Viol.
II
Viola
D.G.
Tisch! Le-po-rel-lo, her ge-schwinde, laßaufs neu die Ta-fel de-cken!
trò! Le-po-rel-lo, un'al - tra ce - na, fa che su-bi-to si por-ti!
Leporello [steckt den Kopf unter dem Tisch hervor]
[mezzo fuori col capo dalla mensa]
L.
Gnäd'ger Herr, gnäd'ger Herr, gnäd'ger Herr, wir sind
Ah, pa-dron, ah, pa-dron, ah, padron, siam tut -
Vc.
Cb.

451
Fl.
Ob.
Clar. in B
Fag.
Cor. in F
Tr. in D
I. II Trb.
III
Timp.
451
I Viol.
II
Viola
Don Giovanni
D.G.
Fort, ge-horche...
Van - ne, di - co...
Komtur
Il Commendatore
K.
Nein, blei-be da. Wohl des ir-di-schen Mah-les ent-beh-ret, wer von himm-li-scher Spei-se sich
Fer-ma un po'. Non si pa-sce di ci-bo mor-ta-le chi si pa-sce di ci-bo ce-
[Kommt mit Gebärden großer Angst hervor und will sich entfernen]
[Con molti atti di paura esce e va per partire]
L.
lo-ren.
mor-ti.
Vc.
Cb.
cresc.
p cresc.
a 2
f
p
fp

461
Fl.
Ob.
Clar. in B
Fag.
Cor. in F
Tr. in D
I. II
Trb.
III
Timp.
461
I
Viol.
II
Viola
K.
näh - ret; an - dre Sor - gen und höh - res Ver - lan - gen
le - ste; al - tre cu - re, più gra - vi di que - ste,
Vc.
Cb.

466
a 2
Fl.
cresc.
p
Ob.
ar. in B
Fag.
r. in F
r. in D
I. II
rb.
III
imp.
466
I
iol.
II
iola
K.
führ - ten weit aus der Fern mich zu
al - tra bra - ma quag - giù mi gui -
Vc.
Cb.

*) See Editors' Commentary.

473
Fl.
Ob.
r. in B
Fag.
a 2
r. in F
. in D
I. II
rb.
III
imp.
473
I
iol.
II
iola
D.G.
willst du?
vuo - i?
Re-de, re-de, du siehst mich be-
Par-la, parla, a-scol-tan - do ti
K.
Hör mei-ne Wor-te, nur kurz ist die Zeit,
Par - lo, a - scol - ta, più tem - po non ho,
L.
schüttelt, al-le Glieder schon zittern an mir,
sem-bra, e le membra fer-mar più non so,
al - le Glieder schon zit-tern an
ah le mem-bra fer-mar più non
Vc.
Cb.

479
a 2
Fl.
cresc.
p
Ob.
Clar. in B
Fag.
Tr. in D
I. II
Trb.
III
Timp.
479
I
Viol.
II
Viola
D. G.
reit.
sto.
K.
hör mei - ne Wor - te, nur kurz ist di
par - lo, a scol - ta, più tem - po no
L.
mir, wie vom Fieber, so werd ich ge - schüttelt, wie vom Fieber, so werd ich ge-schüttelt, al-le Glieder schon zitter
so, la ter-za-na d'a-ve-re mi sem-bra, la ter-za-na d'a-ve-re mi sem-bra, e le membra fer-mar più
Vc.
Cb.

482
Fl.
Ob.
r. in B
'ag.
in F
in D
I.II
rb.
III
mp.
I
l.
II
la
G.
Re-de, re-de, du siehst mich be-reit.
Parla, parla, a-scol-tan-do ti sto.
Zeit.
ho.
Du ba-test mich zum Mah-le,
Tu m'in-vi-ta-sti a ce-na,
mir.
so.
c.
b.
cresc.

490
a 2
Fl.
Ob.
Clar. in B
Fag.
Cor. in F
Tr. in D
I. II
Trb.
III
Timp.
Viol.
I
II
Viola
Komtur
Il Commendatore
K.
kennst du auch dei - ne Pflich - ten? Gib Ant - wort mir, gib Ant - wort mir: Wirst mein Ma
il tuo do-ver or sa - i; ri - spon - di - mi, ri - spon - di - mi: ver - ra - i
Vc.
Cb.
fp
cresc.
f
p

500
a 2
Fl.
r. in B
Fag.
r. in F
I.II
b.
III
500
I
ol.
II
la
[div.]
G.
Don Giovanni
Wer hätt einmal im Le - ben wohl
A tor-to di vil - ta - te tac-
K.
du auch wohl tei - len?
tu a ce - nar me - co?
Leporello (von fern, zitternd)
(da lontano, tremando)
Nein, nimmermehr, sagt, daß Ihr kei-ne Zeit habt!
Oi - bò, oi - bò, tem - po non ha, scu-sa - te!
c.
b.

506
Fl.
Ob.
Clar. in B
Fag.
Cor. in F
Tr. in D
I.II
Trb.
III
Timp.
506
I
Viol.
II
Viola
D. G.
je mich feig ge-sehn? Ich bin entschlossen.
cia - - to mai sa - rò! Ho già ri-sol - to.
K.
Ent-schließ dich: So kommst du?
Ri - sol - - vi: Ver - ra - - i?
Zu Don Giovanni)
(A Don Giovanni)
L.
O sagt doch nein, o sagt doch nei
Di-te di no, di-te di no.
Vc.
Cb.

513
Fl.
Ob.
Clar. in B
Fag.
Cor. in F
Tr. in D
I.II
Trb.
III
Timp.
513
I
Viol.
II
Viola
D. G.
nie___ hab ich ge-zit-tert, ich fürch-te nichts, drum sei's!
fer- - mo il co-re in pet-to, non ho ti-mor; ver-rò!
Nimm sie denn!
Ec-co-la!
Komtur
Il Commendatore
K.
Reich mir die Hand zum Pfan- - de!
Dam-mi la ma-no in pe- - gno!
Vc.
Cb.
a 2

521
Più stretto
Fl.
Ob.
Clar. in B
Fag.
Cor. in F
Tr. in D
I.II
Trb.
III
Timp.
521
Più stretto
I
Viol.
II
Viola
D. G.
O weh,
Oi-mè,
wie kalt faßt sie mich an!
che ge-lo è que-sto ma-i?
K.
Wohl-an?
Cos' hai?
Beug_dei-nen Sinn, be - reu-e,
Pen- - ti-ti, can-gia vi-ta:
dir schlug die letz-te Stun-de!
è l'ul- ti- mo mo-men-to!
Vc.
Cb.

528
Fl.
Ob.
ar. in B
a 2
Fag.
or. in F
r. in D
I. II
rb.
III
Timp.
tr
528
I
Viol.
II
iola
sich vergeblich freizumachen]
sciogliersi, ma invano]
D. G.
nein, nicht kenn ich Reu - e, he - - be dich weg von hier!
no, ch'io non mi pen - to, van - - ne lon - tan da me!
K.
Denk an den Tod, be-
Pen - - ti - ti, scel - le -
Vc.
Cb.

535
Fl.
Ob.
Clar. in B
Fag.
a 2
Cor. in F
Tr. in D
I.II
Trb.
III
Timp.
535
I
Viol.
II
Viola
D.G.
Nein, nein, du alter Schwätzer!
No, vecchio infatuato!
Nein!
No!
Nein!
No!
K.
reu-e!
ra-to!
Beß-re dich!
Pen-ti-ti!
Beß-re dich!
Pen-ti-ti!
Vc.
Cb.

542
Fl.
Ob.
ar. in B
Fag.
or. in F
r. in D
I.II
Trb.
III
Timp.
a 2
542
I
Viol.
II
Viola
D.G.
Don Giovanni
Nein! No!
Nein! No!
Nein! No!
Nein! No!
K.
Komtur
Il Commendatore
Ja! Sì!
Ja! Sì!
Ja! Sì!
Jetzt Ah,
L.
Leporello
Ja, Sì,
ja! sì!
Vc.
Cb.

550
a 2
Allegro
Fl.
Ob.
Clar. in B
Fag.
Cor. in F
Tr. in D
I.II
Trb.
III
Timp.
I
Viol.
II
Viola
D.G.
K.
Vc.
Cb.
Don Giovanni
[Flammen von verschiedenen Seiten. Erdbeben
[Foco da diverse parti; tremuoto]
Welch un-gewohntes Angstgefühl,
Da qual tre-mo-r in-so - li-to
(Geht ab)
(Parte)
naht dein Straf - ge - richt!
tem - po più non v'è!

557
a 2
Fl.
Ob.
r. in B
Fag.
r. in F
r. in D
I.II
Trb.
III
Timp.
557
I
Viol.
II
Viola
Don Giovanni
D.G.
höl - li - sche Gei - ster na - hen sich, es stürmt das wil - de Flam - men - meer der Höl - le her zu
sen - to as - sa - lir gli spi - ri - ti, dond' e - sco - no quei vor - ti - ci di fo - ce, pien d'or -
Vc.
Cb.
cresc.

563
Fl.
a 2
Ob.
Clar. in B
Fag.
Cor. in F
Tr. in D
I.II
Trb.
III
Timp.
Viol.
I
II
Viola
D.G.
mir!
ror!
Chor [aus der Tiefe, mit dumpfer Stimme]
Coro [di sotterra, con voci cupe]
Coro
Schwer ist die Schuld zu süh - - - nen,
Tut - - to a tue col - - pe è po - - - co,
Vc.
Cb.

567
Fl.
Ob.
r. in B
Fag.
r. in F
. in D
I.II
Trb.
III
Timp.
I
Viol.
II
Viola
Don Giovanni
D. G.
Was fol - tert so die See - le mir, was
Chi l'a - ni-ma mi la - ce-ra, chi
Leporello
L.
Wie be- - ben ihm die
Che cef- - fo dis- - pe -
Coro
schlimm - res noch har- - ret dein!
vie- - ni, o'd un mal peg- - gior!
Vc.
Cb.

571
Fl.
Ob.
Clar. in B
Fag.
Cor. in F
Tr. in D
a 2
I.II
Trb.
III
tr
Timp.
571
I
Viol.
II
Viola
D.G.
tobt in al - len A - dern mir, ich füh - le Höl - len - qua - len, welch Schre - cken, wel - ch
m'a - gi - ta le vi - sce - re, che stra - zio, oi - mè, che sma - nia, che in - fer - no, che te
L.
Glie - der, Ver - zweif - lung reißt ihn nie - der, sein Kla - gen und sein Jam - mern
ra - to, che ge - sti da dan - na - to, che gri - di, che la - men - ti,
Vc.
Cb.

576
Fl.
Ob.
ar. in B
Fag.
r. in F
r. in D
I.II
Trb.
III
Timp.
a 2
576
I
Viol.
II
Viola
D.G.
Pein,
ror,
was
chi
L.
dringt mir durch Mark und
co - me mi fa ter -
Bein, durch Mark und Bein,
- ror, mi fa ter - ror,
Coro
Schwer ist die Schuld zu
Tut - - to a tue col - - pe è
Vc.
Cb.

580
Fl.
Ob.
Clar. in B
Fag.
Cor. in F
Tr. in D
I. II
Trb.
III
Timp.
a 2
f
sf
tr
580
I
Viol.
II
Viola
D.G.
fol - tert so die See - le mir,
l'a - ni - ma mi la - ce - ra,
was
chi
L.
wie be - ben ihm die Glie - der,
che cef - fo dis - pe - ra - to,
Coro
süh - - - - -nen,
po - - - - -co,
schlimm - res noch har - ret
vie - - ni, c'è un mal peg - -
Vc.
Cb.

584
Fl.
Ob.
lar. in B
Fag.
or. in F
r. in D
a 2
I.II
Trb.
III
Timp.
584
I
Viol.
II
Viola
D.G.
tobt in al - len A - dern mir, ich füh - le Höl - len - qua - len, ach,
m'a - gi - ta le vi - sce - re, che stra - zio, oi - mè, che sma - nia, ah,
L.
Ver - zweif - lung reißt ihn nie - der, sein Kla - gen und sein Jam - mern, sein
che ge - sti da dan - na - to, che gri - di, che la - men - ti, che
Coro
dein,
gior,
Vc.
Cb.

589
Fl.
Ob.
Clar. in B
Fag.
Cor. in F
a 2
Tr. in D
I. II
Trb.
III
Timp.
tr
589
I
Viol.
II
Viola
[Die Flammen wachsen, Don Giovanni versinkt]
[Il foco cresce; Don Giovanni si sprofonda]
D.G.
o Qua - len, Höl - len - pein!
che in - fer - no, che ter - ror!
L.
Kla - gen und sein Jam-mern dringt mir durch Mark und Bein!
gri - di, che la - men - ti, co - me mi fa ter - ror!
Coro
schlimm - res, schlimm - res, schlimm-res noch har - ret
vie - ni, vie - ni, vie - ni, c'è un mal peg -
Vc.
Cb.

594
a 2
Fl.
Ob.
Clar. in B
Fag.
Cor. in F
Cor. in D
in G
I. II
Trb.
III
Timp.
Viol.
I
II
Viola
(Wird verschlungen)
(Resta ingluviato)
D.G.
Ach!
Ah!
L.
Ach!
Ah!
Coro
dein!
gior!
Vc.
Cb.

Letzte Szene

[Leporello, Donna Anna, Donna Elvira, Don Ottavio, Zerlina, Masetto mit Gerichtsdienern]

Scena ultima

[Leporello, Donna Anna, Donna Elvira, Don Ottavio, Zerlina, Masetto con ministri di guistizia]

612
Fl.
Ob.
Fag.
in G
a 2
Viol. I II
Viola
D. A.
D. E.
Z.
D. O.
M.
Vc.
Cb.
tr
mfp
p
Donna Anna
Erst wenn der
So - lo mi-
schon stehn die Rächer für ihn be - reit, für ihn be - reit.
tut - to il mio sde-gno sfo - gar io vo', sfo - gar io vo'.
621
Ket - ten Last fest ihn um - span - net, ist ü - ber - stan - den mein schwe - res Leid.
ran - do - lo stret - to in ca - te - ne al - le mie pe - ne cal - ma - da - rò.

632
Fl.
Ob.
Fag.
Cor. in G
Viol. I II
Viola
Leporello
L.
Ihr hofft ver - ge-bens, ihn noch zu fin-den, laßt al-les Su-chen, er ist schon weit, er ist sch
Più non spe - ra - te di ri - tro - var - lo, più non cer - ca - te, lon - ta-no an-dò, lon - ta - no
Vc.
Cb.
641
a 2
f
p
[f]
Donna Anna
D. A.
Was ist ge-sche-hen, re-de, er-zäh-le, re - de, er-zäh-le doch,
Cos' è, fa-vel-la, cos' è, fa-vel-la. Via, pre - sto, sbri-ga-ti,
Zerlina
Z.
Was ist ge-sche-hen, re-de, er-zäh-le, re - de, er-zäh-le doch,
Cos' è, fa-vel-la, cos' è, fa-vel-la. Via, pre - sto, sbri-ga-ti,
Donna Elvira
D. E.
Was ist ge-sche-hen, re-de, er-zäh-le, re - de, er-zäh-le doch,
Cos' è, fa-vel-la, cos' è, fa-vel-la. Via, pre - sto, sbri-ga-ti,
Don Ottavio
D. O.
Was ist ge-sche-hen, re-de, er-zäh-le, re - de, er-zäh-le doch,
Cos' è, fa-vel-la, cos' è, fa-vel-la. Via, pre - sto, sbri-ga-ti,
L.
weit. Da kam ein Rie-se... da kam ein Rie-se... doch, ach, ich
dò. Ven - ne un co-los-so... ven-ne un co-los-so... Ma se non
Masetto
M.
Was ist ge-sche-hen, re-de, er-zäh-le, re - de, er-zäh-le doch,
Cos' è, fa-vel-la, cos' è, fa-vel-la. Via, pre - sto, sbri-ga-ti,
Vc.
Cb.

651
Fl.
Ob.
Fag.
in G
a 2
Viol. I
Viol. II
Viola
re - de, er - zäh - le doch!
via, pre-sto, sbri-ga-ti!
Schnell doch, er-zäh-le re - de doch!
Pre-sto, fa-vel-la, sbri-ga-ti!
Schnell doch, er-zäh-le, re - de doch!
kann nicht... nein, nein, ich kann nicht, ich kann nicht wei-ter, ich kann nicht wei-ter, ich kann nicht wei-ter!
pos - so... ma se non pos - so, ma se non pos-so, ma se non pos-so, ma se non pos-so!
Vc.
Cb.
660
Leporello
Rau-chen-de Flammen... ich ring nach A-tem... der Mann von Stei - ne... halt, halt, nicht wei-ter... gleich hier... dort
Tra fu-mo e fo - co... ba - da-te un po - co... l'uo - mo di sas - so... fer - ma - te il pas - so... giu - sto... là

669
Fl.
Ob.
Fag.
Cor. in G
Viol. I
Viol. II
Viola
D. A.
Z.
D. E.
D. O.
L.
M.
Vc.
Cb.
cresc.
f
p
a 2
Donna Anna
O Gott, was hör ich!
Stel - - le, che sen-to!
Zerlina
O Gott, was hör ich!
Stel - - le, che sen-to!
Donna Elvira
O Gott, was hör ich!
Stel - - le, che sen-to!
Don Ottavio
O Gott, was hör ich!
Stel - - le, che sen-to!
un-ten... furcht-ba-res Kra-chen... dort hat der Teu-fel ihn zu sich ge-holt.
sot-to... die-de il gran bot-to... giu-sto là il dia-vo-lo se'l tran-gu-giò.
Masetto
O Gott, was hör ich!
Stel - - le, che sen-to!

678
a 2
Fl.
Ob.
Fag.
in G
Viol.
Viola
cresc.
Donna Anna
Das war der Schat - ten, den sie ge -
Ah cer - to è l'om - bra che l'in-con -
Zerlina
Das war der
Ah cer - to è
Donna Elvira
Das war der Schat - - ten, den ich ge -
Ah cer - to è l'om - - bra che m'in - con -
Don Ottavio
Das war der
Ah cer - to è
Leporello
So war's, das schwör ich.
Ve-ro è l'e - ven-to.
Vc.
Cb.

*) For a cut, see Supplement III, page 461.

695
Fl.
Ob.
Fag.
Cor. in G
p
695
I
Viol.
II
Viola
D. A.
sehn, das war er, der Schat-ten, das war, das war der Schat - - ten, den sie ge-
trò, ah cer-to è l'om-bra, ah cer - to, cer - to è l'om - - bra che l'in-con-
Z.
sehn, das war er, der Schat-ten, das war, das war der Schat - ten, den sie ge -
trò, ah cer-to è l'om-bra, ah cer - to, cer-to è l'om - bra che l'in - con -
D. E.
sehn, das war er, der Schat-ten, das war er, das war der Schat-ten, den ich ge-
trò, ah cer-to è l'om-bra, ah cer-to, ah cer- to è l'om-bra che m'in-con-
D. O.
sehn, das war er, der Schat-ten, das war er, der Schat - ten, den sie ge -
trò, ah cer-to è l'om-bra, ah cer - to è l'om - bra che l'in - con -
M.
sehn, das war er, der Schat-ten, das war der Schat - ten, den sie ge -
trò, ah cer-to è l'om-bra, ah cer - to è l'om - bra che l'in - con -
Vc.
Cb.

707
Larghetto
Fl.
Ob.
Fag.
Cor. in G
cresc.
Viol. I II
Viola
D.A.
Z.
D.E.
D.O.
M.
Vc.
Cb.
sehn!
trò!
Da der Himmel, teu-re Ge-lieb-te,
Or che tut-ti, o mio te-so-ro,
714
[div.]
Ra-che hat voll-zo-gen, end auch du nun dein Wi-der-stre-ben, am Al-tar reich mir die
ca-ti siam dal cie-lo, por-gi, por-gi a me un ri-sto-ro, non mi far lan-gui-re

719
Fl.
Ob.
Fag.
Cor. in G
719
I Viol. II
Viola
Donna Anna
D.A.
Gönn, o Teu - rer, mir noch dies Wei - len, laß dem Schmerz ein Jahr mich weihn!
Lascia,o ca - ro, un an-no an-co - ra al - lo sfo - go del mio cor!
D.O.
Hand.
cor.
Vc.
Cb.
cresc.
p
724
Mag dein Herz sich nach mir seh - nen, treu er-ge-ben bleibst du
Al de-sio di chi t'a-do - ra ce - der de-ve un fi - do a-
Mag mein Herz sich nach dir seh - nen, treu er-ge-ben bleib ich dir,
Al de-sio di chi m'a-do - ra ce - der de-ve un fi - do a-mor,

728
vi-
Fl.
Ob.
Fag.
Cor. in G
728
vi-
I
Viol.
II
Viola
D.A.
mir, treu er-geben bleibst du mir, treu bleibst du mir, mag dein Herz sich nach mir seh-nen,
mor, ce - der de-ve, ce - der de - ve un fi - do a-mor, al de-sio di chi t'a-do-ra
D.O.
treu er-geben bleib ich dir, treu bleib ich dir, mag mein Herz sich nach di
ce - der de-ve, ce - der de - ve un fi - do a-mor, al de-sio di chi m'
Vc.
Cb.
733
Cor. in G
733
I
Viol.
II
Viola
D.A.
treu er-ge-ben bleibst du mir, treu er-geben bleibst du mir, tre
ce - der de-ve un fi - do a-mor, ce - der de-ve, ce - der de - ve u
D.O.
seh - nen, treu er-ge-ben bleib ich dir, treu er-geben bleib ich dir, tre
do - ra ce - der de-ve un fi - do a-mor, ce - der de-ve, ce - der de - ve u
Vc.
Cb.

737
Fl.
Ob.
Fag.
in G
in D
-de
Viol. I II
Viola
[div.]
D. A.
bleibst du mir, treu bleibst du, ja bleibst du mir.
fi - do a - mor, un fi - do, un fi - do a - mor.
D. E.
Donna Elvira
In ein Klo - ster laßt mich
Io men va - do in un ri -
D. O.
bleib ich dir, treu bleib ich, ja bleib ich dir.
fi - do a - mor, un fi - do, un fi - do a - mor.
Vc.
Cb.
741
I
Z.
Zerlina
Wir, Ma-set-to, gehn nach Hau-se, setzen uns zum Abendschmause!
Noi, Ma-set-to, a ca-sa an-dia-mo, a ce - nar in compa - gni - a!
zie-hen, dort mein Le-ben zu be-schließen.
ti-ro a fi-nir la vi-ta mi-a.
M.
Masetto
Wir, Zer-li-na, gehn nach Hau-se, setzen uns zum Abendschmause!
Noi, Zer-li-na, a ca-sa an-dia-mo, a ce - nar in compa - gni - a!
L.
Leporello
Einen bessern Herrn zu
Ed io vado all' o - ste-

745
Fl.
Ob.
Clar. in A
Fag.
Cor. in D
in D
a 2
Viol. I
Viol. II
Viola
Zerlina
Z.
Mit dem Teu-fel eng im Bund, büßt er in der Höl-le Grund, büßt er in der
Re-sti dun-que quel bir-bon, con Pro-ser-pi-na e Plu-ton, con Pro-ser-pi-
Masetto
M.
Mit dem Teu-fel eng im Bund, büßt er in der Höl-le Grund, büßt er in der
Re-sti dun-que quel bir-bon, con Pro-ser-pi-na e Plu-ton, con Pro-ser-pi-
L.
su-chen, will ich jetzt ins Wirtshaus gehn. Mit dem Teu-fel eng im Bund, büßt er in der Höl-le Grund, büßt er in der
ri-a, a tro-var pa-dron mi-glior. Re-sti dun-que quel bir-bon, con Pro-ser-pi-na e Plu-ton, con Pro-ser-pi-
Vc.
Cb.
749
Höl-le Grund, a-ber wir, ihr gu-ten Leute, singen froh und glück-lich heute unser
na e Plu-ton! E noi tut-ti, o buo-na gen-te, ri-pe-tiam al-le-gra-mente l'an-ti
Höl-le Grund, a-ber wir, ihr gu-ten Leute, singen froh und glück-lich heu-te unser
na e Plu-ton! E noi tut-ti, o buo-na gen-te, ri-pe-tiam al-le-gra-men-te l'an-ti
Höl-le Grund, a-ber wir, ihr gu-ten Leute, singen froh und glück-lich heu-te unser
na e Plu-ton! E noi tut-ti, o buo-na gen-te, ri-pe-tiam al-le-gra-men-te l'an-ti

753
Fl. I II
Ob.
r. in A
'ag.
. in D
a 2
I iol. II
ola
Z.
schö - nes, al - tes Lied, sin - gen froh und glück - lich heut un - ser schö - nes, al - tes Lied:
chis - si - ma can - zon, l'an - ti - chis - si - ma can - zon, l'an - ti - chis - si - ma can - zon:
M.
schö - nes, al - tes Lied, sin - gen froh und glück - lich heut un - ser schö - nes, al - tes Lied:
chis - si - ma can - zon, l'an - ti - chis - si - ma can - zon, l'an - ti - chis - si - ma can - zon:
L.
schö - nes, al - tes Lied, sin - gen froh und glück - lich heut un - ser schö - nes, al - tes Lied:
chis - si - ma can - zon, l'an - ti - chis - si - ma can - zon, l'an - ti - chis - si - ma can - zon:
Vc.
Cb.
756
Presto
Donna Anna
sotto voce
D.A.
Al - so stirbt, wer Bö - ses tat, wer Bö - ses tat,
Que - sto è il fin di chi fa mal, di chi fa mal,
Donna Elvira
sotto voce
D.E.
Al - so stirbt, wer Bö - ses tat, wer Bö - ses tat,
Que - sto è il fin di chi fa mal, di chi fa mal,

763
Fl.
Ob.
Clar. in A
a 2
Fag.
Cor. in D
Tr. in D
Timp.
Viol. I
Viol. II
Viola
D.A.
Donna Anna
Bö - ses tat,
que - sto è il fin,
D.E.
Donna Elvira
Bö - ses tat,
que - sto è il fin,
Z.
Zerlina
sotto voce
Al - so stirbt, wer Bö - ses tat, wer Bö - ses tat,
Que - sto è il fin di chi fa mal, di chi fa mal,
D.O.
Don Ottavio
Bö - ses tat,
Que - sto è il fin,
M.
Masetto
Bö - ses tat,
Que - sto è il fin,
L.
Leporello
Bö - ses tat,
Que - sto è il fin,
Vc.
Cb.

771
Fl.
Ob.
r. in A
a 2
Fag.
. in D
a 2
. in D
[f]
imp.
[f]
771
I
iol.
II
f
iola
f
.A.
Bö - ses tat, al - so stirbt, wer Bö - ses tat, wer Bö - ses
que - sto è il fin, que - sto è il fin di chi fa mal, di chi fa
.E.
Bö - ses tat, al - so stirbt, wer Bö - ses tat, wer Bö - ses
que - sto è il fin, que - sto è il fin di chi fa mal, di chi fa
Z.
Bö - ses tat, al - so stirbt, wer Bö - ses tat, wer Bö - ses
que - sto è il fin, que - sto è il fin di chi fa mal, di chi fa
.O.
Bö - ses tat, al - so stirbt, wer Bö - ses tat, wer Bö - ses
que - sto è il fin, que - sto è il fin di chi fa mal, di chi fa
M.
al - so stirbt, wer Bö - ses tat, wer Bö - ses
que - sto è il fin di chi fa mal, di chi fa
L.
al - so stirbt, wer Bö - ses tat, wer Bö - ses
que - sto è il fin di chi fa mal, di chi fa
'c.
b.

778
Fl.
Ob.
Clar. in A
Fag.
a 2
tr
Cor. in D
Tr. in D
a 2
Timp.
778
I
Viol.
II
Viola
tr
D.A.
tat, wer Bö - ses tat, al - so stirbt, wer Bö - ses tat, wer
mal, di chi fa mal, que - sto è il fin di chi fa mal, di
D.E.
tat, wer Bö - ses tat, al - so stirbt, wer Bö - ses tat, wer
mal, di chi fa mal, que - sto è il fin di chi fa mal, di
Z.
tat, wer Bö - ses tat, al - so stirbt, wer Bö - ses tat, wer
mal, di chi fa mal, que - sto è il fin di chi fa mal, di
D.O.
tat, wer Bö - ses tat, al - so stirbt, wer Bö - ses tat, wer
mal, di chi fa mal, que - sto è il fin di chi fa mal, di
M.
tat, wer Bö - ses tat, al - so stirbt, wer Bö - ses tat, wer
mal, di chi fa mal, que - sto è il fin di chi fa mal, di
L.
tat, wer Bö - ses tat, al - so stirbt, wer Bö - ses tat, wer
mal, di chi fa mal, que - sto è il fin di chi fa mal, di
Vc.
tr
Cb.
tr

785
vi-
Fl.
a 2
Ob.
a 2
r. in A
Fag.
a 2
r. in D
. in D
a 2
imp.
785
vi-
I
iol.
II
iola
. A.
Bö - ses tat! Wie im Le - ben so
chi fa mal. E de' per - fi - di
. E.
Bö - ses tat! Wie im Le - ben so
chi fa mal. E de' per - fi - di
Z.
Bö - ses tat! Wie im Le - ben so
chi fa mal. E de' per - fi - di
. O.
Bö - ses tat! Wie im Le - ben so
chi fa mal. E de' per - fi - di
M.
Bö - ses tat! Wie im Le - ben so
chi fa mal. E de' per - fi - di
L.
Bö - ses tat! Wie im Le - ben so
chi fa mal. E de' per - fi - di
Vc.
Cb.

*) See Editors' Commentary.

802
Fl.
Ob.
Clar. in A
Fag.
Cor. in D
Tr. in D
Timp.
Viol. I
Viol. II
Viola
D. A.
D. E.
Z.
D. O.
M.
L.
Vc.
Cb.
[div.]
du, ern - test du nach dei - ner Saat, nach dei - ner Saat,
vi - ta è sem - pre, è sem - pre u - gual, è sem-pre u - gual,
ern - test du nach dei - ner Saat, nach dei - ner Saat,
al - la vi - ta è sem - pre u - gual, è sem-pre u - gual,

813
-de
a 2
Fl.
Ob.
Clar. in A
Fag.
Cor. in D
Tr. in D
Timp.
Viol. I
Viol. II
Viola
D. A.
D. E.
Z.
D. O.
M.
L.
Vc.
Cb.
wie im Le - - - - - ben so im To - -
e de' per - - - - fi - di la mor - -

820
Fl.
Ob.
Clar. in A
Fag.
Cor. in D
Tr. in D
Timp.
Viol. I
Viol. II
Viola
D. A.
de ern - test du, ern - test
te al - la vi - ta è
D. E.
de ern - test du, ern - test
te al - la vi - ta è
Z.
de ern - test du, ern - test
te al - la vi - ta è
D. O.
de ern test du, ern - test
te al la vi - ta è
M.
de ern test du, ern - test
te al la vi - ta è
L.
de ern - test
te al - la
Vc.
Cb.

829
Fl.
Ob.
Clar. in A
Fag.
Cor. in D
Tr. in D
Timp.
Viol. I
Viol. II
Viola
D. A.
du nach dei - ner Saat, nach dei -
sem - pre, è sem - pre, sem -
D. E.
du nach dei - ner Saat, nach dei -
sem - pre, è sem - pre, sem -
Z.
du die Saat, nach dei -
sem pre u gual, è sem -
D. O.
du nach dei - ner Saat,
sem - pre, è sem - pre,
M.
du nach dei -
sem - pre, è sem -
L.
du nach dei -
vi - ta, è sem -
Vc.
Cb.
p
I
tr

839
Fl.
Ob.
Clar. in A
Fag.
Cor. in D
Tr. in D
Timp.
Viol. I
Viol. II
Viola
D.A.
D.E.
Z.
D.O.
M.
L.
Vc.
Cb.
I
a 2
tr
f
ner Saat. Al - so stirbt, wer Bö - ses
-pre u - gual, al - la vi - ta è sem - pre u -
ner, dei - ner Saat. Al - so stirbt, wer Bö - ses
-pre, sem - pre u - gual, al - la vi - ta è sem - pre u -
nach dei - ner Saat. Al - so stirbt, wer Bö - ses
è sem - pre u - gual, al - la vi - ta è sem - pre u -
ner Saat. Al - so stirbt, wer Bö - ses
pre u - gual, al - la vi - ta è sem - pre u -

847
Fl.
Ob.
Clar. in A
a 2
Fag.
Cor. in D
Tr. in D
Timp.
847
I
Viol.
II
Viola
D. A.
tat, al - - so stirbt, wer Bö - ses tat, wer Bö - ses
gual, al - - la vi - ta è sem - pre u - gual, è sem - pre u -
D. E.
tat, al - - so stirbt, wer Bö - ses tat, wer Bö - ses
gual, al - - la vi - ta è sem - pre u - gual, è sem - pre u -
Z.
tat, al - - so stirbt, wer Bö - ses tat, wer Bö - ses
gual, al - - la vi - ta è sem - pre u - gual, è sem - pre u -
D. O.
tat, al - - so stirbt, wer Bö - ses tat, wer Bö - ses
gual, al - - la vi - ta è sem - pre u - gual, è sem - pre u -
M.
tat, al - - so stirbt, wer Bö - ses tat, wer Bö - ses
gual, al - - la vi - ta è sem - pre u - gual, è sem - pre u -
L.
tat, al - - so stirbt, wer Bö - ses tat, wer Bö - ses
gual, al - - la vi - ta è sem - pre u - gual, è sem - pre u -
Vc.
Cb.

853
Fl.
Ob.
ar. in A
Fag.
a 2
or. in D
r. in D
a 2
Timp.
tr
853
I
Viol.
II
Viola
D. A.
tat, wer Bö - ses tat, Bö - ses tat!
gual, è sem - pre u - gual, sem - pre u - gual!
D. E.
tat, wer Bö - ses tat, Bö - ses tat!
gual, è sem - pre u - gual, sem - pre u - gual!
Z.
tat, wer Bö - ses tat, Bö - ses tat!
gual, è sem - pre u - gual, sem - pre u - gual!
D. O.
tat, wer Bö - ses tat, Bö - ses tat!
gual, è sem - pre u - gual, sem - pre u - gual!
M.
tat, wer Bö - ses tat, Bö - ses tat!
gual, è sem - pre u - gual, sem - pre u - gual!
L.
tat, wer Bö - ses tat, Bö - ses tat!
gual, è sem - pre u - gual, sem - pre u - gual!
Vc.
Cb.

Ende der Op
Fine dell' Oper

SUPPLEMENT

I

Concert Ending of the Overture

The autograph manuscript of the Overture includes a sheet containing the following concert ending, doubtless also in Mozart's hand:

II

Transposition of the Aria No. 21b

At the first performance of the opera in Vienna on May 7, 1788, Mozart was compelled to transpose the newly written aria for Elvira (No. 21b) to D Major. He had the recitative begin in the original key, and only at measure 20 did he modulate into D Major as follows:

III

Cut in the Finale No. 24

In the autograph manuscript, measures 689–749 are crossed out and replaced on a separate sheet, which can scarcely be by Mozart, though the handwriting is very similar, by the following transition passage:

continues page 444, m. 750

BASIS OF THE EDITION

The present score has been edited from Mozart's autograph manuscript, which today is in the library of the Conservatoire de Musique in Paris, and from the photocopy made for the Preussische Staatsbibliothek in Berlin. Unfortunately Mozart's manuscript is not preserved in its entirety; it lacks the last sheet, which is replaced by copyist's work, and the recitative with the Commendatore's first two passages in the graveyard scene. Nor are the sections composed for the Vienna première preserved in manuscript, except for Elvira's recitative and aria (No. 21b). Furthermore, the wind parts in the sextet and in the two finales are also missing. Mozart was unable to fit them onto the twelve-staff note paper that he used for his clean copies; he wrote them on extra leaves, which appear to be irretrievably lost. For the editing of these wind parts we were able to use a copy in the Prince Fürstenberg Library in Donaueschingen (Mus. ms. 1386a/b) which bears the heading: "Il/ Dissoluto Punito/ o Sia/ Il D: Giovanni/ Drama giocoso/ in due Atti/ Rappresentata [*sic*] nel Teatro di Praga l'Anno 1787./ La Musica è del Signor Volfgango. Mozart. in Prag zu finden bey Anton Grams in Ballhaus No. 239." This copy, which apparently was prepared under Mozart's supervision, contains all the wind parts, in the form used by Mozart in the autograph score, as a supplement, and, in the second finale, also shows the trombone part, the authenticity of which has been so hotly debated up to now.

Also consulted was a copy owned by the Prague Mozart-Gemeinde, known as the "Prague" or "Graz" score, which served as the basis for the wind parts in Bernhard Gugler's first edition of *Don Giovanni* (1869).* In addition, use has been made of photocopies of the Italian manuscripts of *Don Giovanni* in the Istituto Musicale in Florence; further details will be found in the Commentary below.

Although the autograph manuscript is quite legible, it contains numerous inadvertences and small oversights of the kind that easily occur during hasty copying. Most of the errors admit of no doubt as to the right reading and have been tacitly corrected. Where this was not possible and there was no opportunity of comparison with similar passages, the apparently correct reading has been placed in the text, whereas all other deviations from the autograph manuscript, the correctness of which was not sufficiently established, have without exception been included in the Editors' Commentary that follows, in order to give as faithful a picture as possible of Mozart's manuscript.

For the Italian text and the stage directions, we have used the reprint of the original libretto, with the variants from the Vienna libretto and the autograph score, edited by Dr. Leopold v. Sonnleithner (Leipzig, 1865, Breitkopf & Härtel). Mozart wrote Italian very precisely; here for the first time his punctuation, which makes full and varied use of semicolons, colons and dashes, has been precisely retained. Only in the formally rounded-off numbers Mozart becomes more careless; here the punctuation has been altered or completed on the basis of the libretto. When from time to time the text in the manuscript deviates from that in the printed libretto, the version in the manuscript has been taken as the authoritative one, and changes made accordingly.

Mozart transferred Da Ponte's stage directions only partially into his manuscript; on the other hand, he added such notations of his own in many places. All missing directions that are needed for staging have been taken from the libretto, but placed in square brackets, to indicate their origin clearly.

Slurs, ties and staccato marks have been tacitly supplied when analogous passages or other instrumental parts proved them to be necessary.

Mozart's manuscript contains dots and two types of dashes, short thick dashes and long thin ones. Mozart does not use the short thick dash as a staccato mark in our modern sense, but as an accent, a *ben marcato*. In the manuscript, to be sure, the distinction between dots and dashes is fluid; many long dashes occur in places where their significance as accents is indubitable or at least highly probable; at other times dots are abbreviated dashes; and indeed Mozart scarcely seems to make a fundamental distinction between dots and weak dashes. In order, however, to eliminate all doubt, we have here followed the manuscript exactly, in so far as possible, since the pen is subtler than the engraving tool.

**Mozarts Don Giovanni, Partitur. Erstmals nach dem Autograph herausgegeben unter Beifügung einer neuen Textverdeutschung von Bernhard Gugler. Zweite verbesserte Auflage.* Leipzig, Verlag von F. E. C. Leuckart (Constantin Sander).

EDITORS' COMMENTARY

Ouvertura

Meas. 1 ff.: The Drums are not transposed as in the autograph MS [referred to simply as "MS" in this Commentary], but notated at the actual pitch. The Trumpets are called "clarini" in the MS.

Mm. 15–17: In writing the indications *fp* and *sfp* Mozart is rather imprecise, sometimes writing them joined and sometimes separated. Generally it is only discernible with difficulty whether this is intentional or accidental. Here, for example, the strings in the MS have *sf. p.*, but the winds *sfp* (in a few places only *fp*); it cannot be assumed, however, that they are to play *sfp*.

Mm. 18 & 19: In the MS, Horn I and Trumpet I have no tie.

M. 21: In the MS, the First Violins, Violas and bass [Cellos and Basses] have the *p* beneath the first quarter note.

Mm. 34 & 35: In the MS, the First Violins have only one slur over both measures; altered here by analogy with mm. 42 & 43 and 143 & 144.

Mm. 42 & 43: This passage has given rise to many differences of opinion. Either Mozart wanted the passage as it stands in the MS and has been printed here, or else he forgot the flat sign in front of the b^2 in the First Violins in m. 43.

Mm. 47–49 & 51: The staccato dots in the First Violins are added; also in the Bassoons, Violas and bass in mm. 48, 49 and 51.

M. 81: In the MS, only the bass has *sf*, all the other instruments *f*; there is no doubt, however, that *sf* is intended throughout, as in m. 77.

Mm. 193–216: The repeat is not written out in the MS, but is called for by "Dal segno, 24 Takte."

Mm. 252–255: The slurs in the First and Second Violins (also in m. 256 in the Second Violins) are lacking in the MS.

No. 1. Introduzione

M. 43: The fermata in the vocal part is lacking in the MS.

M. 57: The MS gives the bass another *p*.

Mm. 87–90: The MS, obviously in error, gives Leporello: "chi son'io tu non saprei."

Mm. 100 & 101: In the MS, the staccato dots are lacking here and in mm. 118 & 119.

M. 107: In the MS, the Bassoons have no marking (in m. 125, Bassoons and bass).

M. 137: In the MS, the slur and tie in the Oboes are lacking.

Mm. 157 & 158: In the MS, Leporello erroneously has "fuggir" instead of "partir."

Mm. 164 & 165: In the MS, the slurs in Oboe II, Bassoons and bass are lacking.

Mm. 168 & 169: The MS lacks the tie in Oboe I (also in mm. 172 & 173).

Mm. 192 & 193: The MS lacks the slur in Bassoon I.

M. 194: In the MS, the bass has a whole note; Gugler made the alteration here, "to avoid the misconception that the string bass should continue to play longer than the other strings."

No. 2. Recitativo e Duetto

Mm. 47 & 48: The staccato marks are given only for the First Violins in the MS.

M. 60: In the MS, the bass lacks the flat sign.

Mm. 87 & 88: In the MS, the Flute slur is divided into two slurs, in contrast to the Bassoons.

M. 95: The MS lacks the slur in Bassoon I as well as the slur in Bassoon II in mm. 94–96 (also mm. 110–112).

Mm. 103 & 104: The MS lacks the slur in the Flutes here and in mm. 121 & 122.

M. 121: In the MS, Don Ottavio has 𝅗𝅥 ♩ ♩ ; altered here by analogy with m. 103.

Mm. 131 & 132: The MS lacks the tie in the Violas.

M. 152: The MS lacks the Bassoon II slur here and in m. 186.

Mm. 201 & 202: The MS lacks the Bassoon II slur here and in mm. 207 & 208.

Mm. 217–219: The MS lacks the slurs in Flutes and Oboes.

M. 220: In the MS, only the second and third quarter notes in the First Violins have staccato marks; the others have been added.

Scena IV

The MS adds: "poi D. Elvira in abito da viaggio" but has no indication of characters for Scena V.

No. 3. Aria

M. 6: Here and in all analogous passages, we have added the staccato dots on the second and third quarter beats in the First Violins, and the slurs on the fourth quarter here and in m. 8.

Mm. 19 & 20: The tie in Horn I is added by analogy with mm. 65 & 66.

Mm. 20 & 21: The slur in Flute II is added by analogy with mm. 66 & 67.

Mm. 32 & 33: The staccato marks are added by analogy with m. 31 (also in mm. 78 & 79).

M. 42: In the MS, the staccato marks are given only here and in m. 43 in the First Violins; the others have been added.

Mm. 53 & 54: The slurs in the Clarinets and Bassoons are divided into two, one per measure, in the MS (change from one system to the next); also in mm. 88 & 89.

No. 4. Aria

M. 1: The first note in the bass is undoubtedly part of the final Cembalo chord; this is clear from the *p* in the bass in the second measure.

M. 17: The MS lacks the staccato dots in the Flutes and Bassoons (also in the Bassoons in m. 21).

Mm. 28 & 29: The MS lacks the slur in the First Violins and Violas.

Mm. 30 & 31: The MS lacks the slur in Oboe I (also in m. 64).

Mm. 52 & 53: The MS lacks the slur in Oboe II (also in mm. 60 & 61).

Mm. 66 & 67: The MS lacks the tie in Horn I.

Mm. 74 & 75: We have added the staccato dots, except those in the Flutes and partially in the Bassoons (first and second quarter beats).

M. 77: In the MS, Flutes I and II have only b^2 (surely a slip of the pen).

M. 108: In the MS, the *p* in the bass here and in m. 110 is placed under the first eighth note; altered in both measures by analogy with m. 106.

Mm. 131–134: In the MS, the Viola slur is divided into two, one per two measures; altered here by analogy with the bass.

M. 144: The staccato marks are added in the Violas by analogy with m. 129.

Mm. 152 & 153: The MS lacks the staccato dots in the Bassoons.

M. 167: The portato in the Horns is added by analogy with m. 165.

Mm. 168 & 169: The slur in Oboe II is added by analogy with the Flutes.

No. 5. Coro

M. 3: The slur in Oboe II and Bassoon II is added by analogy with the Second Violins.

Mm. 11 & 12: The MS lacks the slur in the Violas (also in mm. 57 & 58).

M. 17: In the MS, the Bassoons are an octave higher (before this, "col Basso").

M. 20: We have added the slur in the second Viola part here and in m. 27 by analogy with m. 43.

No. 6. Aria

Mm. 14–16: The staccato dots in the Second Violins are added.

M. 16: The Horn ties to the next measure are lacking.

M. 49: The staccato dots are added (also in mm. 69–71 in Violas and bass).

Mm. 57 & 58: The slur in Flute II and Bassoon II is added.

Mm. 80 ff: The staccato marks, partially lacking in the MS, are added.

No. 7. Duettino

M. 18: The MS lacks the staccato dots in the bass.

M. 41: In the MS, the *p* in the bass is placed under the first quarter beat (also in m. 43).

Mm. 59 & 60: The slur in Flutes and Bassoons here differs from mm. 51 & 52, as in the MS.

Mm. 67 & 68: The MS lacks the slur in Oboe II here and later.

M. 71: The MS lacks the slur in Horn II here and in mm. 73 and 75; it is added by analogy with m. 67.

No. 8. Aria

M. 1: As in No. 4, the first bass quarter note again belongs to the Cembalo.

M. 32: The MS mistakenly gives the viola 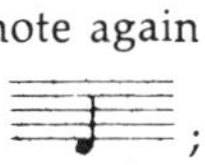 ; here Mozart, beginning a new system, had the Violin clef in mind.

No. 9. Quartetto

M. 1: Again the half note in the bass belongs to the Cembalo.

Mm. 32 & 33: The Bassoon portato is added by analogy with the preceding measures.

M. 33: In the MS, the Second Violins lack the slur to the next measure.

M. 38: The MS erroneously gives the Clarinets and Bassoons:

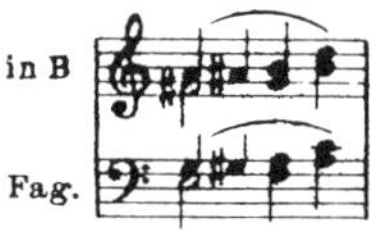

Mm. 41 ff.: The staccato dots in the First Violins are added by analogy with m. 40.

M. 46: The MS lacks the Bassoon slur (also in m. 63).

Mm. 64 & 65: The Clarinet and Bassoon slur is added by analogy with the Flutes (also the Clarinet I and Bassoon I slur in mm. 73 & 74).

M. 85: In the MS, Donna Elvira's last sixteenth note is d^2 instead of c^2.

No. 10. Recitativo ed Aria

M. 10: The staccato marks in the First Violins are added (also in mm. 12, 14 and 39).

Mm. 15 & 16: The MS lacks the staccato marks in Oboes and Bassoons.

Mm. 35–37: The staccato marks in the bass are added (also in mm. 44 & 45).

M. 52: The MS lacks Don Ottavio's quarter-beat rest.

M. 70: The MS shows a note as well as a quarter-beat rest in the bass. It is impossible to say whether the rest or the note was written first or last, but since Mozart composed the aria before the recitative, there is no reason to deprive the bass of its final note.

M. 77: The slur in the Second Violins is added by analogy with m. 107.

M. 83: Here the MS has the bass slur over the entire measure in contrast to all the other analogous passages.

M. 84: The MS has staccato dots only in the First Violins (lacking altogether in m. 114), whereas in m. 123 they are given only in Bassoon II, First and Second Violins and Violas.

M. 105: In the MS, the First Violins have:

 ;

altered here by analogy with m. 75.

M. 109: The slur in Horns and bass is added (see m. 79).

No. 10a. Aria

Mm. 35 & 36: In the MS, the Bassoons have no slur.

Mm. 41 & 42: The slurs to the next measure in Violas and bass are added by analogy with mm. 6 & 7.

M. 48: The portato in the Horns is added by analogy with m. 13 (also in m. 60).

Recitativo

Mm. 33 f.: The measure ends halfway at the end of a system; beginning a new system, Mozart mistakenly begins a new measure. (The usual cut in earlier editions is not adopted here, since it results in the loss of the rest).

No. 11. Aria

Mm. 26 & 27: In the MS, Clarinets I & II are without ties (and without slurs in mm. 28–32).

Mm. 33 & 34: In the MS, Horn I has no tie (also in mm. 35 & 36).

M. 55: The staccato dots in Flutes and First Violins are added.

No. 12. Aria

M. 21: In the MS, the First Violins here have no staccato dots (see m. 17).

Mm. 54 & 55: In the MS, the solo Cello has a slur over both measures (also in mm. 56 & 57); altered here by analogy with mm. 52 & 53.

Mm. 68 & 69: In the MS, the Second Violins have no slur.

M. 70: In the MS, the Bassoons have *b*-flat instead of d^1 (change of page).

Mm. 76 & 77: In the MS, the Horns have no slur (see mm. 73 & 74).

M. 77: The markings in Violas and bass are added.

Mm. 78–85: In the MS, these measures are crossed out in ink—whether by Mozart himself cannot be decided—although the final note of the Oboes is entered in m. 86.

M. 85: We have added the markings in Flutes and Bassoons in the second half of the measure.

M. 98: In the MS, the Bassoon staccato dots are lacking.

No. 13. Finale

Mm. 1 ff.: The Clarinets are lacking in the MS; Mozart wrote their part on a separate sheet—"N.B. 2 Clarinetti auf dem extra Blatt Pag. 1"—which is unfortunately lost.

M. 8: The MS lacks the tie to the next measure in the Flutes.

M. 11: The MS lacks the Flute slur here and in mm. 15 & 16 (see m. 46).

Mm. 15 & 16: The MS lacks the tie in the bass and places the *p* in m. 16.

M. 20: Except for the tie in Oboe I, we have added the wind markings.

M. 22: The MS lacks the slur in the First Violins.

M. 23: The staccato dots in the First Violins are added by analogy with m. 49.

M. 29: In the MS, the *f* in Violas and bass here and in m. 32 is placed on the first quarter beat.

Mm. 84 & 85: In the MS, the First and Second Violins have only one dot after the quarter notes (an abbreviation common at the time).

M. 98: In the MS, in contrast to m. 93, the First Violins have only one slur over the second and third quarter beats.

M. 100: The slurs in the Bassoons are added.

M. 134: The slur in Flute II is added (also in m. 136 in Oboe II).

M. 154: In the MS, the *f* in Flutes and Oboes already appears here on the second eighth note.

Mm. 174–176: The staccato dots in First and Second Violins are added.

M. 189: The slur in Oboe II is added (also in mm. 193 and 197).

M. 209: The MS lacks the slur on Bassoon II.

Mm. 236–242: We have added the slur in the Violas here and in mm. 422–425, 430–433 and 446–449 by analogy with mm. 244–250.

Mm. 248 & 249: The slur in Oboe II is added by analogy with mm. 240 & 241 (also in mm. 426 & 427 and 434 & 435).

Mm. 251 & 252: In the MS, the First and Second Violins have:  . It is impossible to decide which of the three possibilities  ,  or  Mozart intended.

M. 259: The slur in Oboe I is added by analogy with m. 264.

M. 260: In the MS, Elvira's text is notated as follows:

Mm. 264 & 265: The tie in Oboe II is added by analogy with mm. 259 & 260.

Mm. 265 & 266: The tie in Horn I is added by analogy with mm. 267 & 268.

Mm. 273 ff.: From this point, the Flutes, too, are lacking in the MS: "NB. 2 Flauti auf dem extra Blatt Pag. 1"; as mentioned above, the sheet is lost.

M. 311: The Bassoon slur is added.

Mm. 313–316: The slur in Oboes and Bassoons is added.

Mm. 318 & 319: Here and in the following measures, the MS shows the tie in the Violas, but not the slur.

M. 322: The MS lacks the tie to the next measure in the bass here and in mm. 324 and 326.

Mm. 360 ff.: From this point, the Flute part is once more entered in the MS, but the other winds are Lacking: "NB. 2 Oboe, 2 Clarinetti, 2 Clarini e Timpani: Pag. 2." According to Gugler, clarinets in B-flat instead of in C were retained.

Mm. 384 & 385: The Donaueschingen score (apparently in error) here gives the Oboes and Clarinets:

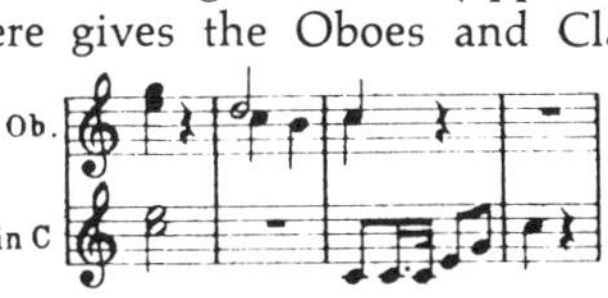

In the MS, Bassoon II lacks the slur.

Mm. 400 & 401: In the MS, the First and Second Violins have:  , and thus originally in the bass, but since Mozart altered the bass to the form printed here, the remaining strings had to be changed as well.

Mm. 448 & 449: The MS lacks the Oboe slur.

M. 458: The staccato dots in the Oboes are added by analogy with m. 442.

M. 463: In the MS, the Violins of Orchestra III have a tie to the next measure.

M. 468: From this point to the end of the Finale, the MS lacks all the winds and the Drums: "N.B.: Tutti li stromenti di fiato Pag. 3 sino al fine."

M. 482: In the MS, the bass's natural sign does not occur until m. 483 (it is impossible to decide on the basis of the Violas playing "col Basso," but see m. 477).

M. 504: The Donaueschingen score gives the winds *f*; here we follow the Graz score's *p*.

M. 507: In the Donaueschingen score, the Flutes have no markings on the third and fourth quarter beats; here we follow the Graz score.

M. 537 ff.: In the MS, the music lines of Zerlina and Donna Elvira are reversed; altered here according to stage practice.

Mm. 562 & 563: The Donaueschingen score lacks the tie in Horn I (also in mm. 591 & 592).
M. 571: In the MS, the Second Violins have ♪. on the fourth quarter beat; in the analogous passages there is a plain quarter note, and we have thus made the change here.
M. 631: We follow the Donaueschingen score for the Horns and Trumpets, thus differing from all previous editions (see m. 639).
M. 648: The Donaueschingen score and all printed editions continue the eighth notes in the Bassoons (but see the bass).

No. 14. Duetto

M. 4: The MS shows staccato dots only in the First and Second Violins.
Mm. 21 & 22: The MS lacks the tie in the Second Violins.

No. 15. Terzetto

M. 2: The MS lacks the staccato dots in the Violas (also in mm. 20 and 55).
M. 18: The MS lacks the slur in Clarinet I, and begins the slur in Clarinet II with the fourth eighth-note beat.
M. 23: The MS lacks the staccato dots in the Second Violins and Violas.
M. 34: In the MS, the bass has staccato dots on the third, fourth and sixth eighth notes (surely a mere oversight).
Mm. 44 & 45: The MS lacks the Bassoon slurs.
M. 69: The MS lacks the slurs in Clarinet II and Bassoon II (also in the first half of m. 70).
M. 72: Mozart indicated another *p* here for all instruments (change of page).
M. 80: Here and in m. 82, the MS places the *p* in the Violas and bass before the third eighth-note beat, but it doubtless goes with the first eighth beat as in m. 13.

No. 16. Canzonetta

M. 1: Mozart inadvertently designated the tempo in the bass as *Allegro* instead of *Allegretto*.
M. 9: In the MS, the bass has *d* on the fourth eighth note; here altered to *B* by analogy with m. 29.
M. 31: In the MS, the bass has  for the first three eighth beats. Beginning with m. 25, only the vocal part and the bass are written out ("Istromenti come prima"). Apparently Mozart fell into error here.

No. 17. Aria

M. 11: The staccato dots in the Bassoons on the third and fourth quarter beats are added (see m. 33); they are lacking altogether in m. 13.
M. 14: In the MS, the First Violins lack the slur to the next measure.
M. 17: The staccato marks in the Oboes and Bassoons are added by analogy with m. 53.
M. 36: The staccato mark on the second eighth note of the First and Second Violins is added by analogy with m. 19.
M. 50: In the MS, the Bassoons lack the slur to the next measure.
M. 54: In the MS, the Horns lack the slur to the next measure.
M. 67: In the MS, the Bassoons rest (but see m. 62).
M. 68: The slurs in the Bassoons are altered by analogy with m. 63.
M. 70: The slur in Bassoon II is altered by analogy with m. 72.

No. 18. Aria

M. 15: The staccato mark in the Violas is added by analogy with m. 91 (also in m. 40; here in the Flutes, too).
Mm. 19 & 20: In the MS, the slur in the Second Violins is divided into two, one per measure; altered here by analogy with mm. 23 & 24, which is the form Mozart used later as well.
Mm. 36 & 37: In the MS, the slur in the Violas covers both measures; changed here by analogy with mm. 11 & 12 and others (also in mm. 87 & 88 in the Bassoons).
M. 38: The Horn slur is added by analogy with m. 5 and others.
Mm. 54 & 55: In the MS, the Clarinet and Bassoon slurs are divided by measure (including the upbeat); the same occurs in mm. 58 & 59; altered here by analogy with the Flutes.
Mm. 64 & 65: The MS lacks the staccato dots in the winds here and in mm. 69–71 and 98 & 99 (also in mm. 66 and 72 in the bass).
Mm. 80 & 81: The MS lacks the Viola slur.
M. 101: The staccato mark in the Clarinets and Bassoons is added.

No. 19. Sestetto

Mm. 1 ff.: Again Mozart wrote all the wind parts and the Drums separately: "NB. Alle Blas-Instrumenten extra."; unfortunately these too are lost.
M. 6: The Donaueschingen score shows no portato in the Horns.
M. 19: The Donaueschingen score gives Horn I another tie to the next measure.
M. 22: In the MS, the bass slur is divided by half-measures.
M. 27: In the Donaueschingen score, Clarinet II has f^1, apparently a slip of the pen; here altered to e^1. In the Graz score it is g^1 (with a tie to the preceding measure).
M. 35: In the Donaueschingen score and all previous printed versions, Oboe II has g^1; we follow the Graz score and print a^1.
Mm. 46 & 47: The Donaueschingen score lacks the tie in Trumpet I.
M. 70: Here the MS does not indicate a new scene, but directly continues the preceding one. This causes the scene numbering that follows, which is based on the libretto, to differ from the MS later as well.
Mm. 86 & 87: Donna Elvira is missing in the MS, but is added here by analogy with mm. 90 & 91.
M. 95: In the Donaueschingen score, Bassoon II has *f* instead of *b*-flat.
M. 97: In the Donaueschingen score, Flute II has d^3 instead of d^2.
M. 137: In the Donaueschingen score, Oboe II here and in m. 145 has a half-measure rest on the first two quarter beats; altered here on the basis of the Graz score.
M. 149: In the Donaueschingen score, the *cresc.* for

Oboes, Clarinets and Bassoons does not appear until m. 150, and the *f* is altogether lacking (also in mm. 194 & 195). In the Graz score and all earlier publications, the *f* for these instruments occurs on the fourth quarter beat of m. 150 (and 195); altered here by analogy with the Flutes.

M. 152: In the MS, the First and Second Violins have only *f* (see m. 197).

M. 157: In the Donaueschingen score, Clarinet I has g^2 (also in m. 202); here altered to e^2 on the basis of the Graz score.

Mm. 229–231: In the MS, the bass has a slur over these three measures.

M. 240: The staccato dots in the First and Second Violins are added from the third quarter beat through the end of m. 242.

No. 20. Aria

M. 1: In the MS, over the vocal line: "a Don Ottavio e Donna Elvira," but at first Leporello addresses all the characters on stage.

M. 40: The staccato dots in the First and Second Violins are added from the second eighth note through m. 41.

Mm. 63 & 64: The MS lacks the tie in Horn I.

Recitativo

M. 3: Mozart wrote incorrectly: 

Zerlina's words "si sottrasse l'iniquo" are followed in the Vienna libretto by the words "Masetto, vien meco," and Zerlina exits with Masetto. Don Ottavio's address begins with "Donna Elvira" instead of "Amici miei," and he too leaves with Donna Elvira at the end of the Recitative, since the Vienna version does not include the Aria No. 21.

No. 21. Aria

Mm. 37 & 38: The staccato dots in the First Violins are added (also in mm. 80–82).

Mm. 49–68: "Istromenti come prima"; only the First Violins in mm. 64, 67 and 68 are shown along with the vocal line and the bass.

Recitativo

Mm. 1 ff.: Of the numbers beginning here that were composed for the Vienna première, only Elvira's recitative and aria (No. 21b) are preserved in the MS. Gugler doubts the authenticity of the present Recitative (Xa), and he is probably right.

No. 21a. Duetto

Mm. 27 & 28: In other editions, the First and Second Violins and the Violas have:

Mm. 36 & 37: The slur in the Second Violins is added by analogy with mm. 60 & 61.

Mm. 67 ff.: The dynamic marks are not the same as in the corresponding passage, mm. 42 ff., but since the autograph score is lost, it cannot be determined which version is correct.

Recitativo

Mm. 1 ff.: For the first time it was possible to consult some Italian manuscripts which were prepared from Mozart's Vienna score by the Viennese copyist Lausch and others. These are the manuscripts P 265/3 and B 117 of the Istituto Musicale in Florence, which give Scenes Xb and Xc with their Mozart music that has never yet been published in any orchestral or piano score. There is no doubt that the abridged and altered versions that have hitherto appeared in this place were smuggled into the score from unreliable sources.

No. 21b. Recitativo ed Aria

M. 16. The MS shows the staccato marks only in the bass; the others are added.

Mm. 77 ff.: Mm. 77–89, and mm. 118–131, are not written out, but called for by an "Istromenti come prima."

Mm. 93 & 94: The MS lacks the tie in the Violas.

Mm. 94 & 95: The slur in the Flutes and Clarinets is added.

Mm. 39 & 40: On transposing the Recitative and Aria to D Major, Mozart had to make various adjustments in the Aria; thus, here and in the corresponding passages, mm. 78 & 79 and 120 & 121, he had to make the change:

M. 102:

M. 115:

M. 135:

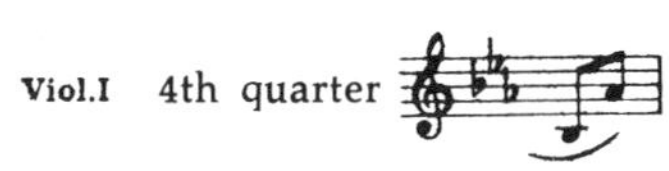

Mm. 139 & 140:

M. 147:

Mm. 155 & 156:

Mm. 164 & 165:

Recitativo

Mm. 1 ff.: The MS lacks the entire Recitative with the two accompanied passages.

M. 8: The vocal line here follows the Donaueschingen score; the version up to now had on the third and fourth quarter beats:

Mm. 51 & 52: The vocal line in the Donaueschingen score:

Although there is merit in having the vocal line follow the Oboe part, nevertheless the traditional version has been retained, since m. 51 is obviously notated incorrectly.

M. 56: In the Donaueschingen score, the vocal line on the second and third quarter beat reads:

Mm. 59–63: Extensively figured in the Donaueschingen score (also mm. 71–73, but there are many errors here).

Mm. 61 & 62: The Donaueschingen score lacks the tie in Bassoon II and Trombone II.

No. 22. Duetto

M. 9: The staccato dots are shown in the MS only on the first and second quarter beats in the First and Second Violins, and are altogether lacking in the Violas.

M. 43: Mozart originally wrote for Flute I:

and this version has found its way into older and newer editions. Later he made the alteration printed here.

M. 52: The MS lacks the Bassoon slur to the next measure (also in m. 53).

Mm. 60 & 61: The MS shows only the slur in the bass.

Recitativo

M. 16: Mozart forgot to indicate the bass.

No. 23. Recitativo ed Aria

M. 6: In the MS, the grace note in the vocal line is an eighth note.

M. 8: In the MS, the First Violins have a slur over the entire measure (see m. 4).

M. 11: In the MS, the vocal line is:

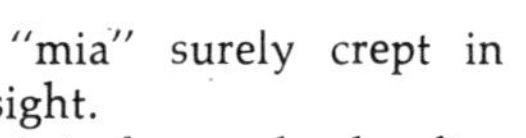

The "mia" surely crept in merely as an oversight.

M. 16: The Aria bears the heading "Rondò," presumably in another hand. But at the end of the Recitative there is also written, unmistakably in Mozart's hand: "attacca Rondò." Yet at the end of the preceding recitative Mozart wrote: "attacca Recitativo Istromentato di Donna Anna col Aria."

M. 28: The staccato dots in the Second Violins are added by analogy with m. 55.

M. 98: Here and in m. 101, the MS has the slur over the entire measure in the Violas (see bass).

Mm. 106 & 107: The slur in Bassoon II is added.

No. 24. Finale

Mm. 1 ff.: In the MS, the Trumpets and Drums are lacking up to the on-stage band music, nor is there any reference to an additional sheet.

M. 7: In the Donaueschingen score, the Trumpets are notated as in the following measure; altered here by analogy with the Horns in the MS.

M. 11: In the Donaueschingen score, the Drums have: 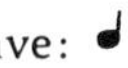

M. 17: In the MS, the Second Violins have:

 ; altered here by analogy with m. 21.

M. 21: The dynamic marks differ from m. 17; thus in MS (change of page).

Mm. 45 & 46: The slur in Oboe II added by analogy with the Flutes.

M. 47 ff.: Gugler writes: "The three pieces played by the band are somewhat carelessly written in the autograph manuscript, especially the first two, which generally lack *p* and *f* indications, and often, slurs and ties. I have consulted the scores of the operas from which they are taken . . ., but merely in order to fill gaps in the notation or to eliminate incorrect insertions in earlier editions, naturally . . . retaining intact . . . all indications originating with Mozart himself." All these additions are clearly identified by smaller size or square brackets.

Mm. 92–94: In the MS, the Cello has only *f*.

M. 165: In the MS, the Clarinets have quarter notes instead of eighth notes on the first and third quarter beats.

M. 213: In the MS, the Violas lack the tie to the next measure.

M. 221: In the MS, the Violas and bass do not have the *f* until the next measure (also in m. 329).

M. 257: In the MS, Horn I lacks the tie to the next measure.

Mm. 344 & 345: In the MS, Clarinet II lacks the tie.

Mm. 372–376: The MS shows only the first tie in Flute II in mm. 372 & 373; the others are lacking.

Mm. 420 & 421: In the MS, the bass slur is divided in two, one per measure (also in mm. 426 & 427).

Mm. 423–425: The slur in the Flutes and Oboes is added.

Mm. 429 & 430: The MS shows the wind slur only in the Bassoon part.

Mm. 433 ff.: The MS lacks the Trumpet and Drum lines as well as the Trombone line, and there is no reference to an additional sheet. But they are present in the Donaueschingen score.

Mm. 441 & 442: The slur in Bassoon I is added by analogy with the Flutes.

Mm. 449 & 450: The MS lacks the tie in Flute II (also the one in Clarinet I in mm. 450 & 451).

M. 453: In the Donaueschingen score, the Trumpets have a whole note.

Mm. 465 & 466: The MS lacks the tie in Oboe I.

Mm. 470 ff.: It is not perfectly clear from the MS how Mozart wished the bass to be executed. The triplets came first and were then replaced with quarter-beat rests—whether by Mozart himself, cannot be ascertained.

Mm. 474–476: The ties in the Trumpets are lacking in all editions, but are clearly shown in the Donaueschingen score.

Mm. 478 ff.: Mm. 478–482 and 503–506 are crossed out in the MS (by Mozart?), and there are corresponding adjustments in the First Violins, Violas and vocal parts.

M. 566: In the Donaueschingen score, the Trumpets have a half note.

Mm. 567 & 568: In the Donaueschingen score, here and in mm. 578 & 579 and 582 & 583, the Trumpets have half notes; altered here by analogy with mm. 563 & 564. Thus also in the Graz score.

M. 570: In the Donaueschingen score, here and in m. 585, the Trumpets have whole notes; altered here on the basis of the Graz score.

Mm. 578–587: In the MS, partially not written out, but called for by an "Istromenti come prima."

Mm. 587 & 588: The MS lacks the tie in Clarinet I and Bassoon II.

M. 596: In the MS, the Flutes and Oboes have only *f*.

M. 602: The opera ended here at the Vienna première. The Vienna libretto reads: "Nel momento stesso [m. 594] escon tutti gli altri, guardano, metton un alto grido, fuggono, e cala il sipario" (At this very moment all the others come out, look, give a loud cry and run off, and the curtain falls).

Mm. 603 ff.: The MS lacks the wind parts.

M. 625: In the Donaueschingen score, Horn II has d^1 instead of *g*.

Mm. 701 & 702: In the MS, Zerlina's words are notated in the following, surely incorrect, way:

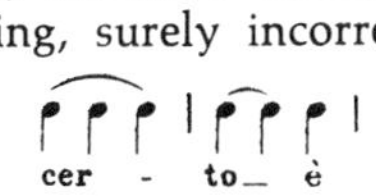

Mm. 689–749: These measures are crossed out in the MS (see Supplement III, page 461).

Mm. 715 ff.: The MS lacks the wind parts, and the additional sheet that had them is lost.

M. 749: In the Donaueschingen score, the winds have a slur from the *g*-sharp to the *a*. In the Donaueschingen score, the Horns play in eighth notes!

Mm. 762 ff.: The MS lacks the winds and Drums all the way to the end.

Mm. 799–803: The notes printed smaller in the Cello part are taken from the Graz score (also in mm. 824–828 and 831–842).

Mm. 813–830: In the MS, partially not written out, but called for by a "Come prima."

Mm. 859 & 860: In the Donaueschingen score and all earlier publications, the Trumpet part follows the Horn part; altered here on the basis of the Graz score.

Mm. 860–871: These measures, which were on the last page of the MS, are lost and replaced in a copyist's hand. But mm. 867–869 were left blank in the Viola and bass parts. It may be assumed that the conjectural version printed here in smaller notes was intended by Mozart.

M. 871: In the Donaueschingen score, the Trumpets have: 

Berlin-Wilmersdorf, Summer 1941

GEORG SCHÜNEMANN
KURT SOLDAN

Recits
rests in accomp
chordal accomp